DR. LAURA

DR. LAURA

THE UNAUTHORIZED BIOGRAPHY

Vickie L. Bane

St. Martin's Press

New York

THOMAS DUNNE BOOKS.
An imprint of St. Martin's Press.

Library of Congress Cataloging-in-Publication Data

Bane, Vickie L.
Dr. Laura : the unauthorized biography / Vickie Bane.—1st ed.
p.   cm.
Includes bibliographical references.
ISBN 0-312-20530-9 (hardcover)
1. Schlessinger, Laura.   2. Radio broadcasters—United States
Biography.   I. Title.   II. Title: Doctor Laura.
PN1991.4.S29B36   1999
791.44′028′092—dc21
[B]   99-22077
                                                         CIP

First Edition: August 1999

10   9   8   7   6   5   4   3   2   1

TO WILMA DEAN NEAL BABNIK—THE MOTHER WE ALL LOVED—
WHO HELPED ME WRITE THIS FROM HEAVEN.

AND TO THE REST OF MY DEVOTED FIRST FAMILY:
JOSEPH W. BABNIK, THE BEST FATHER IMAGINABLE;
JOANN C. DAYTON, THE SISTER, THE WOMAN, EVERYONE
WANTS TO BE LIKE, BEAUTIFUL INSIDE AND OUT;
MICHAEL J. BABNIK, THE BROTHER, THE MAN, WHOSE OWN
INTEGRITY AND KINDNESS ARE A MODEL TO US ALL.

AND, AGAIN, TO THE WORLD'S FINEST HUSBAND, FATHER, AND EDITOR,
DAVID G. BANE, AND THE NEATEST SONS ANY TWO PEOPLE COULD BE
LUCKY ENOUGH TO HAVE: JASON DAVID AND TODD JOSEPH (TJ).

ACKNOWLEDGMENTS

In the fourteen months it took to research and write this book, literally hundreds of wonderful people gave generously of their time and their talents.

My thanks and appreciation to those incredible individuals who helped make this book possible know no bounds. This is as much their book as it is mine.

Sincerest thanks to all the interviewees who so graciously and magnanimously shared their recollections, including those actually cited in the text, those whose words appear without their names (you know who you are), and those I regretfully had to leave out.

With incredible gratitude to:

Madeleine Morel of 2M Communications, my agent, and Thomas

Dunne of St. Martin's Press, my editor, who offered me the project back in 1997, even though I had never heard of Dr. Laura; James Oberman, a world-class research expert who can find anyone who needs to be found, and a gentleman to the core; Barry Staver, a super photographer and even better friend, who saved me on so many occasions I cannot count them; Monica Rizzo, Craig Thomasoff, John Griffiths, Karin Grant, Lorenzo Benet, and all my other confederates at *People* in Los Angeles, who shared their considerable wisdom with me; John Marzullo of Citadel Entertainment who doggedly found me photos; Ellyn Hutt, who spent many hours teaching me about what it means to her to be an Orthodox Jew; Kristen Nardullo and Niklas Arnegren of St. Martin's Press, who keep track of everything; Naomi Shulman, also of St. Martin's, who copyedited the final manuscript; Wendy Goldstein of Cold Spring Harbor Lab on Long Island; the fine ladies at the Long Island Studies Institute at Hofstra University in New York; and Leonard Aschenbrand, who spent hours reading me names of Stony Brook graduates and giving me their phone numbers.

Special thanks are due my extended family: Vera Dawson, our lovely sister-to-be, and my sister's children and grandchildren, who are like my own: Troy Dayton, Kathy Dayton, Tracy Seul, Chris Seul, Debbie Seul, and Cody Seul; John and Pat Bane, my special in-laws; Doug Bane, my brother-in-law in L.A., who knows his real estate and generously shared it with me; my nieces, Alison and Jennifer, and my grand-niece, Madison, and Michael, Mary, Kelsey, and Kevin Bane, who are as dear to me as any blood relatives.

Finally, I want to express my gratitude to the special friends who were always there, especially Jane and Bob Urschel, and Terry, Jim, Matt, and Scott McKerley.

My thanks, my love.

DR. LAURA

FOREWORD

On a hot summer night in 1998, I sat in a Los Angeles Chinese restaurant with the mother of Laura Schlessinger—the mother whom Laura has not seen for over fourteen years.

Over wonton soup and shrimp in lobster sauce, we laughed and traded stories about being afraid. I cannot share her stories with you because I promised her I would not tell her tales, only those factual tidbits already carefully gleaned from the memories of other travelers who shared Laura's path along the way.

But, having spent many hours over several different meetings together, I can share my impressions.

Impressions are fitting.

Lundy, as she prefers to be called, is not your mother's mother. She is a different sort of seventy-plus: petite but not frail, hard but softer than she knows.

Around her neck Lundy wears a gold chain with a Chinese dragon. Her top is a short-sleeved, scoop-necked, black-and-flowered jersey that clings to her bodice. Her figure is good—solid, not meaty. The light yellow linen skirt she wears is short, just above the knees. She eschews stockings, opting instead to slip her feet, which are as tan as her legs, and shapely still, into sandals with three-inch heels.

When the waiter arrives Lundy is abrupt, dismissive, in her sureness of what she wants. The wine must come after the soup, with the main course. Not before.

The soup comes, and she serves, forgoing the fried noodles. Lundy carefully bundles up the extras in a tiny white box for her bird, Sweetie Pie, who likes fried noodles.

Her long fingers with carefully manicured mauve nails are curved around a glass of chardonnay, but Lundy drinks little and talks more, using a toss of her head or a flip of her hands to express a point.

Her green eyes are zesty, taking on added sparkle when she is making a sarcastic remark. They sparkle a lot.

She wears a hint of eye shadow—blue I think—but otherwise her face is makeup-free. There are wrinkles, of course, battle scars from a life that perhaps has not always gone her way.

Wrinkles, green eyes, and a chin that, if Laura were here, might all blend together with her mother's features in a mirror.

Impressions are fitting.

Back in her spacious one-bedroom condominium in an elite suburb near the city, we sit in a nook in front of a television set. The nook is cozy and close, while, to the left, the living room spills over into the dining room. Off to one side in the sunroom is Sweetie Pie's cage, covered with a tattered gray sweater.

Sweetie Pie is a blue-and-gray parrot. Once the feathers must have burst forth from Sweetie's chest in proud array. Not anymore. Sweetie has carefully plucked the fluff from her breast to reveal the pink skin beneath.

The tone in Lundy's condo is light. The carpet is a soft pink, the sectional sofa white, and the windows large. Framed reproductions hang amidst her own oil paintings, signed in large, bold strokes with one word: "Lundy."

There are no pictures, only paintings.

We talk and laugh and argue a bit, while we eat cherries from a bowl. Once more, she is strong in her resolve about what she will not say, and I respect her choice, her fears, her own impressions.

Impressions are fitting.

This is, after all, a book about impressions.

This is a book that tells what other people perceived or observed about the Laura Schlessinger who, for whatever moment, walked through their lives.

Over the years, Laura evolved from a daughter into a mother. She earned a doctorate, got married, got divorced, had her tubes tied, had them untied, got married again, had a baby, embraced Orthodox Judaism, and, in between, became a radio superstar.

This book attempts to fill in the spaces between the commas. It is not a hunt for flaws so much as it is a study of defining moments: those periods of time or those significant life choices that have an impact, that shape the person to come.

We are all products of how we were raised and the times in which we lived.

By walking in Laura's footsteps through a life that has already spanned more than fifty years, perhaps her listeners, fans and critics alike, will more clearly be able to form their own impressions of the person who is Dr. Laura.

CHAPTER ONE

But the true measure of your character is not in your thoughts but in your behavior, especially when you're provoked. Ultimately, you are what you choose to do.

DR. LAURA SCHLESSINGER

APRIL 13, 1997

From the instant Laura C. Schlessinger, Ph.D., stepped out the door of the Dallas–Fort Worth International Airport in Texas, she should have felt the heat.

It was the third of March, 1997, and a sunny 73 degrees. The temperature, it seemed, was every bit as warm as her welcome.

In town to speak at two different charitable events, "Dr. Laura," as she bills herself, left her husband, Lew Bishop, and their eleven-year-old son, Deryk, at home, in the family's sprawling house in Hidden Hills, just across the freeway from Calabasas, California. That, in itself, was rare for Dr. Laura, who prided herself on being, first and foremost, "my kid's mom"—the kind of mom, she told her millions of listeners nearly every weekday, who put family first and career somewhere further down the line. And the kind of talk-radio host who expected the same moral stance from her fans. Without qualification.

"Welcome to the program," Dr. Laura would say at the start of each call to her three-hour, five-day-a-week, interactive, moral advice show. Then, the caller would launch into his or her "moral dilemma."

On a typical day, Dr. Laura would hear from around six to eight fans an hour, most of whom would start out by saying how much they adored Dr. Laura, her show, her morals or all three. But even a warm welcome from Dr. Laura or adoration from the fans could not save some callers from verbal lickings if they were not living up to Dr. Laura's tough moral code of family values, which excludes, among other things, sex out of wedlock, divorce if kids are involved, and leaving children in child care.

If she had ever listened to Dr. Laura, a caller like Jennifer, the un-wed mother of a three-year-old, really should have known better. Jennifer had called in to confess a second pregnancy by another live-in boyfriend.

"So he's not anxious to get married, is that right?" queried the good doctor.

"No, he is actually," claimed Jennifer. "We know we're going to be together—"

"Yeah, yeah, yeah," broke in Dr. Laura, who has heard this all before. "Is he the father of the other kid?"

"That was another infidelity," explained Jennifer, adding, "We are in the nineties and things just happen."

"I see—you woke up in the middle of the night pregnant, not ever having had intercourse with the man you aren't married to," answered Dr. Laura, sarcastically. "I knew that in the 1990s something had to be different. What kind of crap are you handing me, woman? People got pregnant by intercourse since the beginning of humankind. There is nothing new in the 1990s."

"I'm animal [sic] enough to admit how I got pregnant," explained Jennifer. "As things go, people are a lot more liberal now—"

"I'm *not*," chimed in Dr. Laura. "You're pregnant out of wedlock? Liberal is good? Is that in the best interest of the kid?"

"No, that's not what I'm saying," said Jennifer, who then confessed that her moral dilemma was whether or not she should have an abortion.

"This is the nineties, just suck it out into a sink. Kill it. Terminate it. Get on with your life," said Dr. Laura, again sarcastically.

"Jennifer, you came to the wrong house to get this handout. . . . This is a life. . . . That's it," she added, forgoing her usual tendency to use one of her preferred terms, "slut," or her favorite comebacks, "How stupid can you be and still be able to chew your food?"

But this was Dallas, not the airwaves, and although Dr. Laura's radio time was over, her work was not done.

Laura was on her own in Dallas. And, even though she was getting paid $30,000 a pop for two speeches, plus squeezing in a promotional event with the local AM talk-radio station that hosted her show, she did not appear particularly gleeful.

When several women from one of the organizations she was addressing met her plane, she was brusque with them, and in a hurry to be off. At the hotel where she was to address a function that evening, Dr. Laura surveyed the first suite reserved for her and reportedly said the "smell" was not right. Hotel management quickly maneuvered her to a second suite, which she also found unsuitable, as she did a third and a fourth. Finally, at the suggestion of one of the women in attendance that they could find another hotel, Dr. Laura moved to an even more expensive place, ranked among the top ten in America: The Mansion on Turtle Creek. The expenses, per prior arrangement, were being picked up by her hosts.

"One usually goes to the Mansion for the food," explained D. J. Kassanoff, an English teacher at Southern Methodist University (SMU) in Dallas, who attended Dr. Laura's speech the following evening and was familiar with the arrangements. "But, since Dr. Laura keeps kosher, they had arranged with a local kosher catering concern in Plano to bring in food for their guest."

Laura's first event was a speech and dessert, sponsored by the Assistance League of Dallas at the Grand Kempinski Hotel. Made up of 120 women who "do good works for charity," the League signed Laura first to keynote their biggest fund-raiser of the year. Tickets were from $50 to $100, and the proceeds from the event were slated to benefit several local educational and medical charities for children.

Between 2,000 and 2,300 people filed into the Crystal Ballroom at the Grand Kempinski at 7:30 that evening, anxious to see Dr. Laura in action.

Phyllis Davis, a friend of several League officers, remembered being surprised by Laura almost from the moment she walked onstage. Instead of immediately addressing the crowd after what Davis recalled as a "marvelous introduction" by Deborah Duncan, then a Dallas television personality, Laura stepped forward and said she needed the stage setup changed.

"She's short, and I'm short, so I understand those kind of things, but she moved the whole stage around. She had someone come on and move everything [the furniture] over . . . and all of this while we are all sitting there, waiting. Then she ended up kind of walking around with the mike so she could be seen in total.

"She was kind of cutesy," Davis continued. "This was a psychologist supposedly there to answer questions, but at the same time, she is a show person, getting paid to do a job. She talked mainly about herself and how she converted [to Judaism] and how she handled her little boy. Then she opened it up for questions. People raised their hands from the audience, and then someone would take them the microphone.

"There was not one person who asked a question who wasn't put down in the most rude fashion I have ever seen," recalled Davis.

"They were questions somebody my age would never ask. They had to do with marital problems and how to handle things with a husband. These people had paid money to come see this woman, and she absolutely put each one of them down. She said, 'I do things differently, and if you listen to my program, you know those are the kind of things

I'm not even going to address: They are too frivolous.' She was not good.

"I was expecting a more sophisticated attitude towards people who had come. I was surprised that a psychologist would come forth with the kind of answers and treat people the way she did," said Davis.

Even though Davis did not remember anyone saying, "Wasn't that just great?" Laura's appearance on March 3 was received less poorly than her performance the next evening.

The following morning, Laura was guest of honor at a breakfast for advertisers sponsored by KRLD, the radio station in Dallas that hosted her show. Rose Saginaw, a Dallas marketing executive and confessed Dr. Laura fan, attended with around 100 others.

"It was at a lovely restaurant at the Quadrangle, which is normally not open in the morning, but they opened up the whole place. My impression of her, as a person, was that she was even wittier, more caring, and more sensitive than I had even imagined. She was very human. On the other hand, she really said some dumb things.

"She said, 'I'm so glad to be in Dallas. You look so good. I expected to find a bunch of overweight people.' There had been a story in the paper about overweight people in Texas, but, number one, that was about San Antonio. Dallas is a fashion center and we are not overweight. Those people who filter for her didn't background her. It was kind of an insulting thing. Those were her opening remarks," said Saginaw.

Still Saginaw believed Laura was a caring person. "I just thought her ears weren't hearing what her mouth was saying. I just think you pick up the patter and the tongue goes and the ears are slower. I mean, light travels faster than sound. I just don't think she heard herself. It didn't sit well. The reason I'm mentioning it is because it helped me understand why they were so upset in the evening. I think she listens carefully when she does her work. On the other hand, when she is not listening to an individual, she just didn't pick up the vibes within the group. I think that's what happened that evening."

"That evening" was the second speech Dr. Laura was paid to give, this time for the women's division of the Jewish Federation of Greater Dallas. Three women from the federation picked Laura up in a private car at The Mansion on Turtle Creek and chauffeured her to the federation's fund-raiser at the Sheradon Hotel.

"They had worked very hard on this fund-raiser, and this was their reward," said a woman from the federation who was privy to the planning.

"Laura was in [the car] for no more than three minutes. [She] said, 'This car smells. Someone has had on perfume. I cannot ride in it.' Then she got out of the car," remembered the woman. "Then she insisted they get her a cab."

Laura reportedly went through three different cabs before she found one that passed her smell test.

Part of her contract with the federation, which served a kosher meal, was that Laura appear at a reception for large donors prior to the dinner and speech for 1,300 ticket holders. At the reception, Laura was described as "hostile" and answered questions from partygoers "only in monosyllables."

D. J. Kassanoff sat at a front table when Dr. Laura was introduced and remembered her as "thin . . . much thinner than I would have ever expected a nonanorectic person to be.

"Before she even spoke they had a little film interviewing rabbis from all different congregations and people who belonged to the congregations like Mort Myerson. The symphony hall [in Dallas] is named after him. These were big givers to the federation. They talked about what the Jewish Welfare Federation meant to them, and it showed children and the like. It was really a nice presentation.

"They gave [Dr. Laura] a nice introduction, and then one of her first comments was that there was no mention of God in this first presentation, and she said, 'The foundation of Judaism, of course, is God.' She is a recent convert. The reality is, there was no need to mention God; that was a given. This [presentation] was to raise money to support organizations," pointed out Kassanoff.

"I don't know what her message was supposed to be. I assume it was 'Why I am a Jew,' or 'Why all of you who are not Orthodox Jews are not particularly good Jews.'

"She made fun of a Reform female rabbi she went to. She said when she first wanted to convert she went to a Reform congregation to be converted. She said she walked in and told the female rabbi, who said, 'Cool. Sign here.' It took a male rabbi in a Conservative synagogue to lead her in the right path, she said. In one breath . . . through innuendo . . . she had put down both professional women and Reform Judaism. She didn't have the slightest knowledge of her audience."

And things went downhill from there.

"At first I was smiling and thinking it's okay, she can be cutesy," said Kassanoff. "I'm sitting in front. She is making eye contact with me and I will smile. Then I decided, I am not going to do this because I don't like what she's doing up there. She thinks she is being very clever and cute and she's being very offensive.

"One young woman stood up and said, 'I teach school. I teach a minority group and only thirty percent of my parents are involved and I find it very difficult. How could I get those other parents involved? I know they work and they're tired, but I need that involvement.'

"Dr. Laura's answer was 'Thirty percent are involved? Well, you're very lucky. That's more than have ever been involved in the places where I've lived,' and then she said, 'We should all live in a minority neighborhood.' She just flippantly tossed aside the question.

"And, I can't remember exactly what she said, but she talked incessantly about her son, about how proud he is to be Jewish, about how much he agrees with what she says, about how she doesn't leave him, although she left him this time.

"She talked about intimacies that, if I would have done that with my own children, they would have been angry. And if they weren't angry, I would have been angry with myself. She talked about going to [the] mikva and both of them getting undressed to be converted. She talked about her relationship with him. It was practically incestuous in my opinion, her constant reliance on her son, her constant mentioning of her son, not so much as a son figure but as an equal, like one would mention one's husband or one's significant other.

"She talked very little about her husband, although she mentioned her husband was in the process of converting, and very much about her son," said Kassanoff.

Adele Hurst, Ph.D., a Dallas psychologist who also attended the presentation that night—not as a psychologist, but to support the Jewish Federation—remembered thinking "how staged and glib she was at presenting.

"She had instant remarks and a way of deflecting, so if she didn't want to answer something, she put it back on the person. She is an entertainer," said Hurst, who believed that, judging from the applause, the audience was "half and half" with respect to Laura's presentation up until a point when she was "very rude" to a questioner. "The applause seemed to die down after that."

"I heard people were leaving in the back," added Kassanoff. "We would have gone, too, but we were in the front row.

"She didn't ask for questions and answers until the end," said Kassanoff, who remembered the last question asked.

"This woman said, 'I'm a grandmother of intermarried children. What would you say to a grandmother of intermarried children?' [Dr. Laura] responded, 'My grandmother's dead. I wouldn't say anything because my grandmother's dead.'

"And the woman said, 'No, you don't know what I am trying to say. I'm the grandmother. How do you handle—' and [Laura] interrupted and said, 'My grandmother's dead. I don't know how you'd handle it. I have no answer to you. My grandmother's dead.' That was the last question. Now that's somebody who is cracking," believed Kassanoff.

"When she cut off the final lady, and she cut her off so rudely, then she said, 'I've got to go.' And she left. They [the federation women] gave her these presents for her son as she was walking off. The person who introduced her was off the stage, standing to one side. She said, 'Oh, by the way, we have presents from Texas for your son.' Laura was no longer on the stage when they handed them to her. [Laura] left them. I don't know if she set them aside right then and there, but she didn't even take the presents they had made for her son.

"She had two men on either side of her," recalled Kassanoff, "and she whisked by my table and she left. She must have sensed she was persona non grata at the end of the talk. She was no longer smiling. She was rushing. I would say she wasn't embarrassed, but she realized she had been rejected. She sensed that rejection and was eager to get away."

Afterward, Kassanoff was "so angry" that she went home and wrote three letters that night, even though she had never before written a letter to the editor.

"Her tales of her dysfunctional childhood, her fixation on her son, and her recent conversion to Judaism came across as narcissistic musings instead of the informative anecdotes of a professional," wrote Kassanoff to *The Dallas Morning News.* "Many of us believe that she has unfortunately adopted Judaism as one would embrace a cult, not only revealing her problematic and fragile emotional state but also overlooking the obvious—that the inherent beauty of our religion lies precisely in its variety."

"She came with a chip on her shoulder," said Kassanoff. "She is a woman in the middle of finding out something about herself and not liking what she is finding. I got that definite opinion. She seemed to be in self-analysis. And anybody who talks the way she talked to others, especially her fellow women, I think that means there is something inside of her. She is not liking women.

"This woman needs help," concluded Kassanoff. "She probably needs therapy more than anybody I ever listened to."

While the buzz in Dallas was that everyone was "consistently miffed" at Laura's performance, Rose Saginaw did not find the sentiment to be universally true.

"Interestingly," revealed Saginaw, "a crowd has a mentality; if you weren't miffed, you shut up. At a dinner party the next night [March 5], of course that was the buzz. Everybody was asking, 'Were you there or were you not?' I said to a person next to me that I wasn't there, so therefore I'm not offended. I said, 'I understand how she riled so many people, but I'm not understanding why it has taken on such a life.' This woman said, 'Well, I was there and I didn't think she did anything that bad.'

"It was politically incorrect to not be offended," concluded Saginaw, who even after Laura's faux pas at the KRLD breakfast still remained a fan.

"I just loved her. She's very human. She was adorable just before she left [the breakfast]. She said, 'Okay . . . my time's up . . . I'm going shopping!' I identified with her. I can see where she is out of touch sometimes, but I was not irritated at all. I felt for her, because I think she is so smart.

"There's an old expression: 'Smart, smart, smart, smart, dumb.' All of us are smart, smart, smart, smart, dumb. And yet, when you see a celebrity, especially someone who has done what she has done, you expect only smart, smart, smart, smart, smart."

And perhaps, "smartly," the incident in Dallas would have died if it were not for another move, perceived by many as "dumb." On March 12, 1997, on her national radio program, Dr. Laura regaled her audience with what had happened to her in Dallas.

She talked about the "bad experience with the audience at the women's division of the Jewish Federation of Greater Dallas," and "the unbelievable mean lies that Marlyn Schwartz wrote in *The Dallas Morning News*."

In tears, Laura related how Schwartz's column had "gossiped" about how difficult she had been, changing hotel rooms and cars because of the odors. She justified her behavior by saying she has allergies and sinus problems.

Saying she was in a "personal and spiritual crisis" over what had happened, Laura revealed she had spent two hours on the phone with her rabbi. She said the criticism was particularly hard to take as it came from one of her "own people." (Schwartz is also Jewish.)

Then she said that in order to take away "the pain and ugliness of the experience," she was sending her $30,000 fee to charities, with the direction that it be earmarked for homes for unwed mothers.

A second Marlyn Schwartz column on the subject ran the following day. Schwartz noted that her first piece made clear that Laura was bothered by the smells. "But the point was her ungracious attitude in dealing with people about this. She was not being maligned for having allergies.

"I told one reporter," recalled Schwartz, "that if [Laura] had a spiritual crisis over sinus, she has more of a problem than I thought.

"I was not trying to make this a controversy," reiterated Schwartz.

Schwartz said she was particularly surprised when Lew Bishop, Laura's husband and manager, called her that same day and "told me everything was false in my story."

At first, Lew told her that Dr. Laura was not paid for the federation speech, though the federation verified that the fee was $30,000. Finally Lew told her that Laura had not been paid yet, and that the fee was actually $25,000, with $5,000 for the agent who booked it.

"I said, 'Why are you calling me and not your wife?'" recalled Schwartz about that call. "He put her on the phone and she started screaming at me. She yelled, 'Why are you calling me?' And I said, 'I didn't call you; your husband called me.' And she said, 'That was a mistake,' and slammed down the phone."

Thanks to Laura's on-air meltdown, the story of what happened in Dallas became fodder for the national media. Reporters by the dozens called Schwartz for her reaction.

"CNN called me at the end of [Laura's] show," recalled Schwartz, "and said, 'Are you sorry you did this?' I said, 'I don't have anything to be sorry about. I reported her behavior; I didn't commit it.' But I will tell you this, I was so mad that she was pitting a Jewish woman against a Jewish woman, I said, 'There is nothing in the Old Testament that says, Thou shalt be obnoxious.'"

The episode had other repercussions.

"Later in 1997, when her new book *[Ten Stupid Things Men Do to Mess Up Their Lives]* came out, our department [at *The Dallas Morning*

News] was going to do a piece about it. They called the publisher and they set up an interview with one of our writers. Then the publisher had to call back and apologize because Dr. Laura refused to speak to *anyone* from our newspaper. And not only did she refuse to speak to the paper, but she had been setting up these satellite things with bookstores all over the country. She canceled the satellite in Dallas. . . . I think she was afraid someone there would confront her," revealed Schwartz.

"So in this case," wrote Schwartz on March 13, 1997, in the last column she did on the subject, "the only thing I can say to Dr. Laura is what I've learned from listening to Dr. Laura:

"If you are going to dish it out, you'd better learn to take it."

It was, as Mirian Longino of *The Atlanta Journal and Constitution* dubbed it, Dr. Laura's "Publicity Week From Hell."

In retrospect, the events of that fateful week in March 1997 and the attendant national publicity only served to spawn even deeper curiosity about the woman who is Laura Schlessinger.

This book attempts to answer that question. This is the story of the evolution of Dr. Laura.

How shall a man escape from his ancestors, or draw off
from his veins the black drop which he drew from his
father's or his mother's life?

—RALPH WALDO EMERSON

(1803–1882)

The Schlessinger family had a heritage more richly developed in the
heartland of Russia than in the Sheepshead Bay neighborhood they
had come to settle in Brooklyn, New York.

It was a bloodline deeply rooted in Judaism. Their homeland was
Russia, but their life was their faith.

In mother Russia, the Jews were at the bottom of the social order.
Czar Alexander III, following the plan of a trusted adviser, attempted
to eliminate his "Jewish problem" by christening one-third, killing another third, and allowing the remainder to emigrate.

So, like thousands of other Russian Jews at the turn of the century,
the Schlessinger family was forced to relocate or die. It was a painful
transition, not just because they left in poverty, boarded overcrowded,

disease-infested ships, and landed in America where they did not know the language or understand the norms, but because of what it did to their way of life.

In their shtetl in Russia, the entire community was intimately familiar with the Bible and biblical events.

As explained by Abraham Shulman, author of *The New Country: Jewish Immigrants in America,* "the shtetl lived in close relationship with the past, in a state of waiting for the future: the coming of the Messiah."

In the shtetl, no one lived in the present. But in America, the emigrants were forced to come face-to-face with the present, and suddenly survival came first.

Landing in America was just the beginning of their struggle.

In those days, most of New York's garment workers were Jewish, making their living in the city's sweatshops and coming home to small tenement apartments in crowded neighborhoods. They worked so life could be better for their children. And, at the same time, they were surpassed by their children, who learned English more quickly, assimilated into the community more easily, and, because of that, did not always hold their parents in quite the same esteem they had come to know, and expect, in their Russian shtetl.

For a Russian Jew like Ralph Schlessinger and his bride, Dorothy Singer, religion permeated their existence. And together, they raised their sons and daughter in a household they hoped would be wedded in Jewish tradition.

In the five books of Moses that make up the written Torah (the Jewish Bible) are the general laws that, together with the oral laws codified in the year 200 of the Common Era, guided how Jews lived their daily lives.*

There were, in all, 613 commandments to live by: some just for men, some just for women, some for kings, and some for all.

---

*Because "anno domini" (A.D.) means "year of our Lord," Jews, and others who want to avoid sectarianism, often use "Common Era" (C.E.) instead.

But tradition does not always mean the same to a son as it might to his mother or father. The moment Monroe Schlessinger, then a young boy, walked out of the family Passover seder, reportedly appalled at the thought of celebrating the slaying of Egyptian babies, he started on a life path toward apostasy that would eventually lead him to forsake his family's heritage.

Monroe was an eighteen-year-old college engineering student when he joined the U.S. Army on December 9, 1942, two days after the first anniversary of the bombing of Pearl Harbor. The Holocaust was more whispers than cries in most news accounts of the day, and Monroe, who was not particularly devout despite his parents' teachings, probably joined the army less to fight the tyranny faced by his European brothers than to help his homeland, while seeing a bit of the world at the same time.

In subsequent years, Monty, as he was known to his friends, would recount with pride his tenure in the armed services.

"He was very proud of his military record," confirmed John Fernandez, who worked with Monty many years later. "And proud of being an officer."

Monty was officer material. He began life in the army as a corporal, but made first lieutenant in July 1944.

Monty told his friends that he met his future wife, Yolanda Ceccovini, during the American occupation of Italy, while he was serving in a disputed territory of Yugoslavia.

Tomorrow has never come with guarantees, especially for soldiers close to the battle lines during World War II. Monty was not thinking as much about the future as about the present when he met Yolanda—known as Lundy.

Lundy was the fiery and vivacious green-eyed daughter of a restaurateur in Gorizia, Italy, located not far from Venice. Raised above her parents' restaurant, Lundy had spent much of each day with her grandmother because her mother, Catherine, and father, Joseph, did not always have time for her.

Athletic as well as intelligent, Lundy's favorite sport then was basketball, which she played with an energy that belied her five-foot-four-inch stature. Just seventeen when her forty-five-year-old mother died of cancer, Lundy was left to help her father, who was then near sixty, and a brother who was two years younger than herself.

From the beginning, Lundy was attracted to Monty, a handsome, intelligent American officer who spoke Italian and was encamped near her town.

Shortly before the end of the war in 1945, Italian partisans killed Benito Mussolini, the Italian dictator who came to power with his Fascist government twenty years prior. Then, with the suicide of Adolf Hitler on April 30, 1945, the German army holding the Italian front surrendered, and the war, at least in Europe, ended.

Monty and Lundy married on August 18, 1946, just two months before Monty was scheduled to be shipped back to the United States for discharge. Lundy was already nearly four months pregnant.

Like many other war brides, she eventually moved in with her new husband's family. From the start, Monty's Jewish family, still living in Brooklyn, was less than taken with his new Catholic bride, regardless of her beauty.

For Dorothy Schlessinger, her son's marriage to a non-Jew was an embarrassment, a calamity. Their family life centered around Shabbat—the holy day of rest—as well as holiday traditions and rituals that helped bind the family. Lundy was clearly outside that loop. Monty's marriage undoubtedly made it more apparent to his family that their son, who had strayed from their faith in the past, was probably not going to return to his roots.

The Jewish prohibition on interfaith marriages had its origin in the Bible.

"Neither shalt thou make marriages with them; thy daughter thou shalt not give unto his son, nor his daughter shalt thou take for thy son (Deuteronomy 7:3)" is the directive followed by the Jewish faithful. It was a law that helped to hold intact the solidarity of the Jewish people, as did all the laws that had been created when Moses first brought together those brethren who believed in one God. And, over the years, the law remained to help maintain a unified Jewish population.

The Schlessinger family, particularly the female members, may have made life miserable for Lundy in hopes that she would weigh anchor and eventually free Monty to remarry within his own faith.

But if indeed Monty was forced to choose between his birth family or his bride, his bride won out.

The couple moved to 532 Flatbush Avenue in Brooklyn, and on January 16, 1947, barely two months after Monty was discharged from the army, Lundy gave birth to the couple's first child, a girl. They named her Laura C. Schlessinger.

Monty returned to school at the City College of New York and earned a bachelor's degree in civil engineering on February 1, 1948. He went to work for Anaconda Copper, transferring to Dayton, Ohio, for a year, but returning to New York in 1952. Once again, Monty settled his family in Brooklyn, not far off Avenue U.

"When I was very young and we had no money at all, my Mom would not, no matter what, stop being at home with me. She wouldn't go to work and leave me. So when I was a little bit bigger, she got a job at a tiny station, and I was right below at a little school. I'd get a hotdog and go up to my Mom's room and say 'hi.' So she never left me," Laura once told Suzanne Singer of the *Ethnic Newswatch*.

Still, growing up on Avenue U in Brooklyn, New York, in the early fifties was not a happy experience for little Laura Schlessinger.

Speaking with *People* magazine's John Griffiths, she blamed the "rejection and punishment" she received from kids she grew up with in her Brooklyn neighborhood on the fact that her mother was Catholic and her father Jewish. "She told me she would get beaten up for being one faith or another," recalled Griffiths.

At the same time, she was also being beaten up, mentally as well as physically, at home.

Laura confessed to Griffiths that when she did something her father perceived as being wrong she would get it "in spades." "She said she was afraid to open her mouth because he would scream at her and smack her," recalled Griffiths.

Laura also told Rebecca Mead of *Redbook* that her father was "real good at getting angry, but he was also good at telling me what was right and what was wrong. I think he could have cared more about the impact of his behavior, instead of feeling entitled to act because that's what he felt or thought." She went on to describe her father as "angry, critical, argumentative. He would argue you into the ground to win."

Still, Monty's moral views must have had an impact on Laura even then. She reported to *U.S. News & World Report* that, even at a young age, she responded to actions she knew to be wrong, like "racing to the principal's office in her Brooklyn grade school when she saw kids ripping pages out of library encyclopedias."

And, even though she felt the threat of religious persecution in her neighborhood, her home was not filled with any religion at all.

"My father was a Jew in name only," she told the *Ethnic Newswatch*. "I don't think he was proud. So there was no Jewish information, no Jewishness in the house. Nothing. Zero."

Laura acknowledged to a *New York Times* reporter (and repeated on ABC's *20/20*) that her parents' marriage was not happy, partly due to the fact that her father's Jewish family would not accept his Catholic wife: "Most of the family was not generous in embracing my mother," Laura told *20/20*'s Bob Brown. "So it was all of that isolation, and loss and anger and hurt."

In 1997, she told the Long Island newspaper *Newsday* exactly how awful her father's family was to her mother:

"The bigger part of my Dad's family was pretty hideous about the fact that he married outside the faith," she said. "They'd call the house and say to my mother, 'Why don't you go back to Italy, and maybe the boat goes down and you and your daughter drown.' That had to be difficult for my mother, whose parents and sister died in the war."

Although she was not quite correct about the family history, it was, nonetheless, a difficult situation.

By the mid-1950s, the flight to the suburbs had begun. Monty, who was working as an engineer for Parson Jurgens at Twenty-sixth Street and Broadway in Manhattan, moved his family, when Laura was eight years old, to a new house in a Long Island suburb: the village of Westbury.

It was 1955, and although Westbury was only about thirty miles from New York, the community was light-years removed from what the Schlessingers left behind in Brooklyn, where both Italians and Russian Jews had solid footholds. The village traced its roots to an early Quaker settler, one Henry Willis, who grazed his cattle and grew crops there during the mid-1600s. It remained essentially a Quaker farming enclave until the New York upper crust discovered the lush countryside in the late 1800s and began to construct lavish estates. With names like Morgan, Phipps, Whitney, and Winthrop, this group was more attuned to polo and horse breeding than to raising grain for human consumption. Accordingly, the economy changed; merchants in the area derived 75 percent of their income from the care and feeding of the well-to-do.

In 1927, the world focused on Westbury as Charles Lindbergh, embarking on the first solo transatlantic flight, started his engines at Roosevelt Field, just outside town. And although the crash of 1929 led to the demise of Westbury as a haunt for the rich and famous, the town continued to grow thanks to the opening of the Roosevelt Raceway in 1940.

The fact that the village sent one-fifth of its population to war in 1941 did not stem the tide of future growth. And by the mid-1950s, Westbury had redefined itself once again, this time as a thriving community of 14,000 residents, the ninth largest in Nassau County. It had become a New York suburb, a bedroom community for an increasingly affluent middle class.

Monty, Lundy, and Laura moved to 17 Oakdale Drive, a three-bedroom tri-level house, with a two-car garage on a tree-lined lane. Years later, Laura would tell Janet Wiscombe of *The Los Angeles Times Magazine* that her parents were "combative and angry," and not "Ozzie and Harriet." Yet they had moved to a community that had all the trappings of a 1950s TV show. While Monty commuted to New York City each day, Lundy dutifully played housewife, and Laura, the dutiful if not always happy third-grader, attended Drexel Elementary School.

From the beginning, there were expectations put on Laura by her family. Laura admitted as much in a February 1997 column, where she talked about being forced as a child to practice the piano one hour a day because her mother "would yell if I didn't.

"But I was persnickety about just when I'd begin practicing," Laura wrote. "It had to be on the hour, a quarter past or half past—exactly. If for any reason I wasn't sitting on the stool on time, I had to wait until the next quarter hour.

"This was my form of rebellion. It was the only way I could postpone the hated inevitable without my parents yelling at me. They actually accepted it as an odd form of self-discipline," she concluded.

Laura would later tell a number of different interviewers that she was a very serious child who worked on science experiments in her basement rather than spending a lot of time with other children.

Barbara Russell, who attended school with Laura both at Drexel and later at Westbury Junior High, remembered her smile.

"I can see her face as if she is standing in front of me," said Russell, an elementary school teacher living in Westbury. "She had a great big smile, like mostly all teeth." Yet, like many of Laura's former classmates, Russell does not remember much else about her.

"She just doesn't stand out," admitted Russell. "She must have been a lot like me back then: very shy, and a person who kind of held back."

"As far back as I can remember," Laura revealed to *The Los Angeles Times Home* magazine in 1979, "I had the distinct feeling of being out of sync with the rest of the world, just as if I had landed from another planet. While my peers were outside skipping rope and playing games, I stayed in the home where, like a hilariously precocious child, I wore an ill-fitting lab coat and crooked glasses.

"Science was my thing. My parents were tolerant of my eccentric withdrawn behavior. They called me the mad scientist and they let me use the basement to carry on all kinds of nutsy research often with milk bottles and fruit flies."

Laura once described her mother to Griffiths as "extraordinarily bright and creative," but a person who did not see her own potential. And, because of that, Laura said, her mother was full of negativity, blaming everyone except herself for her unhappiness.

Years later, Laura told *Ethnic Newswatch* that their Jewish neighbors on Long Island were "very unaccepting" of her mother because "she was a shiksa [a non-Jewish woman] and because she was gorgeous.

"I think the gorgeous was more important than that she wasn't Jewish. My mother was Sophia Loren–like. I mean a body and a face. I'm sure all the husbands were after my mother. A lot of problems came from the Jewish women. I got into fistfights because they called my mother a dirty refugee."

An old neighborhood acquaintance said that Lundy called the neighborhood they moved into "the Golden Ghetto."

Laura was ten and a half years old, and just starting the fifth grade, when Lundy gave birth on September 18, 1957, to a brown-haired girl with apple cheeks and a pretty little smile. The Schlessingers named their second daughter Cindy, and brought her home to a sister who, for better or worse, had become used to life as an only child. So in a household where, as Laura later told interviewers, she was not getting much emotional support, she now had to vie for attention with a new baby.

In a tearful episode of ABC's *20/20* in January 1996, Laura told Bob Brown that "there wasn't a lot of love in my family."

When Brown asked her what she would have said on a talk show when she was a twelve-year-old, she replied:

"I would have said—I would have said my parents are always angry and I don't feel loved. It's hard to feel loved when there's anger all the time. I think I would have said and I would have hoped for some feedback to make it all better.

"I think I always did school and stuff to be smart. That way I'd be special. And then I will be loved," she added.

At the same time, Laura said that she did not admire her parents, especially her mother.

Laura told writer Irene Lacher in 1994 that her mother was both "frustrated and angry" about her life. "But, in my opinion," said Laura, "she complained about it but didn't take any risks. And I don't admire that. . . .

"Taking on the responsibility and the job of being a mother and a wife is something to enjoy," she added, "not to use as an excuse for one's own weakness and fear of taking the risks for doing other things."

But, although theirs was not, by any account, a happy marriage, Monty and Lundy stayed together, probably as much for their children as for themselves.

In a 1997 column Laura wrote, lambasting "so-called children's advocates" for "watching how elected officials vote on issues important to children" such as preschool child care, after-school programs, safe schools, and good discipline, she lauded her parents for seeing "raising and caring for their children as their responsibility and obligation."

Blaming children's problems on parents who divorce or who place them in child care because they work, Laura concluded that such parents would "rather challenge the government to clean up their mess so they can retain their freedom to pursue fulfillment."

Something that, in retrospect, her own mother did not do.

CHAPTER
THREE

At fifteen, I remember thinking everything is always forever.

—DR. LAURA SCHLESSINGER
NOVEMBER 11, 1997

When Laura started her sophomore year at Westbury High, the school had a diverse, eclectic populace of 800 students. The campus itself was part of the former Phipps estate, deeded to the school district as a gift from the Phipps family.

Petite, brown-haired, and attractive, Laura was already heavily invested in what was then the love of her life: science.

It was, after all, the *Sputnik* era, when the United States, egged on by the success of the USSR's space program, began to push the sciences in school. And, although she did not aspire to space flight herself, Laura was aware of the early successes of U.S. space heroes like John Glenn, Alan B. Shepard, Jr., and Virgil Grissom.

At Westbury, she promptly joined the Biology Club, becoming the group's secretary-treasurer and helping to put together a science project for the North Nassau Science Teachers Congress.

Besides Biology Club, her only entry into student life was signing up for chorus, and she sang with the group of sixty-plus students at the New York State Music Fair in Port Washington, New York.

"As a little girl," Laura once revealed to *Psychology Today,* "I [felt I had] to do something meaningful. And I wouldn't talk to anybody about that because I thought it sounded odd. All the kids talked about getting a boyfriend or a car, and I kept struggling with why I was alive, what life means. Psychiatry can explain certain things, but it cannot give you answers to the questions of purpose and meaning. I kept struggling."

Ron Estroff, a fellow Biology Club member from Westbury, did not know Laura well, but recalled her as a stickler for detail.

"People kind of intersect in life," he explained, "and our intersection was that I took care of the greenhouse [for the Biology Club] and she was the treasurer.

"We lived a couple of blocks apart, and when Laura was ready to move from Westbury she called me and told me she wanted me to come to her house," said Estroff. "She gave me all the money for dues. She made sure all the records were kept. She always was a devil on detail. She said, 'Here is this,' and 'I want you to give this to this person.' And I did. She was very responsible."

At the end of Laura's sophomore year, she was uprooted from Westbury High School when the family relocated.

The problem, according to former neighbors, was Lundy.

Laura's mother, who had actually attended parties with several of the neighbors, "liked to do things her own way."

Things came to a head during the Christmas of 1961, when Lundy decorated a tree in front of the family home with lights. A predominantly Jewish enclave, some neighbors supposedly felt Lundy's act was an intentional slight. Word got back to Lundy, who, from that moment on, apparently wanted to leave Westbury.

This time the move was less than three miles away, farther east of New York, down the freeway to the Long Island village of Jericho.

Like Westbury's, Jericho's heritage was Quaker; in fact, one of the hamlet's major claims to fame was a Friends Meeting House constructed in 1788. Jericho was a farming enclave, and remained so through the early 1950s. In 1958, with the city continuing to push outward, potato farms gave way to housing developments and the community began to change.

Richard Pasqualetto's family was one of the first to move into the new neighborhood.

"I remember the change in the community," he said. "Jericho had a general store with a post office and a gas station next door when we first moved in. Then, with the housing development, they put in the shopping areas and strip malls. Jericho had some sort of history as being a way station on the Jericho Turnpike, a toll road from the colonial days. I kind of feel we moved in and made a great change to the community. We destroyed a lot of history."

The Schlessinger family's house in Jericho was a previously owned redbrick tri-level with white siding and a one-car garage. It stood on a quiet lane just two blocks from George A. Jackson Elementary School, where Laura's sister, Cindy, would start first grade. The neighborhood was saturated with teenagers who attended Jericho High School and rode the school bus together.

Remodeled from an elementary school into a high school in 1959, Jericho High School had just graduated its first senior class in 1961, yet by the fall of 1962, when Laura started, it was already bursting at the proverbial seams. Designed for 1,200 students, it had a September 1963 enrollment of a hundred more.

For a new kid on a bulging high school campus, where the middle and high school classrooms were intertwined because of space problems, it was tough to get noticed, even in a junior class of just 160 students. It was tougher still for a girl who, most of Laura's classmates recollect, did not quite fit in.

"Laura was a quiet girl," recalled Helene Spitzer, a New York travel specialist who back then was co-captain of the school's cheerleaders. "She was very shy and tended to stay to herself. Laura was all academics, and she did not have any other life in high school that I can think of other than academics."

Bob Raiber, a New York City dentist and former neighbor and classmate of Laura's, confirmed Spitzer's assessment. Although Raiber always believed that Laura wanted to fit in, it just never happened.

Each school day, Raiber would climb on the bus with Laura, most times sitting with her since they got on at the same stop.

"My first recollection was that she was always well-spoken," said Raiber, "and always very articulate."

The two would carry on long conversations that, oddly enough, did not transcend beyond the bus. Still, Raiber recalled that Laura was hurting.

"I do remember having lots of long conversations with her on the bus going home about the way kids were. My sense was that she was not welcomed by the other kids and she felt that.

"She was just not that social," continued Raiber. "Everyone went out on weekends to parties or football games and I can't remember her doing that. I can't remember her being that social with everyone else."

Arthur Kaminsky, the salutatorian (and wit) of Laura's graduating class, now a successful New York agent and attorney, recalled Laura as academically confident and socially uninvolved. "She was very smart. She was attractive. She was pretty intense, and pretty quiet. Sarcastic. Kind of hung to herself."

Kaminsky knew how hard it was coming in as the new kid. "I came in eighth grade, and I had a hard year making the transition, so I didn't have very many friends [then]. I'm a pretty social guy, pretty outgoing and extroverted, and it took me a full year to crack the scene and become part of the group and really establish friendships. That was a real effort. I remember it was very hard on me. I remember being very upset and kind of disappointed and constantly thinking of strategies to try to make friends with people. That was in eighth grade. [Laura] came in eleventh grade and it was much harder.

"A lot of people don't understand that the early 1960s were really the 1950s," said Kaminsky. "So social life consisted of going to birthday parties. People would have birthday parties and you would get invited to that week's birthday party, and that would be in somebody's finished basement in the suburbs. Social life consisted basically of make-out parties. People would kind of dance. There wasn't what you would call any real dating . . . and there certainly was very little sex. The only way you had a social life was to be part of the group.

"Basically, if you were in the group that got invited to each other's birthday parties, that was your social life," continued Kaminsky. "I think partly because [Laura] came there late and partly because she was, I think, fiercely shy, and partly because she sort of erected a bit of a barrier between herself and others, she never got into that group that I recall. I never went to her house or met her parents that I can remember.

"It was a pretty heavily Jewish community . . . about seventy-five percent Jewish, I would say," explained Kaminsky. "This group that were friends, almost all of them were Jewish. I don't think anyone sat around and said, 'Let's keep her out.' Kids are kids. Had she tried harder to get in, it probably would have been accomplished."

Kaminsky recalled two others who came to Jericho in tenth and eleventh grades and still managed to crack the inner group—both of them male. Kaminsky allowed that sports probably helped them break the barrier. "But," he added, "they kind of worked at it. There were more barriers for her, but part of it was just her own personality, and what she was willing to do and not to do."

Richard Pasqualetto, who did not remember Laura at all, did recall what it felt like being one of very few Catholic kids in a Jewish neighborhood.

"The local public schools used to close on Jewish holidays because the attendance was low. Because of my last name, I was very easily targeted as Catholic, whereas I don't think Laura's name was ethnically different. Still, I never felt there was any prejudice. Everybody got along well.

"I saw us as a community, not divided by ethnic or religious lines at all. I had Christian and Jewish friends. If there was adversity there, it surely didn't affect me."

One of the things Laura was not willing to do was concentrate too much time on her physical persona. She was pretty, but not glamorous.

"In fact, her attractiveness, I think, was very natural and very wholesome," explained Kaminsky. "It was a benefit to her, but she didn't do a lot with it, so to speak. It was almost like [she was] the Amish girl in the middle of sophisticated, suburban New York."

Raiber thought so too.

"I thought she was attractive, but she definitely did not do anything to enhance. She didn't dress stylishly." Indeed, years later, when Raiber's mother saw a picture of a now grown-up Laura, she remarked that she had not really changed.

"My mother said [Laura] kind of looked older even when she was in high school," said Raiber. "Maybe she didn't dress the way kids normally did in high school. But I think the reason people didn't ask her out was because she was sort of an outsider. And in class she might have been threatening to the other girls because she definitely was smarter than the average girl in the class."

But Laura did have two close friends from Jericho.

Donna Wolper, a potter in Quebec, Canada, was one of at least two friends who used to hang out at Laura's house in Jericho.

"I think there was a lot of resistance [to Laura] in the beginning," recalled Wolper, who readily admitted she, too, was not a member of the in clique. "A lot of people didn't like her because she was too together. She was kind and nice to me."

Terry Eagle, another of Laura's friends from that time period, remembered Laura as "very much the same then as she is now. Very aggressive. We were all children and she was the adult."

Eagle even remembered Laura handing out advice, and more. "I had a crush on a guy," explained Eagle, "and I think we stalked him that year [they were juniors], with her helping me."

According to Eagle, Laura had several parties at her house as well, "the kind where you turn off all the lights and play Johnny Mathis," said Eagle. "She was fun. She could twist your arm into doing things you didn't want to do, but certainly nothing bad. Back then we hadn't even heard of all the naughty things you could do."

Kaminsky did not remember being at any of Laura's parties, but did recall that she was comfortable with repartée.

"She and I got along well. We'd kind of shoot verbal darts at each other. I remember mostly a lot of sarcastic interchanges between herself and myself. There was a lot of that kind of thing back and forth, which I actually enjoyed.

"We had pretty much [all our classes] together. The way it was organized . . . was what they called tracking. So, if you were in the most academically gifted homeroom, then you had most classes together. . . .

"There was almost a cockiness," said Kaminsky about Laura's attitude in school. "She was very academically confident in the classroom. She was smart and she knew she was smart and she carried herself in that way.

"I think it was easy to see through that in terms of what you call social confidence. I think if she had been socially confident, so to speak, then somehow people would have been drawn to her, and that didn't happen. She was almost shy and introverted in that way and therefore a person who could even be excluded or left outside much easier. I think if she had been socially confident that would have drawn people towards her in a natural, charismatic way," he concluded.

So, instead of forming many friendships, Laura joined clubs—for example, the Physics Club. She ended up president of the eight-member group, which included five boys and one other girl.

David Martin, a physics teacher at Jericho who came in 1962, was the club's sponsor in 1963 and remembered Laura as one of a "very good group of kids," although he could not recall anything about her individually.

Miriam Reff, a popular biology teacher and class adviser at Jericho, remembered Laura as "a nice kid . . . very sweet . . . but introverted.

"I think she was trying to tell us something," believed Reff. "That class was very vocal; it was hard to get a word in edgewise."

Reff described the class as "cliquey."

"Everybody knew everybody else. They were all very self-confident," recalled Reff. "The kids were all anxious to learn. It was a different time. They were very respectful of teachers. It was a very bright class and very opinionated. The very opinionated students were Jewish . . . intellectual Jewish boys."

Reff felt the Laura she knew was not necessarily happy. "There was something there, but I couldn't put my finger on it."

But if Laura had a problem with her mother, Eagle did not recall hearing it.

"Her mother was real quiet, even though [she] was there when we were at her house. Her mother would just say, 'Hello. How are you?' She never talked to us."

In addition to her scientific side, Laura also had an early bent toward both politics and journalism. Although she did not run for a class office, she did serve as campaign manager for a classmate who was running for student body president. And, according to Lois Smith, a teacher at Jericho High School, Laura was also involved in a service organization called Blue Key.

"Blue Key was like an adjunct to the National Honor Society," explained Smith. "It was sort of for students who didn't make Honor Society—one step down. It was a service club. They would do things like help new students, do tutoring, usher at plays and concerts, and do picnics and Christmas parties at a local orphanage.

"When [Laura] was here, she was like one of all the students; she didn't just jump out. Now, as they matured and went on in life, then they really found their niche on the planet and became very special people," said Smith.

"They loved school," she said. "Jericho is a unique community. We didn't have a candy store on the corner because we don't have a corner like that, so the school became the focus of where these kids hung out. As a result, everything emanated from school."

Laura also joined the campus newspaper, *Jer-Echo,* as its assistant editor, a leadership position that she hoped to parlay into the editorship her senior year.

Lawrence Grobel, well-known as a biographer of Truman Capote and John Huston, as well as for articles for many national magazines, was on the newspaper staff with Laura.

"I was writing for the sports section," recalled Grobel, who was also busy with athletics, drama, and campus politics. "There was a day I was absent from school during the end of our junior year. That happened to be the day Mr. Heller, our school principal, called the newspaper staff into his office. Eight or ten kids were on the paper, and he asked them to vote for who would be editor the next year. The kids voted and they voted for me. I don't even know what the vote was. All I know is I got a phone call late one afternoon. One of the kids called me and said, 'You've just been elected editor of the newspaper. Nobody wanted Laura; they wanted you.'

"I did not know about this, and I say this being politically aware. Being editor of the newspaper was never one of my ambitions. Laura was the assistant editor, and she probably should have been named the editor. So I thought, 'Wow, I'm going to have to give this some thought.' . . . I called Laura, or I saw her in school, and I offered her to be associate editor with me. But Laura had stopped talking to me. Laura was angry. She was convinced that I did this behind her back. This never made sense to me, but she believed that I was absent on purpose. Since that time, I really believe that Laura has always felt that I did something to screw her out of something that was rightfully hers.

"The editorship is indicative of the fact kids weren't fully trusting of her," believed Grobel. "She deserved the place as the editor, but the others didn't want her.

"She was so angry that we lost her. The next year, we didn't hear from Laura about doing anything."

"Looking back," Laura herself told *The Los Angeles Times Home* magazine in 1979, "it seems to me I was struggling for some kind of acknowledgment or approval. I didn't feel happy, just driven toward science." And, she said, she reacted by "retreating into the seemingly rational world of science." The childhood experiments with "milk bottles and fruit flies" turned into experiments in genetics and biochemistry when she was in her teens. She even built her own lab equipment in the basement.

So, while most of her peers were worrying about who they would go with to the "Dance" and the "Bohemian Ball," two junior mixers put together by her classmates, or looking forward to the ski trip or the picnic at Belmont State Park, Laura spent much of her spare time in her own "science lab" at home.

In her senior year, Laura was still somewhat involved in journalism, now as editor of the Spanish newspaper. She left the Physics Club, instead indulging her scientific bent with a stint in the Science Research Program, which brought her to the lab at Cold Spring Harbor, and to her very first serious boyfriend.

"The only lab that our kids tended to go to was the DNA lab in Cold Spring Harbor," said Lois. "Our kids during the summer, and also during the school year, would go and rub shoulders with the big guys."

The laboratory was located off Long Island Sound, some thirty-five miles from Manhattan and about five miles from the village of Jericho. Students who wanted to work there joined the Science Research Program.

"Students weren't selected," said Smith about the early Jericho–Cold Spring Harbor partnership arrangement. "It was advertised if they wanted to go and do those kinds of things. There was no pay, but they did get the opportunity to do real, legitimate research with notable researchers."

For someone who, like Laura, had a love of science, working there was a life-altering experience.

Cold Spring Harbor Laboratory's reputation was rooted in its successful history. Established in 1890 as a summer field station where scientists and students alike were actively involved in studying

Darwin's theory of evolution, it became a year-round research facility in 1904.

Throughout the years, scientists at the lab conducted Nobel Prize–winning research that drew together the biological disciplines of biochemistry, biophysics, genetics, microbiology, and physiology.

For example, in 1952, just eleven years before Laura went to the lab, Alfred Hershey and Martha Chase conducted pioneering research in phage genetics that earned Hershey a shared Nobel Prize in 1969. And, at the same time Laura worked there, the geneticist Barbara McClintock was in residence, still researching aspects of her theory on transposable genetic elements, commonly referred to as the theory of jumping genes, which would net her a Nobel Prize in 1983.

As a bonus, Laura met Russell F. Star, the boy who would become her first love, at Cold Spring Harbor. They began dating shortly after they met.

Russell had graduated from Syosset High School on Long Island, and when he and Laura met, he was a student majoring in biology at the State University of New York at Stony Brook.

Laura "was personable," recalled his mother, Virginia Star. "She had an appealing personality."

Laura's experiences at Cold Spring Harbor, including her introduction to Russell Star, undoubtedly abetted her decision to major in biology in college and, later, to obtain her doctorate in physiology.

Back then, even her high school classmates were predicting that science would be the path Laura would soon follow. The *Imperator,* Jericho High School's yearbook, shows a serious-faced Laura, with dark hair, no jewelry, and the same black, V-necked sweater worn by many of her female classmates. And, while the descriptions of the two young women featured on the same page cite their "Dresden loveliness" and "charming ways," Laura's description is more, well, scientific:

"Heredity determines the color of her eyes, but science lights them up. . . . Her assistance is invaluable in any research lab."

Kaminsky recalled Laura signing his yearbook, adding the initial "C" in between the first and last names.

"We have the same middle initial, 'C.' She is 'C. Schlessinger,' and my initial is 'C' for Charles. She would always insist on signing her name Laura C. Schlessinger. I think it was to give herself a sense of importance, or reinforce that she was a serious person. I never used to do that, and she started teasing me about it, so I started doing it. In my yearbook, I don't remember her exact inscription but whatever it was, she added the 'C' in under her name."

She did the same in Raiber's yearbook, but unlike Kaminsky, Raiber knew the initial had more meaning to Laura, and he knew why.

"I remember asking her," said Raiber. "She said the 'C' stood for her mom's mother."

Laura Catherine Schlessinger, the half-Jewish, half–Italian Catholic girl, would forever be caught between her family's diverse heritages.

There are things in my past for which I am now
embarrassed [although they] seemed logical at the time—I
was a child of the '60s.

DR. LAURA SCHLESSINGER, QUOTED IN

THE LOS ANGELES TIMES,

SEPTEMBER 12, 1998

Graduating from Jericho High School on June 23, 1964, Laura was
elated to be moving on.

By her own admission, her high school days were not particularly
joyful. She has confessed to numerous interviewers over the years that
she was a serious kid who spent most of her time studying and achiev-
ing top grades.

Her senior year in high school had been marked by the assassination
of a president, the escalation of the Vietnam conflict, and civil rights
clashes in the streets of Harlem. Many eighteen-year-olds were already
dying in rice paddies or protesting their discontent with a world that
appeared nearsighted, if not blind, to justice.

One of her high school classmates, Jack Feirman, now a New York

attorney, recalled discussions about political matters and civil rights issues he had with Laura in the lunchroom at Jericho. "I was considered
a flaming liberal," said Feirman, "while she went more to the right."

These were just not her fights; her quarrel was within. More inner
than outer directed, Laura was an eighteen-year-old struggling to find
her own self-worth, and education still looked like the proper panacea.
As she told writer John Griffiths, securing top grades helped her over-
come "the big bugaboo of self-doubt."

After a summer spent honing her research skills at the Cold Spring
Harbor Laboratory, college beckoned, and Laura was ready. Yet, while
academically Laura remained confident in her abilities, socially she
was still vulnerable, unsure of herself. And in this, she has said, her
family certainly did not help.

She told writer Janet Wiscombe that she never considered herself
pretty. When she was about to depart for her first year of college, she
asked her handsome father, "Daddy, am I pretty?"

"'No. You aren't pretty,'" she remembered him answering. "'You
don't have the looks to make a guy turn his head twice.' I was devastated," she told Wiscombe.

Then, in what Wiscombe termed "a rare moment of introspection,"
Laura added, "I was always on a treadmill, always trying to prove
something. I'm like a panther. There's always something I have to
jump."

Initially, Laura did not jump far from her roots. She began her first
semester of college at the State University of New York (SUNY) at
Stony Brook, some forty miles northeast of Jericho.

When Laura began classes in the fall of 1964, the university's Stony
Brook campus had only been open for two years. Its seven buildings
were nestled on 480 acres of wooded land not far from Long Island
Sound.

Laura would have applied for admission in 1963, when the university served about 750 students with a faculty of 122; these figures grew
substantially with the freshman enrollment of 1964. In spite of its small
size, SUNY–Stony Brook was strong in its preparation of secondary

mathematics and science teachers, its original charge back in 1956, when the board of trustees of the State University of New York established the Long Island branch, first at Oyster Bay, then moving to Stony Brook.

Laura had a Jericho Faculty Memorial Scholarship from Jericho High School; she relied on this and a Regents Scholarship to help pay her tuition ($1,500 per year) and her room and board.

Laura lived in E-hall, the ground-level section of H-Quad, a brand-new three-story brick building that many students believed more closely resembled a prison facility than a women's dorm. Each room contained two single beds, two desks, two dressers, and two built-in closets. The common bathroom was in the middle of the hall.

But for the women living in H-Quad, most of whom were experiencing their first brush with freedom, even the lock-ins at night and the curfew were livable since boys were allowed in the rooms during prescribed times of the weekend. And, for those living on the first floor, even curfews were bendable because latecomers could crawl in through the windows.

"It was our first chance at getting out of our parents' homes and those parental values," said one woman who attended Stony Brook back then. "We were thinking we could do whatever we wanted, and we relished having all that freedom."

Laura's roommate her freshman year was Joanne Schaedel, who also had grown up on Long Island, although nearer the city. Schaedel was younger than Laura, having skipped her junior year of high school, so when she rolled in to Stony Brook in the early fall of 1964, she had just recently turned seventeen.

"I was very naive and afraid of my own shadow," claimed Schaedel about her early days at Stony Brook, "and somehow I ended up in this room with Laura. I was just in awe of her. She was so all together."

Schaedel recalled arriving at the dorm the first day after Laura was already situated.

"I don't know how she got there. I don't ever remember seeing her family. I guess it was all part of this savoir faire that she had. Here I was, I came with my parents, and they tucked me in. I never met her parents," said Schaedel. "I remember she did talk to her mom on occasion. It wasn't like she was calling home regularly. She was just so very sophisticated."

Perhaps some of what Schaedel was reading as sophistication was, in part, a way for Laura to deal with those who might shut her out before they ever had a chance to try.

So, just as Laura had had trouble fitting in with the group she really wanted at Jericho High School, she seemed poised to experience more of the same at Stony Brook. In the beginning, Schaedel said that Laura would join her and some of the other girls on the floor at meals in the dorm's cafeteria. But not for long.

"She was not the type of person who seemed to need girlfriends," believed Schaedel. "She wasn't very friendly. She just didn't want to be with the girls. Laura was on her own in the fast lane."

Other women on Laura's floor that year felt the same way.

Susan Woulfin, a high school teacher in New York who then lived diagonally across the hall from Laura, agreed with Schaedel.

"I don't think Laura had many friends who were girls," said Woulfin, who also believed that Laura was outwardly more sophisticated than the norm. "Freshmen are lost most of the time, but she always seemed to know what she was doing."

And while Laura felt ugly in her father's eyes, she seemed to more than meet her classmates' standards.

"She was very pretty and very slim," thought Woulfin, and most of her classmates concurred.

One who came to know the inner Laura a bit beyond her other floormates was Marni Elias, a pretty, peppy freshman from Parkchester in the Bronx, who had a roommate who liked to go to bed early. Sometimes Elias ended up sitting in the hallway, her back against the wall, reading a book—usually not one assigned for a class. It was during times like those that Elias sometimes got into discussions with Laura.

"I remember her talking about her parents," recalled Elias. "Her father was Jewish, her mother was not. I don't know whether she practiced any religion, but she liked her father. She did speak about this to me, and I guess I'm pretty intuitive, so I listened. She worshipped her father; she hated her mother. Her mother was supposedly very beautiful. We never really saw her parents. They never came like everybody else's parents to take everybody else out. Anyway, in her eyes, her mother was absolutely beautiful, and she [Laura's mother] flirted with and tried to steal every boyfriend that Laura ever had. It seemed to me there was a competition between Laura and her mother over the father.

"And yet, underlying this, you could see there was this real insecurity about this problem with her mother," concluded Elias, who eventually ended up professionally on the clinical side of special education. Although Elias felt no closer to Laura than her floormates did, even back then she could understand that the conflict with her parents had deep roots.

During these discussions, Laura became more real to Elias.

"She let her guard down. To imagine your mother was trying to steal your boyfriends, to be in competition with your mother for your father, to feel you were not as pretty as your mother . . . that's hard stuff.

"I don't remember her having female friends. I don't think she got along with women. She had this bad relationship with her mother. Laura just didn't know how to deal with women; she was more comfortable with men. She was flirty, because, I imagine, in her opinion, that would be how her mother reacted. I think she was doing the same thing. It was very important to her to be attractive and desired, and she was, in fact, an attractive and pretty girl."

If Laura took no comfort in being with her female classmates, she did, indeed, appear to get along well with the men.

One of the reasons Laura selected Stony Brook probably had something to do with her boyfriend, Russell F. Star, who was just beginning his senior year there, still as a biology major. Approaching six feet in height, Star towered over Laura's five feet, three inches. He was slim of build, dark of hair, and all together quite good-looking. Like Laura, he was studious, making the dean's list in two of his four years at Stony Brook. He was athletic as well. Star participated in judo and fencing, and belonged to the Ski Club.

Richard Gambrell, a classmate of Star's who was also in Judo Club, recalled Star as an all-around great guy.

"Russell was a very nice, decent guy, and extremely bright," said Gambrell, "actually a genius." Yet also a "regular guy" who would lend his TR-4 automobile to pals without even thinking about it.

Elias remembered Laura as being "madly in love with Russell."

"It was a pretty serious relationship," said Elias. "I got the impression she was going to marry him.

"On weekends, she would have Russell over, and she would tie something on the door and Joanne was barred," continued Elias. "In the beginning I think it was okay because . . . Joanne sort of went home on weekends because she had a boyfriend at home. And then Joanne would come back and the beds would be moved together and everything."

"She would bring Russell back to the room, shut the door, and put a scarf on the doorknob. That meant I was not to come in. So I would end up sitting for hours and hours in the room next door," confirmed Schaedel.

"Once my parents and my two younger brothers came up on a Sunday to visit me," continued Schaedel, who said the incident took place in October. "I don't know where I was, but I came back and they met me in the parking lot, and we went to see the room, which looked all right when I left it in the morning. But now, by afternoon, [Laura] had had company. When I got there and opened the door, she wasn't there, but she had been there during the day. I just remember that her bed was a shambles, the blankets were on the floor. It was just a mess, and I was mortified. I was so embarrassed, and my mother was like, 'Who *is* this person?'"

Finally, six months into their freshman year, Schaedel moved permanently into the room next door, leaving Laura with a single.

"Joanne was like this really easy person to get along with," recalled Elias. "Joanne was the kind to keep everybody together and to keep in contact with everybody. Joanne, of all people, would have been easy to live with.

"Laura could be sweet and friendly," continued Elias. "But you just had the feeling she was looking down on you, that she was better than everybody else."

"She was outwardly friendly . . . the kind of person who would be a great acquaintance. But people didn't warm up to her. I know I didn't, and I don't know of anyone who did," said Woulfin.

Except her professors.

Laura was especially intrigued by intelligence and confidence, characteristics more readily available in older, scholarly types like university professors than in first-year college students.

Dr. Edwin Battley, since retired but then one of Laura's freshman biology professors, remembered well his first encounter with the eighteen-year-old biology major who stopped to ask him a question as he was on his way to lunch.

"At that time the dining room for faculty was in what was called the Humanities Building," recalled Battley, "and we would all go over there to eat because there was no other place to go. I was on my way to lunch, and this very attractive young lady came up and asked me if I knew anything about tomato paste agar. She knew that in our biology class we cultured a form of fruit fly for simple experiments in genetics.

"She had apparently worked as a high school student at a private research lab in Nassau County, where she had learned to culture *Drosophila*. They had been doing experiments and she had used this particular medium for the culture of *Drosophila* and apparently it worked very well, and she wondered if I knew anything about it," explained Battley.

"Of course, since I didn't know about it, it aroused my attention, because it was not the sort of question one would normally expect from a freshman. We became good friends, but then she became good friends with everybody, simply because she is very outgoing and not afraid to approach people."

Although Battley believed that Laura was not in awe of her professors, she was respectful, and "in many ways a naturally academically inclined person."

"Often when students appear, you size them up and you can tell almost immediately whether or not they are going to be successful," he added. "I could usually tell from the first hourly exam what grade a student was going to get at the end, because of their approach. She was an A; absolutely great, right from the start."

According to many of Laura's floormates, Battley, who was not married, saw a lot of her outside the classroom and the laboratory.

"He would call, and she would go out to the Coach House to meet him," one said. "The Coach House was a local gathering place where a lot of the professors hung out and a lot of the older students."

Battley refused to comment.

According to other floormates, many of the girls in the dorm were seeing professors outside of class. On Laura's floor alone, one girl dated the dean of students, and two others were dating philosophy professors.

Over time, Laura began to drift away from Star.

"I was pretty surprised she dumped him," recalled Elias about her final split from Russell.

Star graduated from Stony Brook in 1965, and was attending medical school at the University of Pittsburgh when he was diagnosed with cancer. He died in July 1968.

"They had broken up in 1965," confirmed Russell's mother, who does not know why the romance foundered. "They just went their separate ways. Russell was unhappy about it, but he didn't go to pieces. He did like her, but she absolutely was not his only girlfriend."

As she had in high school, Laura put most of her energy into her studies.

"She was a very good student, that I remember," said Mary Bernero, a fellow biology major, now on staff at Stony Brook. "I know she always got good grades, and I know she took very good notes.

"I missed some class or a lecture and got notes from her. They were excellent . . . impeccable. You could tell she stayed awake through the whole class."

Schaedel, however, also remembered Laura as extremely competitive.

"We were both taking biology and calculus together," explained Schaedel. "Calculus at Stony Brook was very, very difficult. I remember one night sitting for three hours. She was at her desk and I was at my desk, and we were doing our calculus. We were all very studious. You had to be a good student to get into Stony Brook at that time.

"We were struggling over the homework. We both finished our calculus except for this one problem, and neither one of us could get it. We did the homework for two hours, and then the last hour the two of us just sat there at our desks trying to figure out this one problem that was just impossible. At the end of an hour I finally figured it out. I will never forget. She came over to me and, she was . . . The only word I can think of was 'vicious.' She was so bent out of shape. She was so angry that I got it and she didn't. She couldn't handle that. She was so competitive that it just killed her that I figured this problem out and she couldn't figure it out."

In addition to her classwork, Laura worked in the laboratory during her freshman year for one of her professors, Vincent Cirillo. Now retired and living in Dallas, Cirillo remembered his former student as "bright and very ambitious."

"I was a biochemistry professor," recalled Cirillo. "I had a laboratory where we used glassware . . . and undergraduates made extra money doing various things. For me, she actually washed the glassware we used during the day for experiments."

Cirillo could not remember much more about Laura personally, but he did recall that her parents came to visit the campus that year, and that she brought both of them to meet him.

"Her father was Jewish and her mother was an Italian war bride," said Cirillo, who was raised Catholic and whose wife, Lilli, is Jewish. "They came to visit the campus and she wanted her parents to meet the professor she was working for. I talked to them for just a bit. Since her mother was from Italy and my parents were from Italy and they were a mixed couple, there was a bit of a reason to talk."

It was, though, one of the few times the Schlessingers visited the campus.

According to Woulfin, Laura rarely went home on weekends her freshman year. "I just had this feeling when she would talk about her parents that they weren't close. Especially her mother," said Woulfin, who did not even know that Laura had a sister.

Schaedel concurred, remembering Laura as "pretty much always there. She was always out with someone, but, no, she didn't go home . . . I remember many weekends not being able to get in the room" because, said Schaedel, Laura had given the scarf-on-the-doorknob signal.

"I seem to remember her not even going home on vacations. I don't think she had that great a relationship with her family. I just seem to remember how odd it was, maybe it was Thanksgiving, that she stayed there and everybody else went home. She really didn't talk about her family. She really was the kind of person . . . she didn't seem to need anybody. It was like she had this chip on her shoulder. She was not an easy person to live with."

Opinionated is also how other classmates recall Laura Schlessinger. "She always had an opinion of things and what people should be doing," said one.

Bernero, however, saw Laura as "a confident person." Years later, she saw Laura's book, *Ten Stupid Things Women Do to Mess Up Their Lives,* and picked it up because she recognized the author's name.

"I also recognized the style," admitted Bernero. "She was always very forward and opinionated with her own ideas. She had her own views, and they were strong views."

Howard Posner, a fellow biology student at Stony Brook who called Laura "his friend," agreed that she had strong views.

"I can say that at Stony Brook in the sixties there was a lot of social unrest, a lot of questioning of morals. Laura was always very well-grounded. She always had a strong anchor in her principles.

"She *was* very opinionated," admitted Posner, "but with very strong moral principles. She was a very interesting person. What you hear of her on the radio is really the way she was back then.

"I remember we were in school . . . when drugs were very prevalent," explained Posner, "and she had a very strong commitment against drugs. It was a very common topic of conversation. It certainly came up, and I knew her opinion that she was very much against it."

And although Laura was doing her share of dating, it was apparent from the get-go that she was at Stony Brook to learn.

"She worked really hard," agreed Woulfin. "She was very bright and her schoolwork . . . her grades . . . were important to her."

While making the dean's list her freshman year, Laura still found time, as she had in high school, to work on the campus newspaper as a reporter and writer. Her first bylined article for *The Statesman* was coverage of a "fireside chat" with the president of the university, Dr. John S. Toll, who was also a physicist.

"She spent a lot of hours there, too, working on articles," recalled Schaedel. "She was a very busy woman."

Over the ensuing years, Laura remained on the dean's list. And by her senior year, she had been made part of the university's Food Committee, charged with "listening to the student body in reference to the food service on campus." But she was still removed from the activities of many of her peers.

At that time, Stony Brook did not have many official social groups, such as sororities or fraternities. Consequently, said Elias, "nobody was really looked down on and everybody sort of drifted to their own kind and made their own friendships." But "it was not an active, easy social life at Stony Brook because it tended to be a commuter school. You really had to make an effort to get to know people."

The sixties were the age of rock and roll, and Stony Brook played host to some of the best. The Doors played a concert date, as did Simon and Garfunkel, Judy Collins, Jefferson Airplane, the Four Tops, and even the legendary Jimi Hendrix. On weekends, most of the students would make their way to a local bar, such as the Gold Coast II in St. James, where they could dance and socialize.

"I remember taking [Laura] to a Simon and Garfunkel concert," said Posner. "We were friends; it was nothing more than that."

"She was," he added later, trying to recall women friends Laura might have had, "a little bit of a loner."

"Stony Brook had more of a small-college flavor," thought Woulfin, who recalled a closeness between the students. "We almost felt like we were experimental or something. We were the first ones to try new things. And they were very open to new things."

"We always wanted to be the Berkeley of the East," agreed Bernero. "There were a lot of students with a lot of ideas. There were rallies and political activism on campus. Even though it was small, it was a very interesting place."

Woulfin, too, recalled being involved in sit-ins, albeit primarily about local issues.

"Safety was a big concern," said Woulfin. "There was a lot of construction going on. Stony Brook was really being built at the time. They would dig up these holes all over and then not put up any lights, and people would fall in the holes."

Woulfin also recalled that Students for a Democratic Society (SDS), a national group of radicals who were responsible for disrupting the 1968 Democratic Convention in Chicago, had a small chapter on campus. The Stony Brook SDS group staged a sit-in protesting the Vietnam War.

These, again, were not arenas in which Laura would have been comfortable.

According to Woulfin, SUNY–Stony Brook got the nickname "Berkeley of the East" primarily for the drug bust in the dorm their senior year.

Laura recalled the same incident in a 1996 newspaper column:

"I remember waking up one morning to a virtual invasion of armed police officers engaged in a major drug raid on campus," Laura wrote. "It was scary and upsetting and, I felt, an insult. However, I knew the reality: There was a major drug problem on campus, mostly marijuana.

"Believe it or not, I had never seen pot and had never used it myself. I'd heard all the arguments about how it really didn't hurt you, it wasn't addictive and it heightened the enjoyment of music, partying, and sex. But I saw there were bad consequences. I saw conformity, out-of-control behavior, conduct outside my value system and a lack of direction toward the long haul of life."

"Laura was just as assertive, just as opinionated, and just as judgmental then as now," said another college classmate, who was in the same dorm, but not on the same floor. "But, looking back, she was probably developing her values. We all were developing our values. It was a very unique place, between 1964 and 1968. That was right in the middle of the whole changing movement of the sixties. People would never have gone to her for advice back then, because we didn't want to hear anybody telling us we were right or wrong. We were exploring our own selves."

And Laura was exploring as well.

CHAPTER

FIVE

Natural abilities are like natural plants, that need
pruning by study . . .

—FRANCIS BACON

(1561 1626)

Laura spent the summer of 1968 in limbo.

Graduation was June 4, and, starting in the fall, she was set to em-
bark on yet another new adventure: graduate school at Columbia University in New York City.

Meanwhile, though she was at loose ends, Laura did not want to
move back home. Her parents had moved out of Jericho the year after
she graduated from high school and into a house in Searingtown, also
on Long Island. So, Laura stayed at Stony Brook for the summer,
rooming with two women she had met her freshman year: Joanne
Schaedel and Marni Elias.

"I don't even remember how we ended up rooming with her," said
Elias. "I guess she asked, and that was fine—'If you want to live with

us, it's okay.' She lived with us, but she really didn't want to be part of us. We maybe made dinner together once or twice.

"Joanne and I shared a double room and Laura had a single. It was a suite: It had a bathroom, a living room and a kitchenette," explained Elias.

"I don't know whether Laura had anybody or not that summer, but both Joanne and I had boyfriends.

"I believe Laura had this really big inferiority complex," continued Elias. "Even then she remained on the outside and tended to put everybody else down. She didn't know how to do common courtesies in dealing with people. In terms of caring and sharing, she really remained apart."

As an example, Elias recalled a time when Laura railed against the roommates for having men in their room.

"She was acting really nasty, accusing us of doing things with [the boyfriends]," recalled Elias. "I mean, the doors were open. Nothing was going on and all four of us were in the room together. I didn't even answer her back, but we were pretty upset by her comment."

The three parted at the end of August without exchanging phone numbers or promises to keep in touch. In the months they lived together during their freshman year and the summer after graduation, neither Schaedel nor Elias could ever remember Laura asking much about either of them—their families, their lives, their hopes and dreams.

"She wanted to be a doctor," remembered Elias. "My recollection [is] that she was always interested in medicine."

"I know she always had big plans," agreed Schaedel, and Elias seconded her remarks. "She was going to do bioresearch. The rest of us, well, we were going to get our college degrees, get jobs, then get married and have babies. Not Laura. She was going to have a career. She was very intense, very focused. We were not on the same wavelength. Laura was going to be somebody."

If one year during the turbulent 1960s can be categorized as their peak, it is most assuredly 1968. The Vietcong and North Vietnamese

Tet offensive at the end of January plunged public approval of the U.S. "police action" to an all-time low. People, especially young people, were incensed at both the war and the assassination, on April 4, of Martin Luther King, Jr. There were riots in hundreds of cities across America, causing $100 million in damages and close to fifty deaths. The violence continued with the assassination of Robert Kennedy on June 5, prison riots, and the police attack on antiwar demonstrators at the Democratic National Convention in Chicago. Concurrently, there were hundreds of violent campus uprisings at colleges and universities throughout the United States.

Columbia University, where Laura earned a scholarship to study physiology after graduating cum laude with a Bachelor of Science degree from Stony Brook, was not immune. Students shut the university down in late April and early May of 1968, just months before Laura was due on campus.

In a look back at that era, Rick Hampson of the Associated Press described what happened.

"For a time it seemed revolution had come to the Ivy League. The dean was held hostage. A professor lost a decade's research when a protestor torched his files. Two students were married in an occupied building by a minister who crawled through the window.

"About 1,000 people, mostly students, barricaded themselves inside five campus buildings for a week, closing the college and drawing international attention to their opposition to racism, the Vietnam War and the status quo in general."

The generation gap, it seemed, was turning into a chasm.

Yet, even though Laura turned twenty-one in 1968, she remained virtually "gapless" in her values, never identifying with or participating in the social upheaval many of her peers were experiencing around her.

In October 1996, Laura told *The Detroit News* that by the time she arrived at Columbia she felt "very out of sync with my peers. They were into drugs and protesting. I wasn't. I was into learning my science and being a responsible citizen."

"She told me she 'worked her ass off'" at Columbia, recalled writer John Griffiths.

Indeed she did.

Graduate students in physiology, like those in many other disciplines at the university, chose advisers on the basis of their interests and the type of research their advisers were doing.

David Schachter, M.D., Laura's adviser at Columbia for her master's and doctoral programs, was working on research related to an area Laura wanted to study: the glucose transport mechanism. Specifically, Laura was interested in finding a reproducible method to more accurately measure the initial rates of sugar "influx and efflux" in the fat cells of rats as they responded to insulin.

"I know she did some work related to glucose transport in yeast during her undergraduate years," explained Schachter as to one reason why Laura was interested in this particular topic.

Laura later told Griffiths she harbored dreams of curing diabetes and cancer, and accordingly spent most of her time "pulling fat pads off rat testicles."

In 1969, Laura spent the summer studying at a research lab in Germany. Dr. Edwin Battley, who was then on sabbatical leave from Stony Brook at Cambridge University in England, recalled that the student he first met as an undergraduate stopped by to visit him on her way to the German lab.

"I'm not sure how she knew I would be in Cambridge," said Battley. "Perhaps I told her. In any event, she came to visit for a day on her way over, sightseeing around Cambridge."

In the fall of 1969, Laura returned to Columbia, and to her research.

"She did her work well," said Schachter. "She was self-starting, and a very good student. She didn't have to be urged along."

Another associate professor during Laura's time at Columbia was Raimond Emmers, Ph.D. He remembered Laura as a student who was "very determined and sure about what she wanted to do." He first met Laura when she came to discuss some thesis writing with another member of the department.

"She was a young, beautiful woman," said Emmers, "and she appeared to be very aggressive. She was very determined in what she wanted with regards to the thesis. There was no talking her out of anything."

Thereafter, Emmers said, he would see her in the lab.

"She stood out because she was so active, going around and talking to people. That's why I remember her," commented Emmers.

During this same period, Laura met another man who would have a major influence upon her life.

Michael F. Rudolph was already a dentist when he met Laura in the early 1970s. He had come to Columbia as a student to obtain a certificate in orthodontics in an intense two-year program.

His classmates back then recalled "Dr. Rudolph" as the classic "nice guy."

Much taller than Laura, with black hair already beginning to be flecked with gray and huge dark eyes, Rudolph was considered both nice-looking and talented.

"He sang and played the guitar, and was very good at it," remembered one classmate, who said that was how Rudolph was helping himself through school.

"We were from all different backgrounds," recalled Viktoria Kohler, a dentist in Indiana who back then was in the program with Rudolph. Although Kohler said the class got along well, they did not all socialize together. Kohler, one of only two female students in their group, saw Rudolph in class and in the clinic where they practiced their skills on human subjects.

"I remember he got along really well with the kids," recalled Kohler about Rudolph's work in the clinical setting. "He was a nice young guy."

Helena Burrell, a New York dentist, agreed with Kohler's assessment. "He was good people."

In 1994, Laura told a *Los Angeles Times* reporter a story about Rudolph, although she never mentioned him by name. It was the tale of a young lady strolling across the George Washington Bridge with a man she had recently met. One of her high heels caught in the bridge, which caused her to fall. Laura apparently injured her kneecap cartilage, and Rudolph came to her rescue.

According to what Laura said then, "He carried her on his shoulders. He came home at noon and put [her] on the potty. And then one night at dinner, he told her his fears. 'I'm afraid of when you get better because I don't think you'll need me.'"

Laura, who healed, said he became "more afraid, which translated into rudeness."

"He created what he most feared," Laura continued. "He was telegraphing that he needed me to be helpless."

Laura also told the same story to John Griffiths of *People,* adding that the fall on the bridge kept her in a wheelchair for a year.

"She told me that when she was in the wheelchair, the guy couldn't do enough for her," recalled Griffiths, "including feeding her, helping her in the bathtub, and hauling her to the movies.

Within a few months of meeting, Laura brought Rudolph home to meet her family, and went to meet his family as well.

"The Rudolphs were Jewish," recalled a friend, "but not particularly religious." So when Laura elected to get married in the summer of 1972, the couple said their vows in the backyard of Laura's parents' home in Searingtown before a Unitarian minister and both families.

A few days after Laura's wedding, Laura's parents left New York for Los Angeles, where her father was starting a new job.

In New York City, Rudolph and Laura shared an apartment on West 171st Street in a largely Spanish-speaking community. It was an area of the city commonly chosen by Columbia students because of its proximity to transit, and also because the rent was cheaper. For two people who were spending most of their time and funds on obtaining higher education, money was definitely a factor.

At that time, Laura's marriage seemed to some friends and colleagues as very happy. Dr. Frank Erk, a former genetics professor at Stony Brook who had Laura as one of his lab students, recalled her bringing Rudolph to his house for dinner not long after they were married.

"I only met him once," said Erk, "but at the time it seemed like a very strong relationship that would last forever. They appeared to be very loving toward one another. It was a good marriage, I would have said."

In June 1973, Rudolph obtained his certificate in orthodontics from Columbia. Although they continued to live in New York City, in early September of 1973 Laura started a job as a professor of physiology at the College of New Rochelle, located in a suburb north of Manhattan.

Founded in 1904 by the Catholic Church, until 1972 the college was a women's school with an emphasis in the arts and sciences, primarily at the undergraduate level. Even in 1973, when Laura started a four-day-a-week schedule, giving physiology lectures and monitoring her students' lab work, there were a fair number of Catholic nuns still on staff as professors.

One such sister, who asked not to be named, recalled that Laura was then known as Laura Rudolph. She was still a year away from receiving her own doctorate in physiology from Columbia, but the sister recollected that Laura came "highly recommended."

"We were a small faculty," said the sister, "so we all knew one another. I remember her as very vivacious and a wonderful teacher."

Professor Richard D. Cassetta, who taught chemistry at the College of New Rochelle, also believed Laura Rudolph was an outstanding teacher.

"She was a young faculty member in the department of biology, but we had to work together with basically the same pool of students," explained Cassetta, who said that back then the class size was about twenty-five to thirty students in the introductory classes and ten to fifteen in the advanced courses. "Her degree was in physiology, so she taught the courses in that in our biology department, plus other courses within the department.

"I think she served on the pre-med committee as well," recalled Cassetta, who described the committee as an advisory group for under-graduate students who were contemplating going into medicine, dentistry, or even veterinary medicine. "And, if she wasn't officially a member of that committee, she certainly had input to it."

On a social level, Cassetta said they and their spouses attended several events with other members of the science faculty, such as receptions or small parties at someone's home. Cassetta remembered meeting Rudolph on those occasions, but it was Laura's "bubbly enthusiasm" that stood out most in his mind.

"She was extremely energetic," recalled Cassetta. "The energy level was incredible. I never remember seeing her in a downtime. It's good to have a colleague like that."

Still, where Laura truly excelled was in the classroom.

"She really had an outstanding command of her field, plus the ability to communicate difficult subject matter in a very logical and clear manner. Students seemed to relate in a very positive manner to her. She was very dedicated to her students," related Cassetta.

Laura told Marshall Berges of *The Los Angeles Times Home* magazine in 1979 that in teaching one freshman class she was "astonished to find how little was known about biology. Some girls in class were pregnant, having abortions, picking up venereal disease. Some didn't even know anything about their menstrual cycle. They were completely in the dark about how their own bodies worked. I couldn't believe it, so I began teaching a course in sex education."

According to Cassetta, she had "very high academic standards" along with the ability to "encourage and motivate students."

Cassetta also remembered Laura as "very research oriented."

"My personal disappointment is that she did not continue on in the field. I felt that Laura had tremendous promise as a scientist. I know she is very successful in what she does, but, in a sense, I view it as a loss to the scientific community that she didn't . . . continue to work with the students both in the classroom and in the research area."

.   .   .

In 1974, Laura finished her thesis: "Effects of Insulin on 3-0 Methyl-glucose Transport in Isolated Rat Adipocytes." It was this 114-page document that earned Laura the Ph.D. behind her name. On October 23, 1974, Columbia University awarded Laura the degree of doctor of philosophy in physiology.

Following graduation, Laura presented her thesis before the Federated Societies of Biology and Medicine during their annual meeting in Atlantic City. Although thousands of scientists attend the meetings, they are able to select among many sessions, so the presentations are not in front of the entire group.

Schachter, Laura's adviser, recalled that her presentation was extremely well-done.

"She was very articulate. She presented her work well," said Schachter about Laura's debut before the federation.

In the front of Laura's dissertation manuscript, one lone sheet of acknowledgments marks the entrance to nearly five years of her life's work. There, Laura wrote:

"I would like to thank my adviser, Dr. David Schachter, for his guidance and patience throughout the course of this study. My gratitude also to Ms. Annabelle Torres for her efficient transcription of my scribbling into readable print. And finally, I thank my husband, Michael, my parents, and my friends for their support and belief in me through all things."

It would be the last public thanks she would give to her husband or her parents, the one and only known published recognition that they had supported and believed in her. Instead, both her husband, and later her parents, were about to become footnotes in Laura's future.

After teaching at the College of New Rochelle through the early summer session of 1975, Laura moved on.

Cassetta said he had no idea why Laura left, although he felt it was because she "was looking for broader horizons in the academic world. In other words, we have a baccalaureate degree here, and it's a solid degree . . . but I think she wanted the opportunity to work in a more advanced setting where she would be working with graduate-level and Ph.D. students."

According to Griffiths, her marriage faltered when Laura's husband grew "cold, punitive and critical."

Laura told Griffiths she left her husband and moved to Los Angeles to teach physiology and human sexuality at the University of Southern California (USC). She told Griffiths she finalized the divorce in 1978 (really 1977) and that the judge was "amused when he brought his parents."

Laura described her marriage to Laura Berman of *The Detroit News* as lasting two and a half years, or "twenty-six minutes in my mind."

Still, she said to Berman that, had there been children born of that relationship, she "would have made a home and been cheerful about it because that would have been my obligation."

The paperback edition of her book, *Ten Stupid Things Women Do to Mess Up Their Lives*, explained in the author notes that one of the rationales for writing the book was her own first, failed marriage. Among the reasons listed for the failed marriage were "fears of autonomy" and "issues of aloneness impacting on identity."

Although Rudolph declined to comment on his marriage or his divorce, acquaintances of the couple back then doubt that there was one critical element that resulted in the demise of the marriage.

"For whatever reason," said one former classmate, "it just didn't work out."

CHAPTER

SIX

Experience is a good teacher, but she sends in terrific bills.

—MINNA ANTRIM

(1856–1950)

The early seventies were fraught with political corruption and turmoil. First it was the resignation of Vice President Spiro T. Agnew in 1973 over charges of income tax evasion, and the resignation of President Richard M. Nixon on August 6, 1974, over the Watergate scandal. Then in 1975, after two decades of U.S. involvement in Vietnam, Saigon fell and Americans departed.

As the sixties had spawned movement toward a nation that questioned authority, challenging both political and social mores, the seventies were a time when people became even more distrustful of government. They also began to question themselves, searching for meaning in their own lives.

And they wanted to talk about it.

Ever a trendsetter, California was ripe to bring something new to the airwaves in America: intimate talk radio. And in 1969 Bill Ballance, a longtime radio announcer, then at KABC in Los Angeles, was one of the men who wanted to do it.

Ballance was an established talent who had been working in the industry since he was seventeen years old. Obtaining a degree in broadcasting from the University of Illinois, he had left school for a time during the Second World War to serve as a captain with the marines in the Pacific theater, where he fought in the Battle of the Philippines on Okinawa. Otherwise, radio was his life.

"Within months," recalled Dr. Norton Kristy, a clinical psychologist and economist originally with the Rand Corporation think tank, who was involved with Ballance from the early seventies, "it [talk radio] evolved into an invitation being extended to women to talk about their most intimate fears and hopes and issues in their lives. Bill did that. He was the first in America to do it, and, within three years, he was widely copied in America and around the world.

"It became apparent there was enormous hunger for psychological information. America, even at that point, had a hundred years of scientific psychology behind it. So in 1970, when Bill and I started doing one five-hour-a-week show together, we brought something added to intimate talk radio: We brought psychological talk radio," claimed Kristy.

By 1975, Ballance was syndicated by Dick Clark on eighty-four major radio stations across the country, with a call-in line that was always blinking.

"America was hungry . . . hungry," remembered Kristy about that time. "Those lights, every light lit up. I believe there were eighteen simultaneous calls that could be put on hold at one time.

"We took them with no screening. We had a seven-second delay so that if some kook or crank set off, we had a chance to edit it. Still, the hunger for that information was obvious.

"My notion was that we would kid and we would joke, but we would tone it way, way down when I was on because this is serious business. I started out each five-hour radio show with somewhere between ten and fifteen minutes of background. If we were going to talk about some area of human fear, sibling jealousies or whatever the topic was, I would start by saying, 'Well, Bill, psychological research tells us that . . .' And then I would do a monologue on what was known, in general terms, about that issue.

"Then when the caller called in with their particular problem, my orientation and response was, 'Well, here's what we know about that,' and then I would relate a particularly interesting study that told us this or that about the issue the individual was raising. I did not attempt to do psychoanalysis. I have never varied from it because I don't think you can significantly help somebody if you are hearing four to eight minutes of their story. You're not getting it in context, and you're not understanding their sociology, the cultural influences and what the person puts up there."

The ever-popular Ballance, who had one of the highest-rated radio programs in America at the time, seemed to get even higher ratings on those days when he was teamed with Kristy to talk about psychological issues, which did not go unnoticed by station management.

"They wanted me to come on [with Ballance] three days a week," recalled Kristy, who had recently started the Center for Counseling and Psychotherapy in Los Angeles and had a busy private practice besides, so he declined.

For six months the station brought in various mental health professionals from Kristy's center, not always with good results. Still, station management recognized that partnering could make for good radio, and they were not averse to Ballance trying out new talent on his own.

Perhaps it was fate or luck, but Ballance was ready for someone like Laura when she fortuitously made her first call to his talk-radio program in 1975.

The moment Ballance began their conversation over the telephone, he was smitten.

It was not that Ballance was unfamiliar with female callers. He had talked to thousands of them, especially during his heyday in radio as emcee of the *Feminine Forum,* first on KGBS for five hours a day, and then on KABC for a two-hour period.

"I started my show on August 7, 1970: *Bill Ballance Feminine Forum.* It ran on KGBS until May of 1974, when the station went all country music. In May of 1975 I went over to KABC. I signed a three-year contract," recalled Ballance, who, like Kristy, has an extremely precise memory, especially as to dates, events, and even conversations.

And, it was not that Ballance had not helped a woman get into broadcasting before. By his own admission, in 1972 Ballance had a hand in introducing, first to KGBS listeners and then to those on KABC, Dr. Toni Grant, a clinical psychologist who earned her doctorate at Syracuse University. Ballance brought Grant on his show as a guest each Wednesday. At that time relatively unknown, Grant would later go on to become a recognized radio talk-show psychologist, considered to be among the forerunners of the therapeutic network gaining popularity over the nation's airwaves.

It was just that Ballance liked Laura's vivacious style.

For Ballance, that summer day in 1975 began normally. The call-in topic was not dissimilar from ones he had used in the past to generate discussion about male-female relationships, such as "If your man loves you for what you are, then why is he trying to change you?"

On this particular day, the topic was "Would you rather be a widow or a divorcée?"

It obviously struck a responsive chord with Laura, who was listening from her parents' comfortable home in Encino. Newly separated from Michael Rudolph, she was looking at divorce from a firsthand perspective. On a whim, she picked up the phone and dialed.

Laura gave the fake name of Cathy to the show's producer, and suddenly found herself on air with Ballance, picking "widow" over "divorcée."

"Then you don't have to second-guess yourself whether you made the right choice in leaving. You don't feel guilt. Everybody feels sorry for you. They come over and cook for you," were some of the answers that Laura told *The Los Angeles Times* in 1994 she gave to Ballance that day.

For Ballance, though, it wasn't so much what she said as how she said it: "She was extremely smart and funny."

He kept her on for nearly twenty minutes, and asked her to leave a number with his producer. Later he called her back and asked her to lunch.

"He asked to meet me. I thought, 'What is this?' I'm a New Yorker. We're very suspicious," Laura would later tell writer Steven Cole Smith of the *Forth Worth Star-Telegram,* adding that Ballance was intrigued "by my personality and wit."

The next day, Ballance came by her parents' house to pick her up, and was even more blown away when he saw her in person: "I was impressed at her intellectually and her good looks and her effervescent personality. She had what I used to call this 'thousand-watt gull wing smile.' I thought, 'Here is a winner. If I can get this woman to take an interest in broadcasting, she would skyrocket right to the top.'"

"He came to my parents' home," Laura told Smith, "and sat across the table from me, and looked me in the eye and said, 'Someday you're going to be an international radio star.' He's in the business thirty-five years, and he's never done this, and this is not a pickup line—we're at my parents' house, for gosh sakes. The closest to radio I'd ever been was turning one on to get the weather report. I had no interest in it, no designs on it."

At lunch at Musso and Frank Grill in Hollywood, they talked, said Ballance, "about ordinary things," which included Laura's future.

"She was married at the time I met her," recalled Ballance. "I didn't know that until halfway through the first date. She said they were in the process of breaking up. There was no attempt to be secret [about it]. Apparently the guy was some sort of rimless zero and cipher compared to her. At least, that's what she said. She couldn't have any fun with him intellectually."

According to Ballance, they discussed the dramatic change of moving from New York City to Encino, California, and her new job in the science department at USC. At that time USC had just given her a summer job and Laura told him she wasn't sure exactly what she would be doing in the fall.

"I said, 'I think you should make broadcasting your career,'" recalled Ballance.

"She said, 'I've never been on the radio.' I said, 'Listen, trust me. You think fast, you have a great sense of humor, you're very resilient when it comes to any type of conversation. You can be serious for a while and then very funny,'" Ballance told her.

"And I think that was a deciding factor," concluded Ballance.

Before Ballance returned Laura to her home, he asserted that the two returned to his apartment for the beginning of what was to become a two-and-a-half-year love affair. This, despite the fact there was, by Ballance's own admission, a difference in their ages. In truth, Ballance was the same age as Laura's father. While both served in World War II, Ballance was a captain and Monty only a first lieutenant.

"Monty always kidded me about that," said Ballance, "and he would salute me."

Ballance also admitted the affair to *Vanity Fair* in 1998, again claiming that he and Laura went to bed that very first afternoon.

Laura denied to writer Leslie Bennetts that this was true, or that she ever had any sexual relationship with Ballance. This despite the fact that Ballance can produce—and has produced—not only intimate, sexually suggestive photos of the two together, but letters and mementos, lovingly signed by Laura.

"That's not true," she told Bennetts, insisting Ballance "was just mentoring me."

In early August, Ballance invited Laura to go with him to Modesto, California, for her first on-air tryout.

"I was sent to Modesto because they were one of my subscribers . . . and I took Laura along," recalled Ballance about that trip. "Her first broadcast, period, was at KTRB in Modesto.

"It was interesting up there. The manager had not told anyone, including me, that we would be working in front of this live audience. Laura was already intimidated at the idea of going on the air. We were working in the round up there—people on bleachers, you know—and there we were at this cheap, cheesy mike, taking phone calls. Her voice was very quavery. I said 'Laura, you've got to project more authority.' So the next hour she was twice as good, the third hour she was four times as good, and by the end of the show, she was really jumping right in, no quavering voice anymore.

"When I brought her back from Modesto, her dad and mom asked, 'How did she do?' and I said, 'She did terrifically.' Laura said, 'No, I didn't. I can do better.' And I said, 'Laura, you did a marvelous job, the way you picked up the pace and your voice projection was just incredible and believe me, I know that big things will happen for you if you follow through and stick to talk radio. You'll be dynamite.' And that's not retrospective wisdom. I really said it right then and there by their swimming pool," recalled Ballance.

As supportive as Ballance said he was trying to be, he also recognized that Laura was suffering from a phenomenon that affects many first-timers, even old-timers, in the radio game: mike fright.

"There are persons who don't experience mike fright a moment," explained Kristy. "Then there are others who are terrified of the mike and remain terrified to some degree through a whole career. The symptoms vary from individual to individual, but they are the result of increased anxiety."

It was Kristy, Ballance's longtime weekly sidekick, to whom he turned for help with Laura.

"The first time I met Laura . . . was on the occasion of her second appearance on the Bill Ballance radio show," recalled Kristy. "Bill asked me to come to the station to talk with Laura because she was terrified on the first show that she did with Bill. He said that she had a bad case of mike fright. He thought that my coming in a bit early and talking with her, and then being there to help take calls, would help."

Walking into the station that morning, Kristy was surprised to see what seemed like a little girl.

"She is a small woman, very slim, with a very youthful appearance and a very winsome smile," remembered Kristy.

When it came to science, specifically physiology, Laura was confident in her abilities. Radio was something new, and she was anxious to do well.

"I said, 'Let's think of [the mike] as a great tiger about to leap on you,'" recalled Kristy about the method he used to help Laura become more comfortable with the mike. "Basically, I began to kid her out of it."

As always, Laura was a quick study. According to Kristy, in less than a half-dozen on-air guest shots, Laura was comfortable with the mike.

"Because of Bill's enchantment with her as a person, he was determined to have her on the show," recalled Kristy. Unlike Dr. Toni Grant, who Ballance also brought on, and who had actively campaigned to get on radio, Laura was there, believed Kristy, "because Bill very much wanted to have her close at hand."

In addition to being interested in Laura professionally, Ballance was interested in her personally.

"They were romantically involved for a long time," confirmed Kristy.

Ballance, meanwhile, continued to help Laura develop her career. "I taught her how to talk while breathing," explained Ballance, "so you don't have to pause to take a breath, and how to pace her voice, and how to use nuances of inflection to get different meanings across. She was a very quick study.

"When I first put her on she was a little timorous. By the next time I have her on, she was more sure of herself," he said. "She's a natural elocutionist and is able to project her voice really well. She can use intonations and tone changes with incredible skill."

Ballance also suggested that Laura contact an old friend of his, Marcia Lasswell, who would become president of the American Association of Marriage and Family Therapists and was a psychology professor at USC, and begin work on obtaining the 2,000 hours of supervised counseling she would need to obtain her certificate. With the certificate, she could then give marriage and family advice on the air. While she was getting her certification, Ballance would bring Laura on his show once a week as a guest.

"I was terrible at the beginning," Laura told Smith, adding that they discussed "the medical aspects of sexuality."

"We always put on a disclaimer that she was not a member of the American Association of Family and Child Counselors, and she was not giving any counseling on the air. She was just giving suggestions based on her own life experiences," said Ballance.

Ironically, Laura had left a bad marriage in New York to start over in California, yet may have gotten a start in her new career thanks to that marriage. It is unlikely that she would have called in to Ballance's *Feminine Forum* that fateful day had the topic not touched on divorce.

Although Laura rarely spoke about her first marriage in any detail, Kristy did recall her commenting that "marriage isn't for me" and that she was "not interested in any relationship in which the guy is seeking marriage."

"I recall that she said, in very global terms, that she was 'never going to be under the thumb of a man again.' I had the sense that she felt very controlled, inhibited, and denied her dignity in her first marriage," revealed Kristy, "and that she was thrilled to be out of it."

But Laura still lacked training with regard to counseling and therapy.

So, at Ballance's request, Kristy also listened to Laura on air to make sure the information Laura was giving was fairly accurate. "To Laura's credit," said Kristy, "she began to pick up on the psychological, emotional, and other dimensions of sexuality. That is what she focused on initially.

"I thought that when she stayed close to the ideological issues, she was very good," recalled Kristy about the times he first listened to Laura. "Then, when she strayed from them, it became rather dubious for two reasons: one, of course, she wasn't trained in the area then, and secondly, I found her, fairly soon after she went on the air, expressing opinions as to behavior and behavioral issues.

"It wasn't so much that they were inappropriate opinions, but they certainly weren't based on science. And secondly, they tended to vary depending on the day or the week that she gave them.

"I remember that she was talking with a young woman for whom sexual incompatibility was the issue. When they had exhausted the physiological issues involved, she began to express and project her attitude and feelings toward men. They were very distrustful of males and there was a clear note of anger in the discussion.

"When I raised that with Laura at Bill's request, because that wasn't the first time—there were a number of such pronouncements, extrapolations from where she started the conversation with the call— Laura's response was to get mad at me. She said she had the right to her opinions and her feelings. And when I pointed out that they varied according to the day of the month or the week of the year, she didn't take it very well.

"I said, 'Laura, I don't think it's fair or appropriate for us to project our own feelings and social sexual attitudes on the caller and to assume that their experiences are similar to our experiences or that their cultural issues are the same as ours.' And she, at best, begrudgingly accepted that and at worst would become angry."

By August 24, 1975, when Laura sent Ballance a letter thanking him for making her his newest "resident sage," she was guesting on Ballance's show every Saturday afternoon from one to three P.M. In her letter, Laura labeled Ballance a "one-man TRUTH-SQUAD," even telling him that she recommended to her students that they tune in to his show.

Then, in February 1976, Ballance also launched a Sunday session at Art LaBoe's Club on Sunset Boulevard in Hollywood. Here listeners could gather from four to eight P.M., and, for $6.50 per person, watch Ballance and his resident sages discuss real-life issues in what was dubbed an "Open Consciousness-Raising Forum" for adults only.

"We did a series of shows, on stage live—Laura, Dr. Toni [Grant], Dr. Kristy, and I—every Sunday afternoon for six months," recalled Ballance, who said he was the one who first introduced Laura and Toni Grant.

"It was 1976, and I introduced them in Studio B at KABC, and Laura gave me hell," claimed Ballance. "Laura said, 'Why didn't you tell me she was so attractive and would be so well-dressed?' and I said, 'Laura, you look fine.' She said, 'Well, I would have dressed up better if you would have told me she was so well-dressed.'"

But it was not Grant whom Ballance continued to promote. It was Laura. Ballance kept her front and center, even over his other sages, at events like the Bicentennial Parade on July 4, 1976, in Los Angeles, where he rode with his arm draped around her shoulders as they both perched in the backseat of a blue Ford convertible.

Those who worked with him or saw the two together had little doubt about how Ballance felt about his newest sage: He was clearly smitten.

CHAPTER

SEVEN

The happiness of most people we know is not ruined by
great catastrophes or fatal errors, but by the repetition of
slowly destructive little things.

—LRNLSI DIMNLI

FRENCH PRIEST, LECTURER, AND AUTHOR

(1866–1954)

Laura was after a new start.

Having filed for divorce and made the move cross-country, she was ready to begin a fresh chapter in her life.

In the acknowledgments section of *Ten Stupid Things Women Do to Mess Up Their Lives,* Laura thanked Dr. Bernard Abbott, former chairman of the department of biological sciences at the University of Southern California, for coming to her rescue.

"After sending me a pleasant, 'Sorry, we don't have any permanent, full-time positions available,' [Abbott] responded with great humor to my follow-up call," wrote Laura, who added that he hired her as a "not-so-permanent, part-time" assistant professor.

To begin with, Laura taught biology and physiology. Later she also taught human sexuality, which she credited with helping her "discover my interest in psychotherapy."

As a teacher, Laura excelled.

Bill Ballance sat in on one of Laura's very first lectures at USC in the fall of 1975.

"I thought she was very good. It was a great big room . . . about three hundred people," recalled Ballance. "It was her very first lecture, and wouldn't you know it, she was horrified because she had a cold sore on her lower lip.

"She said, it will probably be the worst on the first day I do my lecture, and sure enough, it was the worst. I said, 'Why don't you, A, put a Band-Aid across it, or B, cover it with heavy-duty makeup,' and she said, 'No. I'm not ashamed to get a cold sore; everybody gets cold sores.' I thought that was pretty nervy of her," said Ballance, acknowledging that Laura later took to the lectern and ignored her minor malady.

"I think she enjoyed teaching," concluded Ballance.

The summer and fall of 1975 began as a virtual honeymoon period for Laura and Ballance.

"They had this intensely volatile, on-again, off-again, love-hate relationship," explained Dr. Norton Kristy, the psychologist who worked with them both at KABC and knew, through Ballance, the extent of their sexual involvement.

According to Kristy, it was hardly a secret at the station, other employees and on-air personalities also knew that the two were far more than just co-workers.

"It was common knowledge at the station," admitted Carol Hemingway, who at that time had her own talk-radio show on KABC.

Hemingway described Ballance's show back then as "very, very suggestive": "He talked about sex incessantly."

On the other hand, she recalled Laura as a bit of a giggler. "She used to laugh a lot," said Hemingway. "I think she had more of a girlish attitude. I can remember Laura talking about not wanting to be deadly serious. She wanted to have fun."

Ballance's assessment was similar. "She had a great sense of humor at that time," he said. "I kept that woman laughing."

Ballance later confessed to reporters from both *The Los Angeles Times Magazine* and *Vanity Fair* that he had a long-running affair with Laura.

"Actually, [they] had the quote wrong," said Ballance with regards to a reference he made to Laura in the publication. "It should have read, 'Ballance calls her Ku Klux because she is a wizard in the sheets, not a demon.'"

But during the tumultuous two and a half years that Laura and Ballance dated, he said their relationship was not always so pleasant. Ballance recalled that Laura was firm in what she wanted.

As an example, Ballance recalled how Laura would tell him where they were going for dinner.

"I said, 'Where would you like to go to dinner?' She mentioned this new little restaurant, and she said, 'And this is absolutely nonnegotiable,'" recalled Ballance, meaning that that is where they would have to go. "She said it with a chill that would nickel-plate an iceberg."

Ballance found her equally difficult to deal with on the tennis court.

"We used to play tennis together," recalled Ballance. "I remember once we were at this la-di-da hotel in Palm Springs. She would always gloat over the score. I don't think I won once. Of course, it didn't bother me because it was so hilarious. She didn't bother keeping score. No matter where we were, she would point at me and say that I never won a single game."

But, said Ballance, it wasn't he alone who suffered from her lack of sportsmanship on the courts.

"I got her into this L.A. tennis club that I was a member of," claimed Ballance. "She was a very good tennis player. I could take her in as a guest, but she said, 'Oh, Bill, I want to belong to this. I want to be a member.' Then she got into a shouting, screaming match in the ladies' locker room about something I could never find out about. I pulled more strings than a cross-eyed harp tuner to get her in . . . it cost twenty-five hundred dollars . . . but she resigned.

"She would scream things: 'How could you have missed that?' Or 'I will hold back a little bit and make the game easier for you if you want me to.' Just terrible things you just don't do, all sorts of put-downs to everybody. I remember one woman at the tennis club one time. Laura said, 'I like your outfit. I didn't know they were still making those.' Anytime she could needle . . . or make fun of others . . . she would do it. She was terribly, terribly rude."

Many others who worked with Laura, or knew her, also recalled that she was not particularly kind to those who served in any capacity.

Ray Briem, a longtime radio talent who then was working the night shift at KABC, said that although he did not know Laura well, he certainly knew of her.

"I talked to some of the people around her, and she was always rough on the staff. She was very dictatorial," said Briem. "To me . . . she was somewhat arrogant."

"She would be intensely expressive of anything that caused her displeasure," recalled Kristy. "She would shout about it. She would proclaim it. She would verbally beat on anyone . . . secretaries, technical people. That never happened with me, but it happened in my presence."

The psychologist in Kristy perceived that some of Laura's confrontations could, in fact, be a product of acculturation.

"Expressing dissatisfaction vigorously, and volatility, [are] in her culture," explained Kristy, alluding to Laura's mother's Italian heritage.

"You know, Laura came from a family where people did a lot of hollering, and that reminded me of a time in my early twenties. I took a teaching and research fellowship at the University of London, and a friend of mine who had completed his doctorate at Columbia came over just at the spring term. The two of us went to Italy. He had spent time in Italy, and his doctoral research was on some aspect of medieval culture. He spoke Italian quite well.

"We were only about an hour out of Rome and stopped at a station at a middle-sized town. It was summer and our windows were open, and just outside our window, there was a large man and a small man. The small man approached and started shouting at the big man, and they started screaming at each other. I thought there was going to be brutal violence. My friend said, 'It's okay, Kris. They're going to walk away banging each other on the back and laughing.' And that was exactly what happened."

Not everyone, however, took Laura's behavior so benignly. Once, when Laura jumped all over an eighteen-year-old who was helping produce Ballance's radio show, Ballance took her to task.

"I said afterwards, 'Laura, let's not forget whose show this is. I don't ever again want you yelling at my producers,'" recalled Ballance. "Laura said, 'They should have better judgment,' and I said, 'They don't all have Ph.D.s from Columbia.' Then I said, 'You know what Ph.D. stands for, don't you? Parrots, Horses, and Dogs.' I finally got a laugh out of her over that.

"Laura hated Kristy because I was always quoting him," said Ballance. "'I am so . . . sick of hearing about him,' she would say. 'He's not all that smart.' She loathed him; she was jealous of him.

"Laura said, with some indignation and hands on her hips—this is when we were standing out in the corridor, getting ready to go on the air at KABC—she said, 'I heard you and Kris the other day, and you gave him a whole minute and a half in his introduction, giving all his credentials. I timed it very carefully . . . in fact, it was a little over a minute and a half, and you only gave me forty-eight to fifty seconds.' This is when she was a guest on my show, before she was even qualified to be a guest!" said Ballance.

"The only thing I could think of to say was that he has impeccable credentials," continued Ballance. "He's done much more . . . he was senior adviser to the Shah of Iran and spent several years in the Middle East, he was senior analyst for the Rand Corporation. I said, 'He's lived a longer life than you, so there is more to talk about in the introduction.' She said, 'Well, I don't think it's fair.'"

Together, the couple traveled to the Grand Canyon, Hearst Castle, and Yosemite National Park. "I started out liking her a lot," revealed Ballance, "but the more I knew her . . . Well, let's just say I never saw her reveal any outcroppings of magnanimity.

"Oh, she was a great demander of things. We would be strolling through a mall or a store and she would say, 'Wouldn't I look great in that cashmere sweater?' and of course I would have to buy it for her. . . . One time, she wanted something particularly expensive, and I said, 'There will never be enough, will there, Laura?' And she said, 'No, there is never enough, never.'"

Another time, Ballance said, they were walking by a jewelry store where Laura spotted a beautiful, two-carat diamond ring.

"'I would just love to be surprised by that someday, Bill,' she told me. So I was looking around for one of those magic shops, and trying to find a three- or four-carat ring . . . the kind that squirts water. But I never did," recalled Ballance.

Laura, on the other hand, did not reciprocate when it came to great gift-giving.

"I love black licorice," confessed Ballance, who also said he gave up eating it after his doctor told him it would ruin his liver. "Anyway, for Christmas one year, my gift from Laura, beautifully wrapped, was a round pound of black licorice. It was the fanciest thing she ever gave me."

Except, perhaps, for the dictionary Laura gave him for Valentine's Day in 1976. She inscribed it with these words:

"'Happy Valentine's Day,' Ballance read, "'To My Pillow Plum-sicles'—I used to call her my little plum—'With respect, admiration and much devoted love, Your Tottle Bug, Laura.'"

"Plum" was apparently a pet name that even Laura recalled, although not in the exact same context.

Laura said on her radio show in early February 1997 that Ballance had actually given her a cat. The name of the cat, she said, was Plum.

Still, it was as her boyfriend that Ballance said he found Laura the most offensive.

"She had just plain bad manners," said Ballance, relating an incident that happened repeatedly when he dropped her off after a date at her downtown Los Angeles apartment in Bunker Hill Towers.

"I am still offended by it," recalled Ballance. "She said, 'Just pull around in front and drop me off at the front steps of the Towers.' About fifteen steps up was the doorway, a big swinging doorway. Normally, a woman would turn around and wave good night to her departing date. Not Laura, not once. Even though we had a congenial evening and hadn't quarreled once, there was no farewell wave, no adieu, no affectionate, 'Had a swell time' or anything like that. She wouldn't even look around, for godsakes.

"I had all these warning signals, but the sex was so fabulous, at the time, I guess I thought it was worth it.

"She was so rude to everybody, particularly those who could not do anything to her . . . waiters and waitresses. One time I took her to a fancy new restaurant, the top of one of the hotels. I've seen this done in movies, but I'd never had a date do this. I asked if she would like to have some champagne, and she said, 'Only Dom Pérignon.' The wine steward . . . came with the bottle and had her take a little taste the way they do. 'Oh no, no, no,' she said. 'That's sour,' she said. She made them send it back twice just to show her power. The wine steward was absolutely furious."

Others recalled, however, and Ballance himself admitted, that he often baited Laura, and sometimes not nicely.

"After a while I found her so vicious, not just to me but to everyone, that I would purposefully needle her . . . in areas she was sensitive about," claimed Ballance. "For example, she had psoriasis. We were sitting in the Musso and Frank Grill on Hollywood Boulevard one day and I said, 'You're scratching your head and a cloud of dandruff is floating over into my consommé.' Talk about gnashing your teeth; it was an actual snarl. She said, 'Don't you ever tell anyone I have psoriasis.' I said to Laura, 'If it weren't for your psoriasis you wouldn't have any character at all.'

"That got to be one of my favorite needlings, about her psoriasis. It was cruel and unusual punishment—but, I thought, well-deserved."

Although Ballance admitted he did not spend a great deal of time with Laura's parents, he did note that they, too, had a very volcanic relationship.

"It is one of those odd situations where you, personally, like both the husband and the wife, but they hate each other," recalled Ballance. "It was sort of embarrassing, when they would fight right in front of you.

"I have asked psychologists off the air repeatedly about this situation. They have said that if her parents were always squabbling and battling, then [Laura] was probably brought up as a child with the idea that this is the way human beings treated each other, particularly husbands and wives. It gets imprinted on their minds [that] that's the way life is."

Kristy also saw Laura's anger projected into her private life. "I very quickly learned that Laura was a very emotionally explosive personality, especially about her expressed feelings toward her parents."

Kristy remembered that the animosity was hard to miss. "She would side with her mother or side with her father, sometimes hate both of them.

"Laura, back in the time I knew her, was a troubled person. She was volatile."

Having met Laura's parents on several occasions, Kristy said he also had, from the beginning, a very clear impression that they were unhappy in their relationship.

"It was my impression that neither one of them felt loved, felt safety [or] security, or took any clear pleasure in the presence of the other. It was a love-hate relationship. There were periods, according to Laura, where her parents appeared to really care about each other and other times where they did not.

"When a child is born in a home devoid of love between the parents," explained Kristy, "the child has to cope. First of all, the child feels guilty. If Mommy and Daddy don't like each other, I must be bad. The child doesn't develop the emotive and expressive ways of sharing loving feelings and kind, warm feelings. Those things are largely absent in the home where parents aren't truly, warmly affectionate with one another.

"I have no ax to grind with regards to Laura. When I first met Laura, in the first several years I knew her, I thought she was basically a good kid, emotionally underdeveloped with a goodly bucket of pain with regard to her own childhood and her own feelings. I knew that she hated her sister. I knew she had powerful, ambivalent feelings toward her parents, and that she could be very hostile toward either one of them with what appeared to be, on the surface, very moderate provocations on their part.

"My own observations were that Laura had experienced a great deal of childhood insecurity and need, and that it had left her with a rather hard outer shell in which she was sardonic and humorous, and pretended to a degree of tough-minded strength that really did not go very deep.

"I got the feeling there was intense sibling rivalry. I learned from her that her parents had a divisive, stormy relationship, and that doesn't encourage us to develop a strong trust in other people. That distrust was evident right from the beginning."

Ballance, too, recalled Laura's animosity toward her sister.

"She introduced me to her sister, Cindy, as 'Here is the family beauty.' [Laura] was snarling. I can just hear that now," said Ballance.

After the introduction, Ballance said Cindy "sort of ducked her head, shyly, and her face got red."

"[Cindy] was a very sweet, highly intelligent girl," believed Ballance, who admitted he only saw her "two or three times."

He saw Cindy the last time in 1976:

"I drove Monty, Laura, and Cindy to LAX [Los Angeles International Airport]. Yolanda wasn't with us. [She had given Cindy a last hug back at the house.] Cindy was flying somewhere, I think going off to school. I never saw her again.

"I'd ask Laura about her, and she would say, 'I don't want to talk about her. I don't want to hear any more about Cindy, so don't bring her up again,' in that stern, schoolteacher voice. I wince at using the term 'sibling rivalry,' but certainly [Laura] was jealous of Cindy."

Laura continued to live with her parents for several months, however, while she began teaching at USC and, at the same time, started classes herself to obtain what is the equivalent of a master's degree in marriage, family, and child counseling (MFCC).

"In addition to the coursework," explained Kristy, who has supervised countless MFCC and psychology students as both a clinical psychologist and university professor, "she had to take two thousand hours of supervised training. That is, you have to spend two thousand hours either in research or with clients.

"I remember that Laura became warm friends with Marcia [Lasswell] and she kind of idealized Marcia while she was in the training program for her MFCC," said Kristy.

Within a year, Laura had her own show on KMPC in Los Angeles, hosting the ten A.M. to two P.M. slot.

"I don't want to take too much credit for that," said Ballance. "She was very ambitious and auditioned. But I am the one who, in effect, discovered her.

"[Having your own show] is totally different from being somebody's guest—mine—for a year. [As a guest] you're sort of in a second position. She really began to shine and glisten and glitter when she had her own show, and was totally different. She tended to defer to me when we worked together, which was a nice thing."

When Laura's divorce became final, she threw a celebration party in the recreation room at the Oakwood Manor Apartments, where she was living.

Then, after moving to California to escape her own first marriage, Laura had to face the demise of her parents' union. Monty and Lundy separated on April 19, 1977, after thirty years, eight months, and one day of married life. They had separated on another occasion, but had tried to reconcile.

"Sometime in the late seventies, when he was manager of engineering services for our Wellington and Burlington plants in Iowa, he took Yolanda back with him. They were trying to get back together, but I guess it just didn't work," said John Fernandez, a friend of Monty's.

Monty, then fifty-two, moved out of the couple's home in Tarzana, California, and into an apartment, filing for divorce on June 4, 1977.

Lundy walked away with the proceeds from the couple's five savings accounts, their stocks and bonds, a 1977 Cadillac, the 1976 income tax returns, and all the household furniture, as well as a portion of Monty's pension from Parson's, a former employer.

Monty, on the other hand, retained his pension from Borax, $1,047 from the Parson's pension, and the proceeds of a settlement with another former employer.

Their divorce was final on August 17, 1977. The next day would have been their thirty-first anniversary. Laura was thirty and Cindy was just nineteen.

In a syndicated newspaper column Laura wrote in July 1997, she revealed to her readers how her parents' unhappy marriage and subsequent divorce affected the family.

"I did not grow up in a happy, healthy home. While it is not morally correct for me to gossip about family members," wrote Laura, "I can say that there was little love, affection and bonding shown in our home.

"When my sister and I became adults," she continued, "our different styles of coping with those familial challenges resulted in our having little in common. After our parents divorced, the stresses worsened to the point where all four of us evolved into completely isolated entities."

But the isolation was not just from her family; she was icing Ballance out as well.

"Finally, I was losing pride and self-esteem so much, almost to the point of dreading every encounter with her on dates and dreading the fighting," claimed Ballance.

"I actually was the one who began to phase myself out of the relationship. I knew that she and Lew were having at it. I could tell the way they looked at each other, their body language and everything," maintained Ballance, who said he and Laura finally split in 1977. "[The breakup] was through mutual agreement. We didn't actually have a screaming breakup; it sort of deteriorated and that was that."

Once again, Laura was ready to start anew.

Laura C. Schlessinger at seventeen years old.

Laura C. Schlessinger at twenty-one years old.

Russell F. Star, Laura's first love, at twenty-one years old.

Laura and Lew Bishop
prior to a tennis match, 1979.
(PHOTO CREDIT: ROB LEWINE)

Lew Bishop, Laura, and their son, Deryk,
stand in the tub of their newly remodeled house
in Woodland Hills, 1994.
(PHOTO CREDIT: MARK SENNET)

Proudly displaying a sweater she both designed and knitted,
Laura stands in front of one of her knitting machines in 1994.

(PHOTO CREDIT: MARK SENNET)

The Schlessinger family home in Westbury, N.Y.
This is where Laura spent her childhood.
(PHOTO CREDIT: VICKIE L. BANE)

Where Laura grew up in Jericho, NY.
(PHOTO CREDIT: VICKIE L. BANE)

Jericho High School, Jericho, NY. Laura graduated in 1964.

The Woodland Hills home where Laura and Lew were married in 1984.

The Schlessinger family: 1975–76 (clockwise: Laura, Lundy, Cindy, and Monty).
(PHOTO CREDIT: BILL BALLANCE)

From right to left: Bill Ballance, Dr. Laura Schlessinger, Dr. Norton Kristy, Dr. Toni Grant.
(PHOTO CREDIT: DR. NORTON KRISTY)

CHAPTER

EIGHT

If someone is in a relationship, you leave them alone.
Don't interfere with relationships.

—DR. LAURA SCHLESSINGER

FEBRUARY 10, 1998

When Laura first met Lewis G. Bishop in the fall of 1975, he was like her, teaching at USC, and, also like her, he was married. The big difference, however, was that Lew had three children, who back then were nineteen, seventeen, and thirteen years of age.

Laura told *People*'s John Griffiths that she liked both Lew's brain and his "sexy shoulders." Lew, on the other hand, confessed to Griffiths that, as hokey as it might sound, he was attracted to Laura's mind and her energy.

"He said he was initially put off by Laura's sense of humor," recalled Griffiths. "He said that he was a straitlaced type who gave scholarly lectures, while she cracked jokes about kidneys."

Laura and Lew, who was an associate professor of biology to her assistant professor of physiology, had adjacent lab rooms, separated by glass.

"The first time I met him, he was dissecting a fly," recalled Bill Ballance, who was dating Laura at the time and recalled that she introduced them in 1976 in Lew's USC lab.

Lew and Laura shared a love of science. And once Laura arrived on the scene, Lew took up tennis, although colleagues said they don't remember him ever having played the game before. They socialized in groups as well, with Lew even attending the "divorce party" that Laura threw at her apartment complex in early 1977. Laura was there with Ballance as her date, and Lew was with his wife, Jeanne.

Both professionally and personally, Lew was well-liked by almost everyone.

Born in April 1933, Lew was raised, along with his younger brother, in Massachusetts. Their father was an executive with an insurance company in Boston, but Lew was not interested in business back then. Lew liked science.

He did his undergraduate work at Brown University, earning a degree in physics on June 6, 1955, the same year that Laura Schlessinger graduated from the third grade.

Lew met his first wife-to-be, Jeanne, while she was employed as a secretary in the same insurance company as his father. A friend described Jeanne as "bright, pretty, and a fun person to be with."

The couple married on September 1, 1955, in Dedham, Massachusetts, and shortly thereafter moved to Troy, New York, where Lew went to work for General Electric.

Their first child, Diane, was born in October 1956, while Lew was working toward his master's degree in physics from Rensselaer Polytechnic Institute.

Stephen, their second child, was born two years later, in March 1958. Jeanne and Lew moved to southern California that same year so that Lew could work on his doctorate at the University of California at Los Angeles.

David, their third and last child, was born in January 1962, while Lew was still doing research for his thesis. In June 1964, Lew finished his thesis, entitled "Physical and Biochemical Studies on Temperature Adapted Amphibians," and obtained his doctorate in zoology.

The family lived in a comfortable house in Fullerton, where Jeanne worked part-time as an admissions clerk for the local Cal State campus. Lew got a job as an associate professor in the biology department at the University of Southern California.

It was, by all accounts, both a happy and a liberal household.

"Jeanne," said a family friend, "even worked on the McGovern for President campaign in 1972, and Lew helped."

Another close friend of the family who knew the couple during the Fullerton days recalled, "I thought Lew and Jeanne had a very happy marriage."

Happy, that is, until Laura Schlessinger stepped into the picture.

Laura told *Vanity Fair* in a 1998 interview that she started dating Lew while he was separated from Jeanne.

"I do know that Lew was married at the time he and Laura got together," claimed Bill Ballance, Laura's mentor in talk radio, who also dated her. When Laura's relationship with Ballance ended, she "peeled off into the arms of Lew," as Ballance put it.

Ballance also told *Vanity Fair* that Laura "always used to complain about how [she and Lew] had to sneak around."

Other colleagues from USC, who wished to remain unnamed, recalled the same thing.

"Laura chased after him," affirmed one colleague. "They used to play tennis together. Some men are like putty. You know how strong she is? Lew didn't stand a chance."

Still, said a close friend of the Bishops from their Fullerton days, Jeanne hoped they could keep their marriage together. At the end of 1977, the Bishops left for Europe, where Lew was to attend a conference paid for by the university. They were gone approximately six weeks, and, by all accounts, had a great time together.

"I thought it would save their marriage," said the friend, "but it didn't. Someone called Lew on the night they returned to report that Laura was not feeling well, and Lew rushed to see her."

"Lew was obsessed with Laura," said a friend who knew them both very well. "I believe it was Jeanne who finally asked him to leave, because she realized things were not going to change."

Jeanne and Lew Bishop officially separated on January 18, 1978, twenty-two years, four months, and fourteen days after their marriage began. In April 1978, Jeanne petitioned to officially dissolve their union.

Since California is a no-fault state, the reason for the divorce did not have to appear in court papers, but two sources, both extremely close to the family, confirmed that Bishop's involvement with Laura was what precipitated the filing.

"Let's just put it this way," said one of these sources. "That relationship [between Lew and Laura] was pretty much what the divorce was about."

Lew moved directly from his house in Fullerton, where Jeanne lived with their then sixteen-year-old son, David, into Laura's high-rise apartment in Bunker Hill Towers near downtown Los Angeles.

In a 1979 interview with *The Los Angeles Times Home* magazine, Laura even went so far as to describe Lew as "her companion." The two were pictured together riding bikes and walking arm-in-arm. That article ran nearly two weeks before Lew's divorce from Jeanne was final.

Rob Lewine, who photographed Laura for the piece, remembered her as "a pain in the ass."

"She was troubled and overemotional," he said. "And she threw a tantrum, not directed at me."

Lewine confessed that, after having been in thousands of people's living rooms over his twenty-year career, what he remembers is what's most distinctive, "for better or for worse."

"For example, I photographed Jimmy Stewart years ago and I came away overwhelmed by a sense of the man's decency and his kindness.

He was an extraordinary gentleman. What I came away with from Laura Schlessinger was her tantrum," explained Lewine.

"In those days you would get a direction from the people at the magazine. They would say, 'We want some of this and some of that.' 'Some of that' included some shots of her on the tennis court. She lived with whomever she lived with at the time [it was Lew Bishop] in some complex downtown on Bunker Hill, so there were communal tennis courts. We went down to photograph her on the tennis courts, having put [in] some time in the apartment, only to find that the tennis courts were occupied.

"At which point, Laura said to whomever was on the courts, 'I'm here with a photographer for *L.A. Home* magazine and we need to take some pictures.' To which they said, 'Well, fine. We'll finish our game and you can have the courts.' And then Laura said, 'You don't understand. I'm here with the photographer right now.' And they said again, 'Well, fine. We'll finish our game and you can have the courts.' She said, 'No, no, *no,* you don't understand, I'm here with the photographer right now.' And they said, 'You don't understand, we're playing a game.'

"And here's where she started to lose it. She said, 'This is outrageous.' She said, 'This is a very important situation for me, and I need to have the tennis courts.' They said, 'Well, the game is an important situation for us, and we've got the tennis courts.'

"And she started ranting and raving in such a fashion that I was embarrassed. I was well aware this was a [therapist] I was dealing with, and I felt she should be patient."

According to Lewine, the people finished their game and then gave up the court.

"It was an outrageous request," continued Lewine. "I was not asking for the tennis court. I was willing to wait; that is part of what I'm paid to do. Anybody with a reasonable amount of integration and maturity could have solved that for themselves.

"Now, to her credit," added Lewine, "later she kind of came to her senses ... and said something like 'I shouldn't do this. . . . I should know better.' She recognized it, and she said, 'This is so embarrassing, and I've made a fool of myself' and all that.

"And I thought that was even funnier; presumably you know that [from her therapy training] from the beginning, and you don't fly off the handle like that," said Lewine. "I'm not saying she's a bad person, but she was certainly neurotic and out of control.

"She was perfectly cordial over the rest of the experience, but it spoke a certain naiveté on top of everything else, because I represented the media," concluded Lewine. "Whereas I was not a reporter, it still registered an impression with me that was not real impressive."

Although reporters have repeatedly asked Lew Bishop to talk about his divorce, he has always refused. Laura, however, told *Redbook* in 1997 that Bishop's children were thirty, twenty-eight, and eighteen when she "got together" with their father, although she did not specify what she meant by "got together." In reality, the Bishop children were twenty-two, twenty, and sixteen when Lew and Laura moved in together.

In an interview with the *Toronto Sun,* Laura was asked about some of her basic beliefs, and her first answer had to do with commitment.

"People don't understand that a commitment is actually a promise," Laura said. "Marriages are broken up too often for not very good reasons. There are only a few very good reasons for getting a divorce. I call them the three 'A's: Addictions that are out of control and the other person refuses to do anything about it; affairs that continue and undermine the vows and the family; and abuse."

She continued by saying: "On the other hand, the reasons that do not justify a divorce are when people feel or say, 'I don't feel in love anymore.' Or 'I'm not happy.' These people want constant stimulation of something new in their lives: They really don't appreciate how much they are being destructive to their kids."

Laura, too, has refused to address Lew's divorce, although she has admitted to past behaviors she is not proud of, without ever acknowledging exactly what they were.

"I admit to past behaviors about which I now have regret and shame," Laura wrote in her June 1997 syndicated newspaper column.

"One important reason for my current perspective is that as an adult, I moved from following subjective morality to embracing an absolute: the Ten Commandments and Jewish law. While I am not, nor can I ever be, perfect about it, I work at it all the time."

But back in 1978, it was Jeanne Bishop who was doing most of the work.

Jeanne was awarded custody of the youngest of the couple's three children, David A. Bishop, who was sixteen years old at the time.

According to the divorce papers, she also received half of the net proceeds from the sale of their house in Fullerton, half the household furniture and furnishings, a 1970 Chevelle, fourteen shares of General Electric stock, half of one savings account and all of another, a life insurance policy on Lew, and most importantly, "her community interest in his pension and retirement plan at the University of Southern California as of the date of separation."

In addition, Jeanne was granted all attorney's fees, $150 per month in child support for David, and $200 per month in spousal support "until death, remarriage, or until further order of the court." The divorce decree was finalized on July 24, 1979.

On August 3, 1979, Laura and Lew purchased a house together at 126 North Irving Boulevard in Los Angeles. The grant deed, which is an official county record, listed an equal, fifty-fifty interest in the property belonging to "Lewis G. Bishop, an unmarried man . . . and Laura C. Schlessinger, an unmarried woman."

While Jeanne was laboring through her divorce, Laura was continuing her postdoctoral work at USC Human Relations Center, obtaining her certificate in marriage, family, and child counseling on January 11, 1980.

There was, however, fallout from Laura and Lew's relationship at USC. Although officials cannot and will not discuss personnel issues, colleagues who were there at the time have confirmed that Laura was not fired, just not rehired to teach in the biology department. Lew, who already had tenure, retired at about the same time.

Once Laura got her MFCC license, she set up shop as a family therapist. And from the beginning, she advertised herself as "Dr. Laura C. Schlessinger, MFCC, and Associates." Laura's listing appeared in the Los Angeles central telephone book in 1981–82.

Yet, in 1996, when she appeared on CNN, she told anchor Miles O'Brien that she was "very clear on my books and when anybody asks me, you know, to give any information about that, the Ph.D. is in physiology. I have a medical science background. I have a postdoctoral certification in marriage/family. That's where the psychology comes in."

Meanwhile, back in the early eighties, Lew and Jeanne were busy addressing new problems.

In 1980, their oldest child, Diane, was in a horrific automobile accident and lay in a coma for four days. Diane would spend the next six weeks in the hospital. According to two close friends of the family, Jeanne was with her daughter every day. Lew came to the hospital after the accident, with Laura. It was obviously a tense time, and painful for Jeanne on many fronts. In the ensuing weeks of hospitalization, Lew regularly came to visit, although less and less frequently with Laura.

Then, in October of 1981, Jeanne Bishop was back in court, attempting to get her half of Lew's pension, as stipulated by court order in the divorce agreement. In the decree, Jeanne was to have received half the pension at the time Lew retired and started drawing from it.

"It has come to my attention that my husband commenced drawing on his pension on or about August 1, 1980," Jeanne wrote in her declaration to the court. "To date, he has paid me ZERO dollars as my community share in said pension and I am asking for an order from this court directing the 'PLAN' to pay me directly my fifty percent (50%) interest in said distribution.

"At the time my husband and I agreed to the Dissolution, we had agreed that we would be co-tenants in the family residence and that I would remain there for a period of years," continued Jeanne, adding that no provision had been made for who would pay for major repairs.

In addition to her share of the pension, she asked the court to rule that Lew should pay a 50 percent share of the repairs.

Besides not legally informing his former wife when he had retired, Lew was behind on his spousal support payments. From July 1, 1981, through October 1981, when Jeanne petitioned the court, Lew had paid her only $200 of the $800 owed. He was held in contempt of court for violating their divorce decree, and the judge issued a bench warrant. Bail was set at $500, and Lew was scheduled to appear in the Superior Court of the State of California to address the charges.

It was just the sort of behavior Laura would deplore on her radio show and in her writings in years to come.

For example, in her 1996 book, *How Could You Do That?*, Laura wrote about "the Abdication of Character, Courage, and Conscience":

"You see," she wrote, "character really is what you are when no one else is looking."

"Obviously," she wrote later in that same book, "any contract is only as good as the 'goodness' of the people who enter into it, be it marriage or issues of custody and visitation. Courts can dictate, mandate, and hold in contempt. But if the individuals in question have no integrity, and value licking wounds through revenge, they'll even find a way around a legal order to do what they want."

In today's world, Laura wrote, "the choice others make in their behaviors is not within your control. However, the people you choose to befriend and the behaviors you choose to tolerate are a measure and reflection of you and of your character."

In May 1982, the contempt charges against Lew were dismissed after he agreed to pay Jeanne half the monies he received from his USC pension plan since his official retirement started in August of 1980, his delinquent spousal support, and his share of attorney's fees.

Jeanne, on the other hand, agreed to list the Fullerton house for sale no later than June 1983.

.   .   .

In October 1984, Laura and Lew married in the backyard of the home they bought together on Sylvan Street in Woodland Hills. Even though they attended the wedding, Lew's three children from his first marriage were not a significant part of his new family.

In a 1997 America Online interview with Dr. Laura, one questioner asked:

"I have heard you say once that you have step kids? Why did I hear that only once and why do you not talk about them? I have 3 and am very proud to say I have 3 step kids [*sic*]."

Dr. Laura's answer was, as usual, blunt.

"They aren't kids," she responded. "The youngest of the three is 35. They live far away, and though relationships are friendly, they are not present in my everyday life."

"Far away" was, in reality, farther south in Los Angeles for Stephen and David, and Colorado for Diane. In past years, Lew has visited his children and six grandchildren, one of whom is the same age as Deryk, at least at Christmastime, usually taking Deryk with him.

Obviously Laura had not bonded to any meaningful extent with Lew's children. The glue in her life was Lew, and in the months and years ahead she would lean on him more and more and more.

The tragedy is not that things are broken. The tragedy is
that they are not mended again.

—ALAN PATON

(1903–1988)

Laura now had the man she wanted in her life, but it seemed to others
the prosperous career she really coveted was elusive still.

Carol Hemingway, who first met Laura back when she got her start
on Bill Ballance's *Feminine Forum,* and who followed her career path
over the years, described Laura as nothing less than tenacious.

"She is, I would say, one of the most persistent workers to get to
where she wants to go," said Hemingway, who once had her own talk
show on KABC in Los Angeles dealing with women's issues. "She put
a lot of time in the trenches. This is not a woman who started out [on
radio] successful. She was on a roller-coaster ride for years—she got
fired from several stations—but she always stuck with it. I really admire her for that. She was clearly determined and persistent."

That same tenacity enabled Laura to move on with her teaching career as well. Even though Laura was no longer an assistant professor of physiology at USC, she elected to branch out to a neighboring university, this time using her credentials in marriage, family, and child counseling.

Laura's first contact at Pepperdine University was L. James Hedstrom, a professor of psychology who rose to head the department before retiring after the winter semester in 1997. Hedstrom, who had started as a student at Pepperdine in 1948, taught there for forty-two years and helped establish the doctoral program in psychology.

Hedstrom hired Laura in January 1982 to teach "Fundamentals in Counseling and Abnormal Psychology" at the Encino campus in the San Fernando Valley—far from the beautiful main campus, which lies among the hills of Malibu, overlooking the Pacific Ocean.

Because the Pepperdine University master's program in clinical psychology and counseling was made up of students who worked during the day, most classes were held in the evenings or on weekends. Pepperdine also utilized a good number of adjunct professors, teachers who do not have regular faculty status and are not on a tenure track.

"We liked to have people working professionally in the field come in and teach their specialty," explained Hedstrom. "Usually [adjuncts] don't get paid a good deal. It was not really a lucrative thing, so I would do my best to make it a positive experience for [them] because they were really making a contribution to our program."

Hedstrom recalled with clarity Laura's job interview in late 1981, primarily because of one unusual feature: She came with Lew.

"I still remember it. She showed up with her husband. I must admit that was rather unusual," recalled Hedstrom. "In fact, I can't remember [another] time an adjunct prospect showed up with their spouse, but I had no objection."

Hedstrom, of course, assumed it was Laura's husband, although in fact, the two were involved but not yet married.

"She was a very articulate, I would almost say charismatic person. I liked her vivacity," recalled Hedstrom about the interview with Laura.

"We are looking for good teachers, people who not only know their stuff but who can transmit it in a palatable fashion to the students, and she just seemed to be a lively, vivacious, intelligent, dynamic type of person who could do that."

She also came with what Hedstrom termed "a rich background," with teaching experience and licenses in both MFCC and sex therapy. Laura's private practice was thriving, and she was continuing to do her local talk-radio show. But just how much she enjoyed that private practice is a matter of debate.

"I think it was fairly important to her during the years she was try-ing hard to make it on radio," said Dr. Norton Kristy, the clinical psy-chologist and economist who knew Laura from when she first got her start on radio. "She was on small stations and on at odd hours, so she had to make a living somewhere."

Still, Kristy was not sure working with patients in a practice was something Laura truly enjoyed.

"It's hard work to speed the growth, change, or maturation of a pa-tient or client," said Kristy, allowing that it can take "years and years" to make a difference.

While Laura had moved away from USC, she had also moved away from her former mentor, Marcia Lasswell.

"I'm not sure exactly why," said Kristy, "except that one day Marcia, to her astonishment, found herself cut. She was persona non grata in the life of her former student and young friend. You'll find Marcia very discreet. Marcia said, in my presence, that she was not going to . . . say anything about the dramatic change in their relationship, but Marcia was very hurt. Marcia was not only Laura's professor but supervised her two thousand hours of clinical work."

According to what Bill Ballance told *Biography* magazine in 1997, there was a party given for Laura and Lasswell supposedly came with-out a gift, and "the guest of honor exploded, chewing out her mentor on the spot."

Ballance and Kristy both confirmed that this was true.

"I don't think she had many women friends," said Kristy of Laura when he knew her in the mid-seventies. "She is an exceedingly volatile person who projects onto her friendships with women the painful business that she had with her sister and the painful business she had with her mother growing up. I don't think that Laura fundamentally likes women. When I knew her, she directed much more of her emotional attention toward men, and very much sought the company and approval of men."

One of the woman friends Laura did have was Donna Wolper, who went through high school with her in Jericho. After graduation in 1964, Wolper said the two did not talk until their tenth class reunion, in 1974. (Laura attended with her then husband, Michael Rudolph.)

A few years later, however, Wolper was breaking up with her husband, and flew to California to visit a cousin. While she was in town, she got in touch with Laura.

"She took me and my two young children out to lunch," remembered Wolper. "She was very helpful and compassionate. She gave me advice and told me how to handle things. I do remember her parting words were, if there is anything she could do to ever help me, just let her know.

"I think she has a very compassionate heart," concluded Wolper.

When Wolper met Laura for lunch, Wolper remembered Laura was off the air, but looking for a new show.

"It was before her son was born. She was practicing. She was at her office. She had had a program, but she was off the air then, and was trying to put together another package. Somebody had approached her and they were trying to put something together. Actually, I think it was for television."

In the meantime, each Thursday evening Laura would rush from her private practice office on North Highland Avenue to Encino, where she taught a two-hour, weekly graduate-level course, "The Foundations of Psychology."

From the start, Laura was a popular professor. Granted, most students took courses in sequential order and therefore selected their classes and times before they selected their professor. Still, Hedstrom remembered that Laura got good evaluations from her students.

He was especially impressed that, unlike some adjuncts, Laura spent out-of-class time with students, sometimes even bringing them to her private practice office for visits. Even then her Los Angeles radio programs, while she had them, had given her some added notoriety.

Cheryl Saunders, at the time a graduate student in psychology, knew the radio show, and asked Laura to be the featured speaker at a banquet held by Psi Chi (a national honor society in psychology) in the mid-eighties. Laura spoke for free.

"She had a good sense of humor," recalled Saunders. "She didn't have a planned speech. We distributed little cards to the audience members and they could write down questions. She just answered questions off the cuff. I remember it was a lot of fun and that she had a lot of funny things to say about the profession and what she had done."

Radio also helped contribute to the client base for her private practice.

"When she had her radio show, she had a thriving business," noted one source who asked not to be named, "but when she didn't have her radio show, things were tougher. She had to get smaller office space to cut down on the overhead."

Interestingly enough, at the same time Laura was teaching at Pepperdine, her sister, Cindy, was attending as a student in the master's program, though at a different campus. Cindy graduated from Pepperdine in August 1983, earning a master's degree in psychology. Like her sister, she also applied for her marriage, family, and child counseling license.

By this time, however, Laura and Cindy had drifted apart—so far that most people did not realize Laura even had a sister. Although Cindy elected not to be interviewed for this book, Laura has told interviewers that their family relationship more or less started to dissolve when their parents divorced in 1977. Cindy eventually moved to the San Francisco area with her husband, Brad Harris, and their two children.

In truth, Laura and Cindy spent little time together growing up. With more than a ten-year age difference, they shared little in common. By the time Cindy was entering elementary school and playing with Barbie dolls, for example, Laura was nearly finished with high school and looking for a real-life Ken. Then, by the time Cindy was getting into high school, Laura was nearly 3,000 miles away, married, and in graduate school, doing research for her doctorate. Even though Laura was not pursuing a relationship with her sister, she never stopped pursuing her career.

In the early 1980s Laura had begun soliciting guest appearances on a number of television programs, including *AM Los Angeles, Mid-Morning LA, The John Davidson Show,* and *The Merv Griffin Show.* She was also the resident therapist on *Alive and Well,* a program on USA Cable.

Then, in September of 1983, Laura took a one-year spot on the nationally syndicated program *Breakaway,* once again as a resident therapist.

"*Breakaway* was kind of like an *Hour Magazine* show," explained Shelley Herman, who started out as a secretary there and eventually became one of the writers, and through that, a friend of Laura's. "It had several different 'experts' in different topics along with celebrity interviews. Laura was on Monday, Wednesday, and Friday, and she would do a segment where people would write to us, then she would read their letters on the air and answer them.

"Her mother was with her almost every day when we did that show, and Lew was always there too," recalled Herman, who said at that time Lew was working in sales for a biomedical company.

"I . . . had the idea it was like if you were going to do a television show and you brought your mom with you because you . . . wanted her to share in the excitement," explained Herman about Lundy's appearances. "It [the show] wasn't like a big-money thing or a big-deal thing, but it was something different and fun. I . . . had the impression that it was a nice, fun, inclusive thing. I don't think it was a strain for [Lundy] to do it physically or emotionally . . . she wanted to be part of her daughter's life.

"If anything, it seemed like Laura was being kind to her mother, having her mother be there all the time," she said.

Meanwhile, Laura continued to teach. By the fall of 1983, she ran a "Practicum in Peer Counseling," which met Tuesday and Thursday evenings from 5:30 to seven P.M. at the Sherman Oaks campus, in the Sumitomo Bank Building. Somewhere in that same time, Hedstrom recalled that Laura moved to a new office and hosted an open house at which he, too, met Laura's mother.

Lundy, who was fifty-two at the time of her divorce in 1977, did not have a substantial résumé, since most of her years had been spent as a housewife. Laura has told several reporters in recent years that after her parents' divorce she hired her mother as an office receptionist. Although she has never said how long her mother stayed, she has said, repeatedly, that they parted ways when she tried to get her mother, who could not type, to take lessons.

"I said, 'I need somebody to type,' and she said, 'Then you need somebody else,'" Laura told *The Washington Post* in 1995. "She packed up her stuff and exited my life."

Biography magazine, however, reported that Lundy did not walk out, but was fired.

By the time John Griffiths of *People* interviewed Laura in 1994, she told him she had not spoken to her mother for over eight years.

"Laura said her mother's refusal to learn to type or to do any office things stemmed more from arrogance. She said her mother was afraid of failure," recalled Griffiths.

Laura also told Griffiths she had no idea where her mother was living, but she thought in New York. In reality, Lundy was living alone in a first-floor apartment in an exclusive suburb of Los Angeles, less than a half-hour's drive from Laura's front door. She has steadfastly refused to talk about her daughter.

Laura has been angry with interviewers who ask about Lundy, and has termed what they write "gossip and innuendo."

Her latest book, *The Ten Commandments: The Significance of God's Laws in Everyday Life,* includes a long chapter on the fifth commandment (Honor thy mother and thy father). Yet she wrote about her mother in the introduction of the same book:

"Her only contribution to my religious training was that American Catholics take it all more seriously than Italians and that she hated the priests because, as they walked around well-garbed and fed, the people starved."

She went on to say that the next complication in her own religious and moral struggle was realizing that "my main authorities, Mom and Dad, were imperfect, inconstant, sometimes troubled, and oftentimes very difficult. This weakened the notion of concerning myself with their pride in my activities."

And, while Laura stated in her July 27, 1997, syndicated newspaper column that she eventually reconciled with her father, she added: "My mother and sister still prefer to be disengaged from each other as well as from my family. My door is open."

As Laura broke further away from her family roots, the *Breakaway* show went off the air as well. Still, Laura and Herman remained friends and business associates, and explored other television projects they could do together.

One of the ideas Laura and Lew conceived together was *Conflict,* a television pilot.

"It was something different," explained Herman. "It was a show where people would come on with some sort of conflict. The object was for them to present their problems, have Laura offer up a sugges tion as to how to resolve it, and then they would come back six weeks later and tell, if they took Laura's advice, how it worked, or if they found another way of doing it. The idea of the show would be, in place of everybody just yelling and yakking, that there would be some conflict resolution.

"I got us a free facilities arrangement," recalled Herman about the first taping of *Conflict.* "For the purpose of the pilot, we had actors portraying the couple in conflict. We actually had several different couples who were there who were friends and business acquaintances. We did the pilot and then a teaser—'here is more of what you could expect on the show.'"

Lew and Laura then arranged for a man, someone they thought had connections in television production, to help market the concept. According to Herman, the man was not generating any initial interest in the project.

"They were still pursuing it as this mom-and-pop shop, and I'm saying, 'Let's go to ICM, let's go to CAA, let's package this one,'" recalled Herman. "But they were reluctant to give up control of the project."

Then, suddenly, Laura pulled the plug.

"It was all their idea for the show," said Herman, "and she pulled out. She just didn't feel comfortable with it.

"It was a good show. I don't know why she pulled out of it."

Lew, of course, was managing Laura's career, although many people saw him more as a mouthpiece.

"As a manager, Lew did not know what he was doing," said one person who was close to both Laura and Lew back then. "Basically, he was just puppeting what she was saying. He had no business savvy. And it wasn't even a matter of his business savvy. If she didn't want to do something, or changed her mind, he would have to make the phone call. He had to hear a lot of people being upset with him."

"She is a very formidable force and very intimidating," agreed Herman. "At times, she will cry at the drop of a hat, so I'm sure [Lew] felt his role in their relationship was to continue to try and comfort her and encourage her. She is a bright woman and very ambitious. If I was going into heart surgery and she was a cardiologist, I would want her.

"Against everybody's advice, they pursued things their own way," said Herman, who acknowledged that they certainly did succeed, if not at first. "It was commendable, because she really did it her way."

CHAPTER TEN

A baby is God's opinion that the world should go on.

—CARL SANDBURG

(1878–1967)

Nearing thirty, recently divorced, and looking more toward a career in therapy and teaching than a family, Laura went through a tubal ligation.

She has told numerous interviewers over the years that she was totally consumed with her profession, and not interested, back then, in having children.

"I was a professor at the University of Southern California," Laura told *The Detroit News* in 1996. "I thought I was going to win the Nobel Prize."

Meanwhile, the bellwether state of California was downsizing itself, veering toward a more conservative view of government's role in people's lives. In 1978, the state's citizens passed Proposition 13, slashing property taxes by 57 percent. It was, in many ways, the start of a movement that would later catch fire in other parts of the nation, and not coincidentally, result in the rise of conservative messengers like Rush Limbaugh. The message was clear: Cut taxes, cut government.

At that point, however, Laura was probably not thinking about government's role in the family because she did not want a family.

She was dating, and sleeping with, her radio talk-show mentor, Bill Ballance, who recalled being with Laura at the hospital after her tubal ligation surgery.

"We were going together at the time that she decided to have her fallopian tubes tied," confirmed Ballance. "I hadn't had my vasectomy yet."

Ballance remembered being at the hospital with Laura during most of her recovery period.

"Before she received any visitors, she would have her hair spread out dramatically on the pillow and set herself up as if for a photo session," recalled Ballance. "I was there every day.

"I remember one time we were left alone, and I said 'Laura, I want you to look me in the eye and tell me the truth. If it's true that you fantasized about the operation being bungled and you dying in the hospital and the mourners and the things people would say about you at the funeral and the eulogy I would give and the size of the wreaths people would give at the grave site, give me a little smile.' Her lips turned up, and she roared with laughter and said, 'How did you know?' I said, 'Laura, because I know you.' It was one of the few times I was able to nail her on her own characteristics," said Ballance, chuckling at his own memory.

By thirty-five, however, Laura had changed her mind about having a baby. She was no longer seeing Ballance, but instead was cohabiting with Lew Bishop.

On a 1998 video for PBS spotlighting her book, *The Ten Commandments,* Laura told the story of how she discovered she wanted to be pregnant.

"Watching PBS, the *Nova* series," Laura related, "there was an egg, and they went in with the fiber optics and they saw the egg coming down the fallopian tube. And then they showed one egg. Then they showed the millions of sperm. Millions. And then they showed the moment where that one sperm connected with that one egg and forty minutes later, there is a baby. I figured, 'Okay, sounds good to me.'"

For Laura, it was a telling moment.

"I realized," she told the *Ethnic Newswatch,* "that I had been living a stultifying, limited sort of life. I was just a brain and didn't think about what blessings could take place in my body."

Laura, by her own acknowledgment, went through the surgery to reverse the tubal ligation, and then underwent fertility treatments, specifically artificial insemination, to get pregnant.

According to Shelley Herman, the Los Angeles writer who had been friendly with Laura since they worked together on *Breakaway,* Laura saw a specialist at Cedars-Sinai Medical Center in Beverly Hills. More than one friend recalled Laura struggling to get pregnant.

"She was trying for well over a year to conceive," recalled Herman. "Every month, if she hadn't conceived, she was in tears for days and depressed, and searching. Even to having African fertility gods in her office; anything it took to try and get her pregnant. She really was very consumed by all this."

During this period, Laura had a small white dog she considered her child-in-waiting.

"Laura used to carry around this little teacup-size white dog as a substitute child," acknowledged Herman. "She was the first to admit it."

So Laura was, naturally, ecstatic in the late summer of 1984, when she found out she was pregnant.

"The fact that she was pregnant made her want to get married," recalled Herman, who said Laura told her during a conversation that she was going to have a baby. "Having lived with Lew all these years, I think she would have been perfectly content just living with Lew forever, until there was a baby on the way.

"It was a joyous occasion and we were all very happy for her because she had struggled for so long," added Herman.

Laura and Lew, who had been living together since 1978, had just purchased a new house. As with their first house in Canoga Park, the grant deed listed, as joint tenants, Laura C. Schlessinger, a single woman, and Lewis G. Bishop, a single man, when they closed August 29, 1984, on the Woodland Hills property.

In October 1984, they were married by a justice of the peace in the backyard of their house. Neither Laura's parents nor her sister attended the wedding. The only close family in attendance were Lew's three children from his first marriage.

Herman was among the guests who came to what was billed as a tennis wedding.

"We were all in tennis togs," recalled Herman. "There was a nice barbecue, and then we played tennis on the tennis court afterwards. It was not a religious ceremony. She wasn't a practicing anything in those days."

Not long after the wedding, according to a source who knew her then, Laura went into Cedars-Sinai for a routine pregnancy checkup and ultrasound. Later that evening, while she and Lew were out with friends, Laura received a frantic page from her doctor, telling her to return immediately to the hospital: She had a tubal pregnancy.

Medically known as an ectopic pregnancy, the condition arises when a fertilized egg becomes implanted someplace besides the uterus—in this case, within the fallopian tube itself. There is no chance a fetus can survive, and the condition is life-threatening for the mother as well.

Her doctor immediately scheduled Laura for surgery.

"She was joyous about the pregnancy," remembered Herman. "It was just devastating. It wasn't even just the idea of losing the pregnancy. There was still the fear she might lose her tube."

During her radio show on November 20, 1997, Laura confessed to a caller who was wondering how to address the question of whether to say he was the father of six or the father of five since one of his children had died that she had suffered the loss of an unborn child. She then explained to the caller that she had gone through fertility treatments to get pregnant, and ended up with a tubal pregnancy.

"They had to remove it or I would die," Laura told the caller, adding that, "in my heart, I am the mother of two."

After recuperating from her surgery, Laura resumed fertility treatments, and in early 1985 was thrilled to learn, once again, that she was pregnant.

While Laura was going through the first trimester of her pregnancy, her sister, Cindy, got married. Then twenty-seven years old, Cindy married Brad Harris on April 13, 1985, in Los Angeles County.

Most of the people Laura was friendly with at the time cannot recall Laura talking about her sister's wedding; even if she knew about it, they doubted that she attended.

In the fall of 1985, Dr. Rhoda Marcovitch, a therapist who had shared, along with Judith Friedman, an office suite with Laura, threw a baby shower at her home in Sherman Oaks for the mother-to-be.

Herman watched as Laura picked up someone else's baby and held it awkwardly. "'I haven't held a baby in years,'" Herman remembered Laura admitting to the group. "And I remember wondering, 'Then why are you wanting a baby so much? You don't know what to do with these little critters.'"

"When I got pregnant with our son," Laura told Irene Lacher of *The Los Angeles Times* in March of 1994, "I woke [Lew] up at three in the morning and I said, 'I want you real clear on one thing. If I even think you hurt him, I will take you down to the molecular level.' And he said, 'As well you should.'"

As is typical of impending motherhood, however, the baby hurt his mother first.

On the evening of November 4, 1985, Laura's labor began. For twelve long hours Laura, who wanted a natural childbirth, endured the pain in a labor and delivery room at St. John's Hospital and Health Center in Santa Monica, a three-story brick hospital less than twenty blocks from the Santa Monica pier.

By early morning it was clear that Laura's petite body could not deliver the baby, and Dr. M. M. Kamrava, her obstetrician, performed a cesarean section.

Deryk Andrew Schlessinger was born at 6:35 A.M. on November 5, 1985, symbolically under the sign of the Catholic cross atop St. John's. Laura was thirty-eight, and Lew was fifty-two.

Later, she would tell *The Los Angeles Times* that she gave Deryk her own last name because Lew "had a prior family."

"And I figured I went through twelve hours of labor and a C-section. I figured, I'm going to name this thing anything I want, and I said, 'Lew, do you have any problem with the last name Schlessinger?' He said, 'No.'"

"Laura always told me she was an only child," said Herman, "and that the reason she wanted Deryk with the Schlessinger name was to carry on the Schlessinger name.

"She was very, very sick after she gave birth," continued Herman, "and she didn't want any visitors. She had a very difficult time. She was trying to do natural childbirth, and she wound up where she had to take an epidural and she got this real bad headache, so they didn't want anybody there."

It was not until a week or two later that Herman first went to visit the new mother and her son. Lew was helping to care for their baby.

"Again, it was a financial consideration," believed Herman. "And also she wanted to experience all of it. Laura had longed for [a baby] so much."

To her credit, Laura was a quick learner when it came to taking care of a baby. By this time, estranged from her mother, her father, and her sister, she had to rely primarily on herself and her husband to meet the needs of a thriving infant.

Herman remembered Laura as being "as comfortable [with her baby] as any new mother . . . wanting to make sure everything goes all right with the baby. He was so wanted and so cherished. They really did keep to themselves a lot; they kind of had this experience for themselves."

And that even included getting rid of her little white dog.

"The minute Deryk arrived, Laura claimed the dog took a little nip at baby Deryk and she gave the dog to Rhoda. The dog is the sweetest little thing," said Herman.

To this day, Laura considers the birth of her child to be her best production. She told John Griffiths in 1994 that Deryk was "proof of my success as a person."

"She told me she loved her kid to pieces and worked her life around him," recalled Griffiths. "Lew said that motherhood had taken a portion of the focus off Laura and made her 'a broader person.'"

It also made her more generous.

"One of the things Laura used to do that I thought was very nice, because she did have exquisite taste in clothing, is [that when] she had Deryk, and, at the time had gained weight . . . she gave me all her clothes," revealed Herman. "They were all designer-label things, nice suits and stuff."

Laura has repeatedly maintained that she was a stay-at-home mom for the first three years of Deryk's life.

U.S. News & World Report reported in 1997 that a woman from Connecticut had called Laura's show to say that she didn't believe Laura could really "develop and maintain a career such as yours . . . working two hours a day."

Laura "responds to such challenges," wrote the magazine's reporter, Joannie M. Schrof, "with long speeches about how she took three years off to raise her son."

In truth, she may have been off radio, but she was still working part-time outside the home.

Although Laura had been teaching a nighttime graduate-level psychology class at Pepperdine University branches in the San Fernando Valley since January 1982, she took the fall semester of 1985 off to prepare for Deryk's birth. But Lew was left to baby-sit Deryk, then two months old, when Laura returned to Pepperdine in January 1986 to continue her hour-and-a-half-long Tuesday evening "Clinical Practicum" for psychology students.

Laura also maintained a Saturday private practice, again sharing office space on Ventura Boulevard with Rhoda Marcovitch and Judith Friedman.

And in mid-1986, with Deryk not yet six months old, she added another teaching commitment to her work at Pepperdine and her private practice. Through the University of California at Los Angeles (UCLA) Continuing Education Program, Laura taught "Biopsychology of Human Sexuality."

One student who took the class estimated that "a couple of hundred people" signed up. She described Laura as a "nice but tough [teacher]."

"Her attitude was the same from day one, which is 'I'm the greatest thing in the world.' That was what she projected to the class," recalled the student.

Although this student had neither met Laura nor spoken with her in class, she was still impressed enough to phone Laura when she was looking for a private therapist several months later.

"It was November of 1986," recalled the student, "and I was looking for a therapist to discuss some family situations."

From the beginning, she said Laura came on strong.

"It was her way or no way," said the student-turned-patient. "Basically I walked in and she said, 'I want you to tape all your sessions. I expect all my patients to bring in a tape. We'll use my tape recorder, and we're going to tape everything.' Basically I think what she was saying was if you listen to this over and over again, you'll get more out of it."

According to this patient, the tapes were returned to her after each session, and are still in the patient's possession. They document "some boundary-breaking" activities between therapist and patient.

Over the next two and a half years, this patient met with Laura almost weekly, paying her $100 an hour for her work.

"I guess she took a liking to me," recalled the patient, who added, "and I guess at that point in my life I needed the attention. She reeled me in and broke nearly every boundary that there is."

For example, the former patient said, "There was a young man she was seeing right before me, and so we would kind of pass each other there in the waiting room. She would talk to me about what some of his issues were. That really freaked me out, because I wondered if she was telling the next person about me? Then there was a very well-known newscaster who was also seeing her [as a therapist] around the same time I was, and Laura talked a little bit about him as well."

That was not the only ethical boundary Laura crossed. "She asked me to baby-sit her son on several occasions," revealed the former patient. "Laura said, 'I don't talk to my sister, and Deryk doesn't have an aunt. I want you to be his aunt.'"

Despite the patient's qualms, she stayed in therapy, becoming closer and closer to Laura and her family, further muddying the line between patient and doctor. For nearly four years, they shopped together, had lunches together, and even spent holidays together.

Still, her patient admitted it was not always easy being friends with Laura.

"I remember one time we went to lunch and some lady was wearing perfume. Laura said, 'That's it. We can't sit here. Either they have to leave this table or we're going to find a new table. I am not going to sit through this lunch,'" said her former patient, who was embarrassed by this public outburst.

But she felt so close to Laura that she overlooked it, knowing she had to be careful to avoid angering her.

"I felt like we were sisters," said the patient. "She was always calling me and we were always spending time together. I thought it was a true friendship."

But, like many of Laura's other relationships, it was not to last.

The words that a father speaks to his children in the
privacy of home are not heard by the world, but, as in
whispering-galleries, they are clearly heard at the end and
by posterity.

—JEAN-PAUL RICHTER

(1763–1826)

After her parents' divorce in 1977, Laura initially kept in better contact
with her mother than with her father. The big split came with her father when he started dating Raenetta Davis, a personnel executive at
Von's grocery chain in southern California. They married in 1982.

According to her former patient, Laura became distant from her father in large part because "she didn't like the woman he was with.
Laura told me she really despised the woman."

Laura's friend Shelley Herman met Laura's father on several occasions.

"Laura started seeing him after Deryk was born, and she was trying
to get some family continuity going," said Herman. "He was a very

handsome man. He looked like Kirk Douglas with a dimple in the chin and that kind of reddish-blond, gray hair. He was very nice."

In a syndicated newspaper column, published in July 1997, Laura revealed to her readers that she had reestablished a relationship with her father approximately two years before he died.

"It wasn't perfect," she admitted, "but it was something."

Several of Monty's work associates and friends, recalling how proud he was of his daughter, were unaware that they even had been estranged.

Gerry Pepper, who first met Monty in 1955 when they both worked for Parson Jurgens in New York and later worked with him at Parson's in California, as well as at U.S. Borax, said Monty spoke often about his daughter.

"He was always interested when people heard about her on the radio or mentioned something to him about her. She used to fill in for Toni Grant," recalled Pepper, "and he was proud that most people actually liked her on the radio ahead of this Toni Grant."

John Fernandez, a friend and Monty's last supervisor at U.S. Borax, concurred.

"He was a loving father to both daughters," believed Fernandez. "They meant a lot to him."

Andrew Lisowski, a civil engineer who was hired by Monty and worked in his division at U.S. Borax for at least seven years, agreed that Monty was proud of his daughters and spoke of them often, although he might not have agreed with his daughters' opinions.

"I remember going with him driving to a job site in . . . 1981 or 1982," said Lisowski. "We were having a conversation, and he turns on the radio. Laura Schlessinger comes on and he says, very proud, 'Here's my daughter.'

"We are kind of listening to what Laura is saying—she was giving some advice about a complex situation—and after a while, he said, 'She's full of shit,' and turned off the radio. That was the kind of person he was. He was proud of her and all that, but he obviously had different opinions."

For a time, Monty worked in the San Francisco area on a major project for U.S. Borax, before returning to the Los Angeles office. He and Raenetta bought a house on Haverkamp Drive in Glendale, and settled into a lifestyle that for Monty still revolved around work.

Pepper remembered Monty as "very demanding in the work area. Probably more than anything, he was very exacting and precise."

Fernandez, too, recalled Monty's dedication to his job. "You might call him an engineer's engineer. He knew his stuff and he wanted to make sure that whatever came out of his department was of the highest quality. He was a perfectionist.

"He had a work personality and a nonwork personality. He could be a charmer off work, a terrific conversationalist, but at work he was a disciplinarian. He demanded compliance to regulation and perfection at work."

Lisowski also saw Monty's tough side. "I got along with him pretty well, but some people were afraid of him because he was tough and at times he could be abrasive. He had that streak."

Lisowski frequently lunched with his former boss, especially at Chinese restaurants, where Monty would take charge. "He was the boss and he would ask everybody what they wanted, and then he would order [for everybody] what *he* wanted. He used to take lessons in Chinese at UCLA once a week. We would go to a restaurant, and he would order in Chinese to impress everybody, but, of course, none of us knew what he was talking about."

Once, Monty asked Lisowski to recommend a restaurant, with disastrous results.

"I said I had heard of this Mexican restaurant that had a seafood dish made of seven different kinds of seafood," said Lisowski.

Together with three others, the group went to the restaurant, where Monty picked the specialty of the house.

"The rest of us got our meal and he didn't get what he had ordered. We are practically done and he's fuming because he didn't get served. The waiter was very apologetic, and they promised to bring the soup out immediately. They bring out this delicacy—this big bowl of soup—and he starts eating it, very gingerly at first. He starts digging deeper and there is this big piece of aluminum foil in the bowl. He absolutely went ballistic. Everybody thought I was going to get fired after that because I recommended the place," recalled Lisowski, chuckling.

According to Fernandez, Monty was also very concerned about his health. Fit and trim at five feet, eight inches, with a thick head of graying hair, Monty played tennis and watched his diet.

"Both his father and his brother had died of stomach cancer," remembered Fernandez, "and Monty was always on the lookout for stuff that might be bad for his stomach.

"He was very meticulous about what he ate," added Fernandez. "Sometimes he would aggravate his lunchmates by returning stuff because it wasn't to his liking. He was always talking about what not to eat and what to eat."

Lisowski concurred. "He was always very conscious about taking care of himself . . . eating his greens and spinach. It's an irony that it didn't matter."

In June 1988, Monty was diagnosed with carcinoma of the stomach: cancer. Within days of the diagnosis he had surgery, and, at the same time, retired from U.S. Borax.

Fernandez said he and Monty became close during the three months between his diagnosis and his death, and he visited him at home "several times." Fernandez met Laura there as well. "On my last visit to Monty . . . he was there with his wife, Rae, and Laura showed up with her husband and son. Most of the conversation was between Laura and Monty. She asked, 'How are you, Dad? How are you feeling?' and 'What did you do different today in the way of treatment?' The conversation centered around Monty's medical condition."

But, recalled Fernandez, what Monty enjoyed most during the visit was playing with three-year-old Deryk. "He really liked his grandson—of course that was the only grandson he had."

John Griffiths of *People,* who interviewed Laura and Lew in 1994, said she told him that in the year before her father died, their relationship improved. "She said he died in 1990, at age sixty-one, of stomach cancer," recalled Griffiths, who said Laura "skipped over dates," but in a lighthearted manner. "The way she talked was 'Yeah, yeah, yeah . . . whatever . . . 1990 . . . around there' . . . and, like, 'Let's move on.'"

Monroe did succumb to stomach cancer, but he actually died on September 26, 1988, at the age of sixty-three.

He was cremated the next day. Fernandez said he was told that there were "dual funerals" for Monty at Veterans Cemetery in Westwood: one attended by Laura and Cindy and their families, and another by Raenetta, her family, and Monty's friends from work.

"Rae asked me to speak on behalf of U.S. Borax at Monty's funeral," acknowledged Fernandez.

"His brother and his father and his brother's family were very religious," said Fernandez. "But Monty was not a practicing Jew. I remember when he was flying back for his brother's funeral [several years earlier] he said he felt kind of like an outcast because he was not into the ceremony. I think they were Conservatives. When he married, he became a Unitarian."

Fernandez also acknowledged the similarities between Laura and her father.

"I think Laura, from what I read, is very outgoing; she is an assertive type of person," said Fernandez. "Monty was that way. Laura is probably a perfectionist, and so was Monty.

"Since his passing, we have come across projects he worked on and we always say, 'Monty certainly would not have let that [mistake] go by,'" noted Fernandez.

Although Laura had not yet returned to radio at the time of her father's death, she was concentrating on something of a new career: machine knitting. With a computerized knitting machine she first purchased when she was pregnant with Deryk, Laura was able to create her own designs.

"She even had business cards where she had a little sample of her fabric and then her name, Dr. Laura Schlessinger, with a phone number on it," recalled Herman. Laura dubbed the business Knit Names.

"I never thought I was artistic," Laura told the *Los Angeles Times-*

View reporter who did a feature on her latest enterprise in November 1987, "but I am."

In fact, Laura became so adept that she started a custom and special-order business, even making special appearances at one Nordstrom's store to peddle her new products.

"We did several charity fund-raisers where Laura would donate an item to be auctioned off. A couple of times I would model the dress and walk around with it on and pass out her cards," recalled Herman.

"It was beautiful beautiful work; very exacting. I think she even taught a UCLA extension course in it. She was very entrepreneurial, and, in those days she needed the money."

Indeed, Laura did need the money, and the pupils—so much so that she pressured one of her previously mentioned patients into taking the knitting class offered through UCLA: $235 a person for an eight-week class that met once a week, two or three hours at a time.

"I was very, very pressured into taking that class. I was still in therapy with her, and she said, 'I want you to take this knitting class.' She said, 'I don't think I have enough people to keep it open, and if you take it, that will help.' I said I'd never done anything like that, and she said, 'You'll love it; I'll teach you.' I signed up," said her former patient, who took two sessions of classes—the first in late 1988 and the second in March 1989.

"There were probably eight people in each class," recalled the former patient. "She brought in her own machines, and Lew came with her to set them up and take them down.

"She and Lew are sewn together at the hip," added the patient, who said Deryk was not with them during the class. "Lew was there for every single class."

Both Shelley Herman and Laura's former patient remember the setup for Laura's knitting business, which Laura started to incorporate in 1988.

"In the house they had out in Woodland Hills there was the main house, and then a very large lawn with a pool and tennis courts, and behind that there were stables. This had formerly been horse property.

Anyway, they turned some of those stables into her knitting area with all the spools of yarn, and they had special air conditioning and a filtration system because there are a lot of fibers. She had the machines set up out there. It was a real nice workplace," explained Herman.

Laura sold two sweaters to the costume designer for a Molly Ringwald movie. She also told John Griffiths that other sweaters were manufactured for a *Designing Women* episode, as well as for Whoopi Goldberg's *Sister Act,* and for the Lost Boys in *Hook.* Laura ended up winning three blue ribbons for her work and a "Best of Show" award at the Los Angeles County Fair in 1987.

"[Laura] loves well-made clothing," said Herman. "She is a very good sewer herself. I remember her buying this industrial-strength sewing machine. I think she got into [machine knitting] in an effort to find clothes for her and as a way of using her creativity. She just made gorgeous things, like St. John knits."

One reason they resembled St. John knits, according to the former patient, was that Laura modeled some of her designs after actual samples.

"She asked me—and I did this; what a stupid jerk I was—to go to Nordstrom's and put on my charge card four St. John knit suits. She said she had no credit left on her card, and I was going to buy them temporarily and then return them. It was October 4, 1989. I put on my credit card seventeen hundred dollars' worth of St. John knits that she wanted to copy the pattern from. She told me she would get them back to me right away. I kept calling Lew, saying, 'You've got to get this stuff back because I need to return it.' I was afraid if the bill comes in and I don't return this stuff I'll have to pay the interest.

"The St. John knits are very expensive, and when you buy them at the Gallerie Department at Nordstrom's they come on fancy hangers. Laura had kept all the hangers and the St. John knits were just thrown into the bag when I came to pick them up to take them back. I said, 'Lew, where's all the hangers?' She always had him do that kind of stuff for her. She was in her knitting room giving a knitting lesson, so I was talking to Lew in the backyard. I said, 'How am I going to return this?' He said, 'Oh, just return it. They don't care.' I was so embarrassed.

"Then he said, 'Take Deryk with you. He'd like to go along for the ride.' I didn't make eye contact [with the clerk at Nordstrom's]. I was talking with Deryk the whole time because I was so embarrassed to bring back these St. John knits all thrown together in a bag."

While Laura could perhaps supplement the family income with her knitting, it was not the family's bread and butter. Laura continued to work in her private therapy practice. She even said as much to the reporter from the *Los Angeles Times-View.*

"I can make money faster doing just about anything else I do," she said, adding that she would spend "about five hours most days"—with her two-year-old son in view.

Interestingly enough, considering what Laura would later tell her listeners about staying home with her own child, she also saved two days a week for her psychotherapy practice, as well as teaching at Pepperdine. She also said that Lew, who was then employed by Grady Medical Systems as a district manager, "worked at home one day a week to be with their son."

"Laura goes through phases of things she likes," said the former patient. "She goes out and becomes like a total maniac for it—her knitting, her karate, her whatever. I don't know if anything lasted for very long."

Herman noted the same thing.

"She started the knitting business and then a few years later that was gone," said Herman. "She will decide she wants to do a particular kind of fitness program and she will go out and buy all the equipment and the cute little outfits and the personal trainers . . . and then she will wake up one day and all of that will be for naught."

During these years, the late 1980s, Lew continued to have hard luck. The first company he worked for collapsed, and Lew got stuck.

"The company went under and owed him a lot of money," recalled Herman.

Laura's former patient also had reason to notice the couple's money problems. "They borrowed money from me once or twice," recalled the former patient, who then remembered a specific incident that happened when she went shopping with Laura.

"What was really weird about that day was, here I'm in therapy with her. It was a Saturday, and after therapy, we walk out, get in the car, and go shopping. We all went shopping, including Lew and Deryk, and when Laura went to pay for something she wanted to buy, they rejected her credit cards.

"Laura has always been very materialistic," commented her former patient. "Money has always been very important to her. I think she related money to fame and importance. I think she felt there was a direct relationship between the two."

And, even while Laura's patient took her doctor's knitting classes and went on personal outings with her, therapy continued.

"Once Laura arranged for two of the students from her knitting class to drop by something for her at the office at the same time as my [therapy] appointment," recalled the former patient. "What she did was expose that I was in therapy with her, because then I bumped into these two students right when I was going in to see her. [Laura] put her needs about her knitting class before my needs as her patient. She violated my confidentiality. I didn't want them knowing I was seeing her professionally. That was private.

"I said to her, 'Laura, why did you do that? Now these women know that I come to you professionally.' And Laura said, 'They don't care; it's not a big deal.'

"Laura kicked me out of therapy once," revealed Laura's patient. "She said I wasn't working hard enough, and that when I felt like I could work harder I could come back. And then she told me to go on a diet and lose weight."

Finally, in mid-1989, the patient told the doctor she had to quit.

"I said, 'This is not a good thing, because I'm confused.' We agreed to stop therapy and just have a personal relationship as friends," explained the patient.

And, while Laura left Deryk with her former patient or with Lew on many occasions, she sometimes took Deryk along when the situations seemed less than appropriate. For example, Herman recalled Laura bringing Deryk to a pitch meeting with executives about a potential television deal.

"We would be sitting in this pitch meeting, and Deryk would be playing with his dinosaurs, making growling dinosaur sounds. He's a kid. He's supposed to do that," said Herman, who acknowledged, however, that this was not the time or the place. "Laura is one to talk about, 'Don't drag kids to inappropriate places.' That was kind of the final straw for me as far as working with her. It just got to be too much with Deryk."

But the next pitch Laura really wanted to throw was the one that would land her back in the kind of job she coveted most: being a talk-show host.

CHAPTER TWELVE

Competition brings out the best in products
and the worst in people.

—DAVID SARNOFF

(1891–1971)

By the time Deryk was three, Laura was, as she put it, "itching to get back into radio."

As she explained in *How Could You Do That?*, a "very, very small radio station near my home offered me a midday program for very, very small wages. I was so grateful I could hardly spit. My son and I would be together all morning, we'd walk to the station, he'd stay at a play center while I was on the air, then we'd walk home and have the rest of the afternoon and evening together."

Shelley Herman could see how happy Laura was to be back on the air, even on a small station.

"When she finally got this break on KWNK, it was practically two blocks from her house. They had this radio station in this shopping mall. It was like this little station nobody knew of, and she had to talk for four hours a day. Lew and I would call up. I would be in the office at the station, and I would call up to give her somebody to talk to. It was like doing improv.

"She was really, really good at doing that," said Herman, "almost to the point of being psychic. The way she would approach it in those days, she was listening and giving people time. She wasn't as judgmental; she would suggest things to people and be compassionate."

One of Laura's former patients, who later became a personal friend, also went down to KWNK "a couple of times" to answer the calls coming in.

"She really didn't need anybody to sit there [and answer phones] because no calls came in. Laura would cry. Lew would even call me at work to get me to call in. I'd say, 'Lew, I'm at work! How can I call Laura?' He said, 'Please call in. Nobody is calling her and she's all upset.'"

According to Laura, when she first took the position, the station manager had asked that she not "fill in or audition" on other stations while she was working his time slot, and Laura agreed. As she told it in her book, within a week a "big" talk-radio station asked her to fill in as a tryout, but Laura, remembering her promise, refused.

She was thrilled, however, in 1989, when the same West Hills–based KWNK station manager recommended her for syndication to the new general manager of a twenty-four-hour-a-day, seven-day-a-week satellite radio network: Sun Radio, out of the Tampa–St. Petersburg area of Florida.

Sun Radio Network was a hodgepodge of talk-radio programming that (mostly small) AM radio stations throughout the United States could pick up via satellite and funnel out through their own airwaves. The network made its money by selling a predetermined number of advertisements that, in turn, had to be run by the stations picking up the signal. Tom Holter, who was then Sun's general manager, signed Laura on after listening to one of her demo tapes.

"I thought [she] was pretty good and maybe we could get something going with it," recalled Holter about his first introduction to Dr. Laura.

The deal was made by phone, primarily through Lew Bishop, whom Holter described as Laura's "quote-unquote agent."

"Lew called [the network] all the time," recalled Holter. "It got to the point where he got to be real hostile. He was never pleasant. Sometimes if you want something you should be nice. I don't think he knew the meaning of that."

"He actually got in the way of everything she did," believed Holter. "He was a pain in the ass."

According to Holter, Laura's financial arrangement with Sun Network "was a barter deal. She had time she could sell herself, the network had time, and local stations had time. She had to sell the ads herself, although I think her husband was the one who sold it."

In turn, Laura and Lew converted a back room in their home into a radio control room, complete with carpeted walls to keep out the sound, added a second line, and bought a telephone interface device called a Comrex.

"You had to have a Comrex unit, which cost about fifteen hundred to three thousand dollars, and I think Laura bought it. They had to put in a second line, but we covered the phone both ways," explained Holter. "[The Comrex] was a little mixer that had a place for a couple of mikes, and, by wearing a headset, she could hear the callers and she could hear the producer."

Laura's "producer" was essentially whatever operating engineer was on duty that day at Sun's headquarters in Florida. The calls were filtered through Sun's phone lines to Laura in Los Angeles.

"The producer would say, 'Hello, you've got some kook from Tampa on line one,' and she'd take it," said Holter.

Laura broadcast daily from nine A.M. to eleven A.M. Although Sun Network started with about eighty stations and grew to 168, Holter said it was difficult to say how many actually carried her program.

"Stations carried whatever they wanted to," said Holter. "She could have been on as few as ten or fifteen real weak stations, which ran everything we had because they didn't have anything else to run. I don't remember how many people picked her up, but I think she was starting to build. We, of course, had people calling the radio stations and saying, 'Hey, we've got this great radio program and you're going to get a lot of calls.' Our affiliate-relations people were working on new stations all the time to get them to carry the programming.

"I thought she had a lot of ability. She knows all the psychobabble words people will buy, and she is able to get in and out of conversations, and that's not easy. She also had a good sense of what should be on the program. She knew if somebody asked a question that was too pat and boring, one that you could answer with a yes or a no, and she also knew when people might like to have more pulled out, especially in the matter of sex."

But even back then, Laura often laid aside her therapist hat and talked about both morality and the need for parents to be more responsible in raising their children. Laura also believed she could help people.

"I'm limited as to how far I can go, talking to someone for 10 or 15 minutes," she told *The Los Angeles Times* in 1990. "But this is not just a show."

Still, Laura's first syndication deal did not bring in big bucks. Advertising was often difficult to sell, and although Holter allowed that "you didn't have to sell many ads to make a few hundred bucks, it certainly wasn't a great landslide of cash. She was probably taking in a hundred to a hundred and fifty dollars a day, which might have amounted to about five hundred to eight hundred a week," he said.

Holter met Lew and Laura in person when they flew to Florida, at their own expense, in March or April so they could see the network operation firsthand and do her broadcast there.

Holter said his biggest problem with Laura was in her choice of guest hosts. "She was real busy with other things, like a private practice, I think, and she frequently had somebody sit in for her," explained Holter. "That became a problem because some of the people she had sit in were just terrible. I suppose they were friends or colleagues or something, but they were just awful. So the stations would complain."

Still, it was not Laura's show but the network that would not withstand the next change. According to Holter, Sun Radio Network was bought out by the ultra-right-wing Liberty Lobby, a fringe group that published the newspaper *Spotlight*. Holter himself soon departed, and some time afterward, Laura also parted ways with Sun.

"She called me three times after that," recalled former boyfriend Bill Ballance. "She said, 'Please help me. If I don't get back on radio I'm going to kill myself.' This is on my tape message machine. I wasn't at home at the time.

"She even went into one of her spasms—'You could help me if you wanted to'—and then she said, 'You have always been jealous of me,'" remembered Ballance, who said he didn't call her back.

As it turned out, however, Laura found her own space. She interviewed for the coveted noon-to-three spot on the up-and-coming KFI.

A former patient of Laura's arrived one afternoon to go to lunch with her, only to find her crying at her front desk.

"I asked her what was wrong, and she said Barbara De Angelis had gotten the on-air daytime position at KFI radio that she had wanted."

Soon thereafter, however, KFI called to offer Laura a lesser position, a nighttime slot.

"When she was at KFI and they first gave her the evening shift, I think she was making maybe a hundred bucks a night," recalled Herman, who acknowledged that even though the money wasn't great, Laura was happy to be on a bigger station.

"Radio is what her strength has always been," said Herman. "She really gets into her own space there. I think she believes this is what she was put on earth to do."

At KFI, Laura was joined by someone she had worked with before: Tracey Miller.

"I first met her when I was a cub reporter in the 1980s," recalled Miller. "I accidentally said 'Thank you, Laura,' on air, and afterwards she pointedly told me, 'You will call me *Dr.* Laura.'"

But by the time the two met up again at KFI, Miller was herself established as a radio personality, and Laura, she said, "was much friendlier. She treated me more like a peer."

"She got very friendly, very quickly, with everyone," recalled Miller. "She gets close to you, gets to know you very well and then plays on any weaknesses you might have. Laura is so driven, she would go to any length to get ahead."

Barbara Whitesides, another on-air personality at KFI when Laura started, recalled basically the same thing.

"I just remember how friendly she was in the very beginning. She was just kind of trying to make her way," said Whitesides. "At that time, I think Barbara De Angelis was still on and really had everyone's ear. She had a lot of clout at that particular time, and Laura was sort of the also-ran. She did the evening show.

"Laura was getting a little bit of recognition, but not much. At that point, she was really friendly and tried to be a team player. I liked her at first. She seemed a little 'Type A,' but she was likable. And, she had her son, Deryk, who is about the same age as my son, Blake. She immediately . . . wanted to get our sons together and do things with our sons," explained Whitesides, who added that they did do a few things together socially. Blake attended Deryk's birthday party, and on another occasion spent the night.

Laura was also making sure Deryk was with her at the station on a regular basis. She would bring him with her to the KFI studios, often including one of his friends as a playmate. But, remembered many former employees, Deryk was not always supervised.

Whitesides recalled an incident that took place at a local soup kitchen at Thanksgiving, when station personnel were called upon to lend a hand. Laura came with Deryk.

"Deryk was all over the place," said Whitesides. "He was totally out of control. Whatever Deryk wanted, Deryk got. She never saw him as being out of hand. If Deryk did it, then it was perfectly all right."

The same thing appeared true at the station.

"[Deryk] had the run of the place," recalled Miller, who continually saw Laura's son running through the halls of the station. "He must have been about five or six then."

Whitesides, too, found Deryk an annoyance, as he ran "roughshod" through the station. "There was no supervision or no reining in of Deryk."

"Laurie Saunders [a DJ] used to do this 'love songs' kind of music on KOST, the sister station to KFI," continued Miller. "One night [Deryk] had this little pal with him and they ran into Laurie's studio while she was on the air, laughing and screaming real loud. Laurie called the station manager and said, 'This has got to stop. The kid just ruined my show.'"

Miller said the policy by which children were allowed into the station changed shortly thereafter, with Miller herself feeling the blow.

"I used to bring my seven-year-old daughter with me on weekends, and the weekend after that, the security guard wouldn't let her in. He said, 'I'm sorry, but an edict came down: no more children in the building.'"

When Saunders was later let go by the station, Miller remembered Laura being "pleased about Laurie being gone. Laura hated her."

Whitesides recalled exactly the same thing, adding that she actually heard Laura going around the station gleefully singing "Ding, Dong, the Witch Is Dead" from *The Wizard of Oz*.

"We all knew what it was in relation to," explained Whitesides.

While everyone recalled seeing Deryk on a regular basis, Lew had not been as visible.

"He would come in to negotiate her contracts and stuff," recalled Whitesides. "He certainly took care of all the business ends of things for her."

At the same time, Whitesides, like many others who worked with Laura, didn't recall Laura ever speaking about her extended family, including parents, siblings, or stepchildren.

"For all I knew, she didn't have any family, because she never ever spoke about a sister or mother or anything," confirmed Whitesides.

Herman, who was still a friend of Laura's then, was struck by her vulnerability.

"I saw a woman who was trying to have a [career] and keep her family together. I wanted her to live happily ever after. Even though Laura will pooh-pooh feminism, I saw her following the path paved for her," added Herman.

Herman said she had respected Laura then, especially knowing how hard she had worked for her doctorate.

"I didn't know until recently it wasn't in psychology," said Herman.

At the same time, Herman said she was pushing Laura to expand her opportunities and her reach. "I kept saying to her, and I'm sure others did too, that if you want to be Barbara De Angelis or Irene Kassorla or Joyce Brothers, then you have to do books and syndicated columns in newspapers."

About this time, Laura started developing the idea for her first book, *Ten Stupid Things Women Do to Mess Up Their Lives,* which she eventually initiated on her own without even having a publisher in mind.

And, thanks to Herman, Laura also decided to sign with an agent, Fred Wostbrock, now with Kazarian Spencer and Associates, Inc., in Los Angeles.

Wostbrock, who has represented personalities such as Gary Owens, Wink Martindale, Phyllis Diller, and Adam West, was (apart from Lew) Laura's first agent. He signed a one-year contract with Laura and Lew in May 1990.

"I signed her for game [and] talk shows for radio and television. I think Laura was impressed that I represented the legendary Gary Owens and Wink Martindale, because she kind of knew of those gentlemen.

"I have to give her credit," said Wostbrock, "her and Lew, they did it their way. If it didn't meet her standards or if it wasn't what she wanted to do, she wouldn't do it."

Wostbrock booked her on a few national and local talk shows. "I know that she did a talk-show pilot before me, but she didn't like the way it came out.

"When I met her, she was on . . . KFI. She was not syndicated, and she was on weeknights from ten to one A.M. and Saturdays from eight P.M. to midnight—not good time slots. I caught her just before she broke big. She wanted to get on daytime. I remember she kept saying, 'Boy, if I could just get daytime, if I could just be syndicated.'

"That was her big goal, was to get on KFI daytime. At the time there was another psychologist on—Barbara De Angelis. [Laura] wanted an afternoon slot. Why? You got a million listeners, versus a hundred thousand. And, at the time, Barbara De Angelis had a talk show, too. That's why people were talking to Laura about a talk show, but she didn't want to do a schlock show."

Wostbrock said he stirred up some interest for a television show, but "it never went to an offer because she didn't like the format." His agency, along with Lew, tried to get Laura syndicated.

"Lew always said they wanted to do it their way. What their way was, I forget, but in the end it worked, and I think that's great," said Wostbrock.

Laura and Lew did not renew for a second year with Wostbrock.

"We didn't leave on bad terms," said Wostbrock. "She wrote me a lovely letter [on August 15, 1991] that said she would be happy for me to represent her for television and voice-overs on a nonexclusive basis, but I don't do that.

"Again, I applaud them because they did it their way. I think Lew took over as everything: chef, cook, and bottlewasher. And again, did he do a good job? I think he did.

"Every time I worked with her, to me now, she was always professional and sweet and funny. She picked up a couple of tabs for our dinners and lunches, as I did. Lew was always at the meetings, and he was a wonderful man. Their kid, Deryk, was with them and he was always nice," added Wostbrock.

"I have listened to her and she's very opinionated, but she always was. She believes in herself so, that I really felt it was just a matter of time before she was going to become a superstar," he said. "She had that sense of self, and she just needed a break."

A break, some say, that Laura got by researching the credentials of her competition.

Laura's former patient who had become a personal friend recalled a conversation she had on the phone with Laura in the early nineties, shortly after she started on KFI.

"She told me she was having her husband look into the background of Barbara De Angelis because [Laura] was 'going to do whatever it took to discredit Barbara.'" When the friend realized exactly what Laura was saying, "It made me real queasy.

"That conversation really scared me. I responded to her by asking why she didn't get where she wanted to go based on her own merit, without stabbing someone in the back. That was the first time I ever stood up to Laura, as opposed to saying only those things I thought she wanted to hear. Laura became very angry and started yelling at me on the phone.

"I had always been afraid of her volatility. That was the thing, I always had to walk on eggshells with her because everything upset her. She started screaming at me on the phone. The screaming was so intense that I hung up the phone. That was it. That was the last time I spoke to her," said Laura's former patient and friend, who was nonetheless devastated by Laura terminating their personal relationship.

"When I stood up to her, that was it: The relationship terminated. The bond I had developed with her son, and him with me, was all yanked away within seconds of that phone call. She reeled me in to her family; she made me part of her family, and she took advantage of my vulnerability. Knowing Laura, I knew that once she did that yelling, that was the termination of our friendship."

Others also recalled Laura's campaign against Barbara De Angelis.

"When Barbara was doing her 'Making Love Grow' motivational seminars . . . Laura always detested that," said Herman. "Laura never liked the merchandising of psychology. She really hated Barbara for doing that. She had me call up and find out all this stuff about Barbara's seminars, the cost and content, things like that." According to Herman, either Laura herself or Lew did research on where De Angelis got her doctorate.

Other sources who worked at the station back then said that memos were sent to management, alerting them that De Angelis's diploma came from what was said to be a mail-order university. Miller was one of those working at KFI when the memos were circulated.

"She put a copy on everyone's desk of the information gathered by checking on Barbara De Angelis. We knew it was from [Laura]," said Miller.

Whitesides recalled the incident as well. "I know that Laura was very instrumental in making a lot of noise at the station about making sure Barbara couldn't be called 'Doctor.'"

Laura herself admitted to Leslie Bennetts of *Vanity Fair* that she complained to KFI management about De Angelis's credentials.

Barbara De Angelis, now the author of ten books, many of them bestsellers, and a recognized television personality, said she had replaced Dr. Toni Grant on KFI, and had been working there for about a year when Laura started at the station.

"I had met Laura at KFI functions, a picnic or something, after she first came. . . . I didn't socialize with anybody from KFI then. I was minding my own business and doing my own show. Tom Leikus and I were friendly, he was the other big show there, but I didn't really get involved in what was happening day to day in the station.

"I try to stay out of trouble. I'm an extremely spiritual person; I try to stay out of conflict with people because I just don't think it's a good use of energy. I have too much work to do," continued De Angelis.

According to De Angelis, she really didn't know Laura very well. "She'd been a little odd whenever I'd seen her. . . . She just would not speak to me, and I had no idea why." But De Angelis did take a phone call from Laura when she called later that year, "the only time I had actually talked to Laura Schlessinger for any length of time.

"I will never forget, she called me one day and I called her back on my car phone," recalled De Angelis. "She said, 'I really want to write a book, and I have some ideas, but I'm having a hard time getting started.' I very nicely told her everything I tell people about publishing—about how to get started, about agents, about how I divide up my material on three-by-five cards. I must have spent forty minutes on the phone with her. She thanked me so much, and I never spoke to her again."

Laura, however, denied to *Vanity Fair* that she ever asked De Angelis about writing a book.

In 1991, De Angelis got her big break with network television.

"I had just signed a contract with CBS. Nobody knew about it except for my family, and I told, probably, my screener and my producer, and I may have told the head of KFI," recalled De Angelis. "And then, that afternoon, my manager called me and told me that CBS had started getting these anonymous phone calls from somebody—a man—saying that I was a terrible person, a fraud, and that I didn't have a real degree.

"I had always told people I got my degree at an alternative school [Columbia Pacific University] and I never said I was a clinical psychologist and I never made any bones about it. I'm an educator, and I've always been an educator. Before I got my degree, I had already written a book. I've always been a researcher and an educator first," she explained.

"I said, 'You're kidding,' and he said, 'I don't understand it. They [CBS] are very upset.' . . . There were like nonstop calls all afternoon, but from the same man," recalled De Angelis. "My manager said, 'Who could this be?' and I said, 'I have no idea.'

"Because of this, we had to go through this whole process with CBS and lawyers, going back to the school where I had gotten my degree and showing their credentials. It was all fine, of course, but it was ridiculous and it cost me a fortune to straighten it out," claimed De Angelis.

"I had no idea who would do something like that, but I was suspicious, because the only people I had told were at KFI, and I think it was a few days later I found something in my mailbox at KFI. . . . It said something like 'You're a fraud' and 'How can you call yourself "Doctor"?'

"Anyway, I had been working for KFI for about two years. It was time for my contract to be renewed. My show had become the number one show in Los Angeles in that time slot, noon to three. The numbers were incredibly high.

"I forget what I was getting paid at the time, but it wasn't that much money. It wasn't what you would get paid when you have the numbers that I had. It had been two years and my agent at the time said we need to renegotiate for several reasons. Number one, because I wanted way more money. Number two was because, since the time I had started there I had written *Secrets About Men Every Woman Should Know,* and it had become a major *New York Times* bestseller, and I was being asked to do a lot of speaking engagements and touring. I had, like, three weeks' vacation, so I couldn't really go anywhere to promote the book. I had a new contract for a book, *Are You the One for Me,* and my publisher was wanting to do lots of appearances and I couldn't get the time. And, number three, I had just signed a contract with CBS to do my own daily morning talk show. I was overwhelmed. I was shooting the show. . . . I was exhausted. I suddenly had four major careers—the book career, the radio, the television, and my speaking career, and I was still giving my monthly seminars, including evening classes at my center in Los Angeles, so I was burned out. . . . I was overworked to the max.

"So my agent went in and said, 'She needs nine weeks off a year.'. . . We had all these demands. Obviously my thing with CBS, which was national, was way more important than KFI.

"I was not happy with them, anyway, and I was very torn and did not know what I wanted to do. We negotiated and had actually come to some agreement, but in the end they would not come through with what we wanted. It finally got to the point where I was starting my CBS show. I was taping them, and they [KFI] were being difficult with negotiations, and finally I talked to my agent and said, 'You know what? I'm letting it go,'" revealed De Angelis.

"I told them I was leaving; I was not fired. If you were fired at KFI, they would never let you do a good-bye show; if you're fired, you don't show up. I had a week or two and then I had an official good-bye show, which I had announced. . . . People even came and picketed the station the day I was leaving with flyers that said, 'Stop Bimbo Radio—Bring Barbara Back,' because I was leaving.

"To be honest, one of the only reasons I even considered staying was that I knew who they were going to replace me with. Laura was the logical choice. She was on in the evenings, and they needed somebody, so they were going to, I knew, move her up to that slot. I struggled with that for weeks and finally had to do what was best for me," she said, adding that her last show was September 13, 1991.

"I didn't know then what Laura was trying to do or what she was saying to the management. I would come in, say hi to everybody, do my show, and leave. Did she influence them into not paying me more so that I didn't stay? It's possible. But I was ready to leave anyway. I only wanted to stay because I felt really, really responsible to my listeners. I was overworked. It was the right decision to make," she concluded.

At that point, however, De Angelis was unaware that her uproar over her doctorate was just beginning. There would be more to come.

And, in the meantime, Laura had lots of new ideas.

Herman said Laura was looking at doing a children's book and Herman recommended an artist friend, Daniel McFeeley, to do the artwork on spec, with the idea that, if the book was sold to a publisher, he would do the original art for publication. McFeeley, a former actor who is now a full-time artist, recalled first meeting Laura about the project in 1991.

Herman continued to come back to Laura with projects, because "I liked what we were doing.

"I liked the shows we were trying to produce. I liked the way she was thinking in those days. She was thinking very creatively as well as very analytically, and that was very constructive."

Still, Herman remembered that Laura always liked to be the center of attention.

For her own needs, Laura began taking Hapkido karate lessons in a studio not far from her home.

That same year, she moved from the evening slot to the noon-to-three segment that used to be De Angelis's. Concurrently, she gave up her Saturday family and marriage counseling practice—not only to spend more time with her family, but also to avoid potential problems.

"When you're a celebrity and a therapist, either way, you're dealing with people who have difficulties. . . . I got worried that somebody might hurt my reputation because they think I'm a deep pocket," Laura told writer Irene Lacher. "That happened to a friend and I went, 'Whoa.'"

CHAPTER THIRTEEN

Character consists of what you do on the third
and fourth tries.

—JAMES MICHENER

(1907–1998)

Just four years after the death of her father, Laura went through another September misfortune: Her house caught fire in an electrical blaze.

At 6:15 in the evening on September 25, 1992, firefighters were called to the house in Woodland Hills. According to a City of Los Angeles Fire Department field incident report, the blaze began when an electrical unit in one bedroom short-circuited, setting a sheet and comforter on fire. Luckily no one was injured, but water and smoke caused $25,000 in damage to the house, as well as another $20,000 in content loss.

The timing was particularly cruel in that Laura and Lew had put a great deal of money they really did not have into redoing the house—particularly Deryk's bedroom, where the fire started.

"They spent a bundle on it with wood paneling, brass fixtures, and [Deryk] had his own bathroom," recalled Shelley Herman. "It was very nice, including the nice drapes and the designer sheets. And, again, they didn't have a lot of money to really do this, so they had really splurged.

"I also know they were displaced from their home for quite a while," continued Herman. "They were living at the Oakwood Apartments in Woodland Hills. It was very difficult circumstances for them because they were used to a home. They weren't used to this confined living. It was many months until the repairs were made."

Although admittedly "terribly upset," Laura told *People*'s John Griffiths that even though they lost many prized possessions, she was not that heartbroken. "She looked on the bright side, saying the fire enabled her to weed out her closet and go shopping!"

In addition, she also managed to attend to the business at hand: testing for her Hapkido karate black belt. In the ten-hour test, she told Griffiths, she came out "black and blue, but at least I wasn't upset."

By the early nineties, "Dr. Laura" was once more well-established on Los Angeles talk radio, and was being invited to appear on television again. She was on a series of talk shows, including *Geraldo,* where she talked about safe sex, and *Donahue.*

"In all the years I worked with them, and I hooked them up with agents, Laura always had a specific thing in her head about what she wanted to do," remembered Herman. "She did maybe a *Geraldo* and a *Sally Jessy Raphael,* and she said, 'That's it. I'm not doing any more of those types of shows.' She really did have certain scruples.

"At one time she wanted to be as visible as Joyce Brothers, but to be able to keep a credibility factor. [Laura and Lew] did a lot of things as far as trying to get people to hire her. There were a couple of movies—Dolly Parton did *Straight Talk,* and Jane Fonda was supposed to do one where she was going to be playing a radio talk-show host. Anyway, they wrote letters to them saying, 'If you need a technical consultant, hire her.'"

Still, Lew and Laura were not doing particularly well financially. Laura told writer Janet Wiscombe that Lew lost his job when Deryk was a baby, although when Wiscombe questioned Lew, he seemed unable to remember the episode and said, if he had lost his job, it was "not for long." Nor did he mention that part of his USC pension was still going to his ex-wife, Jeanne.

In October 1991, the government placed a tax lien of $6,474 against the couple's house in Woodland Hills. (It took them until April 1992 to pay the debt.)

Lew confessed that much to *Vanity Fair* in 1998; Leslie Bennetts, who conducted the interview, described him as "tearing up and turning his head away in embarrassment." "Six years ago," Lew told Bennetts, "our house was in foreclosure. We had no money. We were in terrible trouble."

But even then, Lew still took care of Laura.

In January 1993, he threw her a birthday party at their house, inviting a number of guests from the radio station, including Barbara Whitesides and Tracey Miller, as well as some highly placed company executives.

"A number of us got there," recalled Whitesides, "and she was playing tennis on the tennis courts out back." After Whitesides and other guests had been there for quite some time, it finally became apparent that the company executives who had been invited were not going to show up.

"Laura got extremely upset and left," recalled Whitesides. "We were all sort of looking at each other and thinking, 'Well now what should we do?' She left her own party because she was upset that station management slighted her by not showing up.

"I went to another birthday party of hers the year before that," said Whitesides. "Lew would constantly throw birthday parties for her. . . . I remember Laura was wearing this dress . . . with green discs all over it. She was truly the center of attention, which is where she feels the most comfortable, when everybody is praising her."

And, once again, Whitesides recalled that gifts were a necessity.

"You absolutely had to bring something for her; you had to lay something at the altar," said Whitesides. "Truly, you just didn't want to piss the woman off. You wanted to do everything that was on the up-and-up because she truly is so incredibly judgmental of everybody."

One of those people Laura had always seemed to judge was the woman she replaced at KFI, Barbara De Angelis. According to De Angelis, over the next few years she had to fight the same accusations that surfaced at KFI over and over again, and they were *always* sparked by anonymous callers.

"In the 1980s, I first got a letter from the Board of Behavioral Science Examiners that said they had a complaint saying I was fraudulently posing as a doctor and asking me to produce my medical degree," explained De Angelis. "I wrote back and said, 'I don't understand, I'm not a medical doctor. I have a Ph.D. in psychology,' and I listed a lot of well-known people at the time who were known as 'Doctor' but did not have medical degrees. They wrote me back and said, 'You are not allowed to use "Doctor" because you don't have a clinical license.' I called up my friends, none of whom had clinical licenses, but well-known Ph.D.s, and I said, 'Do you use "Doctor"?' and they said yeah, and I said, 'Have you had troubles?' and they said no. So I wrote back, and said, 'I'm confused.'

"Then they sent me the statute. . . . It said [that] the only people who can use 'Doctor' . . . are people who have a clinical license given by the State of California," explained De Angelis. "Nobody is allowed to use 'Doctor' unless they are a medical doctor or . . . you are a professor in the psychological field with a clinical license.

"This was news to me. But . . . so I said to them, 'Fine, I'll stop using it.' I wasn't famous because I was a doctor, I was well-known because of my work.

"When my infomercial started to run in 1993, it was a huge success. I was already off KFI, when once again, my manager called me one day and said the local station in Los Angeles had gotten an anonymous phone call claiming they are airing a program with fraudulent information because I'm not a psychologist," said De Angelis, who had been careful not to call herself "Doctor." "I suspected at that point who it was. We had to go into the station and take out the files from Sacramento and do the same thing all over again."

At the same time, according to De Angelis, the Los Angeles District Attorney received an anonymous complaint that she was practicing psychology without a license.

"Then I had to hire [attorney] Bob Shapiro," revealed De Angelis, "to handle the same thing with the City of Los Angeles."

"I just couldn't believe this was rearing its ugly head again," said De Angelis.

"Then [in 1992], several months after I left KFI, I received a call from a woman who sounded very nervous on the phone. She said she had been a patient and a friend of Laura's and she wanted to meet and talk to me because she had some information, and she felt very guilty she hadn't come forward with it before. I was intrigued and met with her. She came out and told me that she knew for a fact it was Laura, as I suspected, who had set out to try to destroy my career and discredit me, because she had heard Laura say it, from her mouth, and not just say it, but scream it.

"She said she had thought several times about calling to tell me, but had her own enmeshment with Laura, and now that had ended terribly, and she was coming forward because she felt awful. We went back and forth and corroborated many details with each other about Laura and her husband, Lew. I was sickened by what I heard, but at least relieved to know that what I suspected seemed to be true.

"So [later], in 1994, when I first got the call about the television station and then the district attorney called, I certainly couldn't prove it, but there was no reason to believe it wasn't Laura. . . . I had never had a problem with anybody else in my life, in my career.

"Shapiro had to go meet with the D.A. . . . . They finally dropped the whole thing.

"I promised again, 'I will put disclaimers on my infomercial that say, "This does not constitute psychological advice."' It was ridiculous. Everybody in the world . . . was using 'Doctor' . . . all of whom were in the exact position I was, including Laura, who is not a clinical psychologist, and they weren't getting singled out. I was."

To this day, De Angelis is extremely careful. "I never call myself a psychologist," claimed De Angelis. "You don't know the lengths I go to when someone calls to interview me and I'll say, 'By the way, under my name on television, do not use "psychologist."' I have to go through this every single time, because even though I have a Ph.D. in psychology, you cannot call yourself a psychologist unless you are a clinical psychologist, licensed by the state.

"It was unbelievable," said De Angelis, who said there were so many incidents that she doesn't remember them all.

"I just got to expect them. The amount of money I spent on this has just been terrible," she said.

According to Sherry Mehl, executive officer of the California Board of Behavioral Science Examiners, the government entity responsible for overseeing the licensing of all marriage, family, and child counselors, "as long as a person has a doctorate, they are allowed to use that title [Doctor]."

Part of the board's jurisdiction, however, comes over "scope of practice," which is the client/therapist relationship. The board is obligated to make sure those relationships meet the guidelines as prescribed by law.

Mehl said that among the board's functions is the duty of ascertaining that there has not been "false or misleading advertising" with regards to a therapist's scope of practice. In other words, the board makes certain that someone is not "intentionally trying to mislead the public or a client" by calling herself a psychologist, psychiatrist, or doctor when she does not have a clinical license to practice psychology or psychiatry.

"We seldom do anything unless a complaint has been filed," affirmed Mehl, "because we don't have the staff to monitor everybody's advertising. But if a complaint is filed, we investigate it in-house first, and then, if it can't be resolved, we send out an investigator."

With respect to Dr. Laura, Mehl said that although her department has received questions in the past about her use of "Doctor," the board has no jurisdiction over her because "what she does over the airwaves is not a client/patient relationship. She is not doing therapy.

"If she were calling it therapy, it would be a different issue," continued Mehl, "but she is really careful not to do that."

The woman whom Laura had treated, on and off, for two and a half years confirmed that it was she who first contacted De Angelis back in 1992.

"Sometime after Laura and I had the last conversation where she told me she wanted to discredit Barbara De Angelis, I was made aware that Laura was getting Barbara De Angelis's spot [on KFI]. I knew then that [Laura] did exactly what she had said she was going to do. I contacted Barbara to see if what I suspected was true.

"I . . . didn't have any allegiance to [Barbara] because I didn't know her. I just wanted to know if what Laura said she was going to do—did she really do it.

"I told [Barbara] what I had heard," said the former patient, "and she said that was exactly what had happened."

In the meantime, this patient had taken action on her own behalf. In May 1992, she filed a consumer complaint against Laura with the Board of Behavioral Science Examiners. The board handed off the complaint to the Department of Consumer Affairs Division of Investigation, which assigned it to an investigator.

"The investigator told me she was confident there was enough evidence," said the former patient, who added that the file was then turned over to the attorney general's office for review to see if the case was prosecutable.

"I talked to Anne Mendoza, deputy attorney general, on September third 1992, at 3:15 P.M.," said the former patient, reading from notes. "Basically what she said to me was the attorney general will only pursue a case if they are ninety-nine percent confident they can win it.

What they said with Laura was she did violate all the boundaries, but boundary violation is not gross misconduct. Yes, she violated the boundaries [between patient and client], but not to the extent that the law states it takes in order for disciplinary action to be taken. Basically what she [Mendoza] said was you must prove extreme and gross negligence. She interviewed Laura, who supposedly told her that 'everything she did was for my best interests.'"

On August 25, 1992, the Board of Behavioral Science Examiners responded by letter to the patient's complaint. It read in part:

". . . As you are aware, the Board conducted a formal investigation into your allegations of unprofessional conduct by Laura Schlessinger. Specifically, she is alleged to have engaged in a dual relationship with you by expanding the professional boundaries of psychotherapy to include numerous instances of personal, social and business ventures. . . .

". . . The Office of the Attorney General has advised us that they believe there is insufficient evidence to prove the case by 'clear and convincing evidence to a reasonable certainty' as required by law. We are therefore closing our file in this matter today. . . ."

According to the former patient, she filed the complaint for two reasons.

"First," she said, "because I found it was very damaging to myself. That whole thing [her relationship with Laura] created more issues for me that I didn't have first going into therapy. And, more importantly, I didn't want it to happen to other people. I felt they needed to know what type of person is out there, spewing out all this advice on the radio and being so contradictory in terms of what she says as opposed to what she does."

Interestingly, the June 11, 1992, "Morning Report," published by *The Los Angeles Times,* featured a blurb that stated Laura had been named by California governor Pete Wilson to the state Board of Behavioral Science Examiners.

According to the governor's office of appointments, Laura's appointment was from May of 1992 to July of 1992, and was marked with the words "resignation."

While the appointments secretary said she had no idea why Laura resigned after less than three months, she said the resignation was accepted and another person appointed to fill the vacancy on the eleven-person board. A short time after that, Laura also terminated her private practice.

Several years later, Laura's former patient ran into Lew at Topanga Plaza in the San Fernando Valley, where Laura was broadcasting her show from the food court. Seeing Lew off to one side, Laura's former patient approached him.

"He looked at me very surprised, and he asked me why I did what I did," she recalled.

"I said, 'Well, look what Laura did to me.' And he said, 'Well, you almost ruined her. She almost lost everything. What you did was very serious.' I said it was the only option I thought I had for what she did to me. I just said to him, 'I didn't feel I had any choice in the matter,' and then I walked away," concluded Laura's former patient.

By 1992, Whitesides, who had originally liked Laura and had gotten her son, Blake, together with Deryk to play, had also decided it would be emotionally impossible to be Laura's good friend.

"I started to back off," admitted Whitesides. "She really seemed like she wanted a friendship, but she was one of those people in your life that . . . to be a friend with them, the price you would have to pay would be enormous. Literally, she would have to control [the friendship], and you would have to act the way she expected you to act. She is easily slighted, extremely easily slighted. You might not even know what you've done until she takes the opportunity later on to *really* let you know, in no uncertain terms, that you have crossed the line. It became apparent to me that there was no way you could be a friend with her and maintain your sanity."

And, by this time, things were deteriorating with Laura's work relationships as well.

Whitesides, who had a seven P.M. to nine P.M. on-air slot at the station, said she also occasionally did a show entitled *The Women of KFI*.

"I'd have a few of the women, like Tracey [Miller] and Marilyn [Kagan] and a couple of others," explained Whitesides. "Well, it got to the point where the other women didn't want to go on with Laura because she was so much the final authority. She didn't want to play fair. You didn't have a good time if Laura was there. She was the definitive answer. If anyone called up and made some comments, Laura would basically sum things up and everybody else [on the panel] was supposed to be in agreement with her. And, if you disagreed with her, I mean she just gave you daggers, like 'How *dare* you disagree.'"

Whitesides also remembered Laura's cutting remarks about many of the other women who worked at the station.

"She put Marilyn down constantly. I think she was intimidated by the fact that Marilyn was better credentialed. She wanted to be supportive of Marilyn when Marilyn first started, but as Marilyn became more popular, all of a sudden [Laura] would throw in little remarks about Marilyn here and there. I think she wanted to see her demise. Anybody who was really successful, she wanted to see their demise, particularly women. For someone who appears to champion women, interestingly enough, any competition whatsoever [by women], she would like to see them not do well."

Marilyn Kagan agreed.

"Oh, she was always on me, always picking on me. On the radio, off the radio," said Kagan about Laura.

A successful television talk-show host in Los Angeles, mother of a young daughter, and a licensed clinical social worker who still keeps a small practice, Kagan first met Laura back in 1991 when she was invited by station management to try out as a substitute for hosts on KFI.

"I had never done radio before," confessed Kagan. "I'd been a successful actress for years, and I'm not stupid, but this was a totally different thing.

"So Laura, not graciously now that I look back on it, consented to let me sit and watch her work the board and talk to callers. This woman was intelligent, driven, quick on her feet, and in my first perception, nice but tough.

"Laura was acerbic, not as acerbic as she is now, but people like that. She could cut to the chase. She wasn't as horrible and as preachy and moralistic as she is now, but she did very well," thought Kagan.

The two began what Kagan believed was a friendship.

"She would call all the time, at home, to ask me to lunch to gossip about Barbara De Angelis, to connect with me. I was so flattered because [starting out in radio] I felt like I was twelve years old again, going into junior high school. I was really scared. I felt like 'Oh God, I have an ally.' We shared a lot," explained Kagan.

Kagan told Laura in detail about her problems getting pregnant. "She didn't share much about her infertility. She did tell me once she had problems, but I didn't know she had a reversed tubal and all that stuff. On the other hand, she sure got a lot out of me.

"I talked about how depressing it was and how painful the procedures were and how I'm a much older mom by now. She would always say, 'I know, but it's a wonderful thing.' I was so grateful she was there, letting me sit in on her show, so I opened up to her very much."

And according to Kagan, Laura "took that information I had shared with her and used that against me."

But at first, Kagan was still practicing her own radio style, sitting in occasionally as a guest host.

"I was terrible to begin with," remembered Kagan, laughing, "but I got better. So I actually sat in for Laura a few times that summer. Still I thought I would have a year or so to sit in. I thought, 'This is great. I'm still working as a family treatment person and I have my own practice and I'll just learn over the years by filling in.'

"Two months later, in September, I get a phone call that De Angelis is out and that Laura is coming to the new time, and could I sit in, and they would try me for a month," said Kagan, who ended up staying in the nighttime slot at KFI until 1997.

"And then, when it became clear I was going to get a job, and Laura was moving to Barbara's place, all of a sudden, the phone calls stopped.

"Then I heard . . . she wanted me to be fired because I was sick.

"I heard through other sources, and later it was validated by my boss, that I was supposedly very ill [because of the infertility treatments] and that I would probably be out for a long time and it was silly to hire me on a full-time basis. And then Laura said, 'Why don't you check out a friend of mine?' She had a male therapist, a psychologist she wanted to have my boss interview.

"That's when I got wise. People said, 'You shouldn't really put your trust in Laura; she will stab you in the back,'" said Kagan. "Laura looks for your Achilles' heel. She finds the place where you are most vulnerable and then she lets you have it. She also has a . . . meanness that frightens people who are kind. There is a certain sense of insecurity with us, and we feel we can't fight back. And then in the next hand, she seduces you with her friendship.

"When I heard she tried to fire me, that really began me opening my eyes to try to take a look at her—her personality and her character," continued Kagan.

"Then in 1994 I got a television show, which really put Laura through the roof. It came to the point where she would pick on me on the air about how disgusting my shows were and all that," said Kagan. "I went to my boss and I said, 'That's slander.' My boss said, 'It's better to just ignore the whole thing.' I think that was part of the problem with Laura, is that people just ignored her and allowed her behavior. Of course, I know why they do it now, because she is bringing in a fortune.

"There was an analyst who once said, 'Righteous indignation gives people a license to be cruel.' That is Laura's bottom line. It gives her license to be mean, to be hateful, to jump on people. She had a right to her own opinion, but the way she expresses herself is so demeaning. I think this righteous indignation she has now supports her in her ability to be hateful. It supports the denial of her hostility," explained Kagan.

"To make it in this business is really unbelievable. You have to really admire that. But there is no joy in Mudville, because she is so hateful and ungracious; people hated her before she had the money. I think they think it's unfair that evil wins out, and that's why people finally started speaking out about her," concluded Kagan.

Whitesides said Laura did not appear to have many friends.

"People kind of stayed away from her. The last thing you wanted to do was ask her advice because she would give it to you, and as far as she was concerned, she had the answer."

Meanwhile, Laura had also picked up a new sideline: acting.

She appeared on *Quantum Leap* as a therapist, and picked up small parts in *Santa Barbara*. She also played an extra in her all-time favorite program, *Star Trek*. Then, in March 1993, she appeared for the first time on the Los Angeles–based soap opera *General Hospital,* as an obnoxious television reporter. She did well enough that she was asked back in July 1995.

Although it is not unusual for *General Hospital* to bring on "real-life people" for cameo appearances, Laura was not playing herself.

"In our story line," explained Scott Barton, the program's former publicist, "we had a girl who played the role of Robin. She met a character named Stone, a kid from the alleys. They fell madly in love—except Stone, at the time, did not know he was HIV-positive. It was Robin's first sexual encounter, and they were cautious because she was a nineties teenager. Anyhow, it turns out Stone finally tests positive for AIDS.

"The scenes Laura did were at a walkathon. She played a kind of snotty, upper-class society person who is not even introduced. The people in the story were walking through the park and she said something to the effect: 'Why do we have to give up our day in the park so *those* people can have their walkathon?' Then it gets worse, along the lines of 'It serves them right. It's God's curse.' She is thinking it's like a gay fund-raiser and they all deserve to get AIDS because they're gay.

"Then Stone and a couple of other people address her and read her beads—like 'Who are you to judge?' and 'What gives you the right?'

The show didn't answer the questions; it just aired two very prominent and deeply rooted opinions.

"The thing that struck me the most about her was that she was so willing to take direction and eager to do whatever she could for the good of the story. I was impressed the way she took on a part that was not a popular role at all. The things that she said were mean-spirited and bigoted, yet she delivered them with conviction. But I know it was really hard for her, because I know it was not at all the way she truly, in her heart, feels about the whole situation," said Barton.

Still, on her own show, Laura would have been even more blunt in expressing her feelings about teen sex and sex outside marriage. And, while some of her listeners might have questioned whether Laura should have appeared in any role on a daytime program that frequently portrays out-of-wedlock sex, Laura's answer would probably have been much as it was two years later, when she wrote an article for *TV Guide* on the subject of morality as it is played out on television.

"Those who create works for public consumption have a responsibility for the content and the intent," Laura wrote.

"The issue isn't that I think no rotten, disgusting or offensive behavior should be shown, but when the context and consequences don't resolve the good vs. evil problem, we help breed crassness, cynicism, and selfishness."

Although Laura obviously enjoyed appearing in dramatic roles, the main thrust of her career was still radio, specifically her daily program on KFI.

In the early spring of 1993, Whitesides recalled an incident while Laura was broadcasting that finished their relationship.

"I came in to pick up one of my final checks," recalled Whitesides, who explained she had been "cut loose" by the station. "Anyway, I came to the station on a day I wasn't working, and I had to leave to go somewhere else.

"At this particular time, the [broadcast] booth was in the center of the radio station, and all the talent's mailboxes were in there too, which was a really strange setup. Most of us were kind of cool about it. It was a *huge* room, so to walk into it you would kind of slide around the back wall and go over to your mailbox, and kind of wave to people [who were on the air]. People were pretty conscientious about not making a big deal or making a lot of noise. Anyway, I am standing outside the booth [where Laura is on the air] and I'm thinking, 'I'll wait until she gets into a commercial break to go in.' Her producer at the time came by and said, 'What are you doing?' and I said, 'I'm waiting to pick up my check.' He said, 'Go ahead and go in.' And I said, 'No, I'll wait,' and he said, again, 'No, it's fine. Go ahead and pick up your check.'

"After him saying it twice, not to worry about it, I walked in very, very quietly, lifted my check out of my mailbox, and was quietly going back to the door. Laura glanced up at me with this look on her face, and gives me the wait-a-minute sign. I thought maybe she wants to say hi. She finished her thought on the air, turned off her mike, and she just unleashed on me. 'How *dare* you come into the booth when I have got the light on? Don't you *ever* do that to me again!' She yelled at me like a harpy. It was the most amazing thing. All I did was kind of look at her like a deer caught in the headlights. I didn't say anything; I just kind of walked out."

Kagan was in the studio when the incident occurred, and recalled seeing Whitesides as she came out.

"Barbara, who is this six-foot-two-inch, big, beautiful woman, was devastated and in tears," she remembered.

"It was so upsetting to me that I cried in the car on the way home," revealed Whitesides. "It was because I was so shocked; I wasn't prepared for it.

"I thought, 'That's it. The woman's too strange; I don't want to deal with her.' Then, a couple of weeks later, there is this strange message on my answering machine from her. At that point, we weren't super close. Our kids had done a couple of things together, but Laura had created such a distance between herself and everybody else at the station.

"Anyway, I had this message from her on my answering machine. It was this sheepish little voice saying, 'I miss our friendship. What's wrong? Aren't we friends anymore?' I thought, This is weird! No apology or 'I was probably a little strong with you' . . . nothing else like that. She really had no clue that she had done something that would be upsetting to me. I didn't respond because I thought, 'I'm going to keep myself away from this woman.'

"It was shortly after that," recalled Whitesides, "that Lew had the heart attack."

CHAPTER FOURTEEN

We don't find meaning in our lives from a lack of challenges
or even misery. We find meaning in our lives by how we
face these challenges.

—DR. LAURA SCHLESSINGER

"THE LAST WORD,"

AUGUST 16, 1998

May 4, 1993, closed hot in Woodland Hills, and Lew Bishop felt strange.

Toward bedtime, Lew told Laura he didn't feel well, and got up to get a drink of water. A few moments later, he collapsed on the floor of the couple's three-bedroom ranch house. He was unconscious and not breathing when his distraught wife rushed to his side. She frantically checked for a pulse, then called for paramedics.

Kneeling next to her husband, Laura tilted his chin backward to open his airways, pinched his nostrils with the fingers of one hand, and, with the other, held his chin as she pumped two deep breaths from her lungs into his. She touched the pulse points in his neck for a moment, feeling for movement, then, with palms overlapped, began to push into his chest just below the sternum. Finishing a count of 15, she once again grasped his chin and pushed air into his lungs. She continued, waiting anxious minutes that seemed like hours, for the paramedics to arrive.

Shelley Herman, a longtime friend of Laura's, said that Laura was truly frightened by Lew's heart attack. At the time, Herman said they didn't want visitors, so instead Herman sent cards and called Laura regularly to check in.

"I knew that Laura was scared," revealed Herman. "It was really the first time she had contemplated life without Lew or life as a single mother. It was really overwhelming to her." Laura told Herman she was actually on her knees in the hospital corridor, screaming in anguish about what she was going to do.

"I was asking about Lew. I thought if I could get her off talking about her and talking about Lew and the recovery, the things medicine can do, it might be more uplifting. I never had seen her as frightened and vulnerable and irrational before, and for so many good reasons. She was finally getting her ducks lined up. They had worked so hard to get her back on the air, to get a family going, to have a nice home that they could share together—and then all of a sudden this happens."

Tracey Miller thought that Laura was "overwhelmed."

"It was all about Laura," said Miller. "I remember she told her producer she could no longer visit Lew [in the hospital] because it was 'too much' for her."

Shortly thereafter, Laura began to suffer panic attacks.

Miller remembered with clarity the first attack she witnessed, when Laura collapsed in the KFI offices:

"She was arguing with her screener," recalled Miller, "and then I saw her go down on the ground. She just folded. Then she was vibrating . . . and had trouble breathing. She was crying and carrying on. Suzanne Whatley [the KFI news director] took charge and told everybody to stand back. I just remember standing there . . . that it looked like an epileptic seizure. When the paramedics arrived, they took her out on a stretcher."

Barbara Whitesides was also present, though she didn't actually see Laura go down. The two were no longer friends by this point, but, said Whitesides, "Regardless of what kind of issues I had with her, I felt really bad for her."

Shortly after Lew's heart attack, Whitesides sent him a plant at the hospital. "I said, 'I hope you're feeling better,' or something like that," she recalled.

A while after sending the plant, Whitesides received what she thought was going to be a thank-you note in the mail. It was typewritten and addressed as having come from Lew Bishop himself.

"He says, 'Because of the way you've been treating Laura, we gave that plant away to some other patient,'" said Whitesides, who added that even though it was typewritten, she assumed it really did come from Lew. "[Laura] didn't respond at all; she just had him do it."

For the next few months after Laura's emotional collapse at the KFI studios, Miller said her producer was commissioned to drive her to and from work. Laura "came back and continued to do the show," said Miller, "but you could tell when you heard her on the air that she was medicated."

Miller left KFI shortly thereafter, but first, she had her own day of reckoning.

"Laura called this meeting between me and her and the general manager to face off about difficulties we were having," explained Miller.

According to Miller, Laura had turned her in to station management for allegedly breaking a company policy that Miller swore to this day she did not break.

"She was constantly telling me to my face what a great mother I was," said Miller, "which was important to me because I was a single mom—those strengths and weaknesses [Laura] looks for again. Anyway, when we had our meeting, I told her, 'What really irks me is how you go on air putting single parents down . . . then you come off and tell me what a great parent I am. What is the truth?' And she said, 'Oh surely you're not going to hold what I say on air against me.'

"I think Laura would like to be the only woman at any given radio station," added Miller.

"Laura has said that anybody who speaks negatively about her is 'just jealous of her success.' That's not true. If you asked me about Laura . . . years ago, before she was successful, I would have answered the same way," said Miller.

John Griffiths of *People* said Laura told him that she sought therapy for six months after Lew's heart attack.

"She told me how terrifying it was for her during the aftermath," said Griffiths. "She said she was fearful all the time and having tremendous bouts of anxiety. One time Lew ran across the room and she said she practically had a coronary."

While her panic attacks had Laura worried that she might be on the cusp of having her own physical breakdown, she didn't consult doctors; instead, Laura retreated to what she knew.

"She sought comfort from her karate instructor," reported *Newsweek*. "His response? A succinct order to 'start kicking.'"

Laura did, and her panic attacks subsided.

Her panic surely had to do, at least in part, with how vulnerable she would be without Lew, especially raising an eight-year-old son. Lew, who would undergo six heart procedures in the next year, was barely up to taking care of Deryk, let alone working a full-time job.

At that point, Laura was a salaried employee, working for KFI as a local talk-show host weekdays from noon to two P.M. She had just turned in the manuscript of her first book, and her show was enjoying superior ratings, but having spent several years "in between assignments," Laura was well aware she was part of a fickle industry.

"Nobody wanted to syndicate me," Laura later told Steven Cole Smith from the *Fort Worth Star-Telegram*. "All the companies that syndicate—I had called them, begged them, written them, faxed them—just about every one didn't return my calls. They were extremely rude. 'It's a woman, it's a shrink, it won't work'—that narrow-minded thinking."

So, when Alan L. Fuller—a longtime radio advertising sales and marketing executive—approached her with a proposition in mid-June 1993, barely a month after Lew's heart attack, Laura was ready to listen. Recognizing Laura's potential, Fuller broached the idea of marketing her as a national spokeswoman for a 900/800 help-line telephone service and, at the same time, syndicating her show. Laura jumped at the offer.

The big problem, as always, was financing.

Fuller knew John M. Shanahan, then the owner of Gateway Educational Products, which marketed "Hooked on Phonics," and approached him about becoming the financial partner. Over the next year, they formulated plans, eventually dropping the 900/800 help-line idea for a full-court press toward national syndication.

On June 27, 1994, they sealed the deal. Shanahan Marketing International (SMI), later renamed Shanahan Broadcasting International (SBI), took over production of *The Dr. Laura Schlessinger Show,* including the rights to syndicate it internationally. Laura's debut was in twenty-five markets.

She was to be paid an annual salary of $250,000 to host the show, and, more importantly, would receive 20 percent of the show's net profits. Fuller was to get $210,000 in salary to manage the show and, after April 1996, 20 percent of the net profits. Shanahan, who put up the collateral for the deal, was essentially the show's owner, so he was set to reap the greatest profit: a full 60 percent.

Back in 1995, between 700 and 800 of the nearly 10,000 AM and FM stations in the United States were airing talk-radio programs. Although not as many people listened as do now, they made up about the same portion of the total radio audience: 16 percent.

Radio stations had a vast menu of talk-show programming to choose from because syndication was not then a major factor, so local hosts had a shot at getting their own program, albeit only in one market.

"In the very, very old days, stations paid cash for syndication," re-

membered Michael Harrison, editor and publisher of *Talkers* magazine, a trade journal for the industry. "In the 1970s, it went to what is
known as the barter system."

Under the barter system, the syndicator would get approximately 50
percent of the advertising minutes available while their "talent" was on
air, and the local station would get the other 50 percent of the advertising minutes to sell.

"'Hooked on Phonics' was her built-in sponsor to begin with," explained Harrison. "It provided the funding to start the syndication.
They [the 'Hooked on Phonics' people] were very successful at advertising. They knew how to use radio to sell advertising."

Also to their advantage was the fact that talk-radio audiences, according to Harrison, tend to be "educated and reactive." In other
words, while listeners who tune in to music tend to tune out ads, talk-
radio listeners pay attention.

"They are likely to respond, especially to a direct response commercial," concluded Harrison.

Still, Laura had to be heard before the money could roll into
anybody's coffers. To help with marketing, Fuller and Shanahan reportedly signed a contract with Radio Today, an established radio
syndication distributor.

"Radio Today was an up-and-running radio syndication company
that had affiliate-relations representatives, and the know-how of advertising and promoting. They had established relationships with stations and a general . . . lay of the land of the industry," explained
Harrison.

By the summer of 1995, just ten months after going national in
twenty-five cities, Dr. Laura was making house calls through 150 stations from Canada to Florida. At that point, her weekly audience was
estimated at between 9 and 10 million people, 9,000 of whom called the
show each day to be put on the air.

Even though the numbers are estimates—syndicators do not release
their entire affiliate lists, which makes it difficult to definitely pinpoint
listenership—Laura's numbers were good, and growing stronger.

"A lot of people never have a shot [at stardom] because they don't have the right backing. Unfortunately, the cream doesn't always rise naturally to the top. There are so many entities vying, that unless you are marketed heavily, you may not be noticed for your talent," explained Harrison about part of the reason for Laura's success.

Laura's talent notwithstanding, Harrison, whose magazine has a readership of more than 90 percent of all businesses in the industry, always believed that much of the credit for Laura's success in syndication had to do with the talents of several individuals, but particularly of one man: Geoff Rich.

"One of the real reasons Laura was going to be big was because of the professional, personal marketing of Laura Schlessinger to the industry and beyond," said Harrison. "Geoff Rich is the president of Radio Today . . . and I credit him with being one of the key people in marketing Laura."

According to Harrison, during 1995 Radio Today put a tremendous amount of time and money into packaging *The Dr. Laura Show* to make it visible to the general managers and programming managers of talk-radio stations across America: the people responsible for deciding which talk-show hosts would get airtime.

"Radio Today advertised and promoted her," claimed Harrison. "They had teams of people on the telephone, talking about her all the time, and they had excellent affiliate service. When a station general manager went to work, there were materials about Laura on his desk. There were ads in the trades, and constant phone calls."

Early on, *Inside Media* reported in May 1996, Rich established a mandate "to limit new affiliates to top markets and grow slowly." This strategy also helped advertising sales. In fact, *Advertising Age* reported in April 1995 that thirty-second spots on Dr. Laura's show were then going for $1,500.

"The number one great reason for [Laura's] success is Laura Schlessinger. But beyond Laura's great talent, Geoff Rich and Radio Today was the combination that started it. [Laura's show] could have died if it had not been for them. They marketed her heavily for at least a year," said Harrison.

Herman, like many people who knew Laura back then, felt the turning point in her career was when Shanahan decided to bankroll her show. "The people I knew were at KFI," recalled Herman. "This is when the business started working for her, because then it wasn't as hands-on in her day-to-day life. She and Lew could turn more of the business over to these professionals.

"Originally, she never wanted to sell out by marketing T-shirts and stuff," said Herman. "She always had a great deal of integrity. She never wanted to be that crass about this stuff. She did a little newsletter, but it was something that was done on her computer and then there was a couple in San Diego doing it for her. It was a very mom-and-pop type of thing, but she really did want to keep the personal touch to it. "I can see where her ego took over with this stuff. Who wouldn't want people walking around with her face on their chests?"

Then on June 24, 1994, nearly a year and two months after Lew's first heart attack and just three days before they signed with SMI, Laura and Lew filed suit in Los Angeles County Court against the Sylmar Medical Center and four of its doctors.

According to the complaint, Lew Bishop, who had an existing cardiac condition when he started seeing the doctors at Sylmar in April 1993 (in fact, Lew's mother died of a heart ailment), underwent a series of tests and treatments to detect abnormalities and decide upon a course of action. The examinations failed to discern that Lew was about to experience a major heart attack. Lew and Laura thus sued, first, for malpractice, asserting that because of it Lew had sustained "injuries" to his body and nervous system, "including mental and physical injury, pain and suffering."

Lew asked for sufficient damages to cover "necessary medical and incidental expenses incurred for the care and treatment following the negligent treatment by defendants" as well as "loss of earnings and future loss of earnings" (Lew was now unable to work), "future medical and incidental expenses," and "future expenses which will be incurred for [his] custodial care and treatment."

The second part of the couple's lawsuit alleged "negligent infliction of emotional distress against all defendants." Laura maintained that seeing her husband collapse and then doing CPR to bring him back to consciousness "sickened and traumatized" her, causing her to "sustain great emotional disturbance, shock and injury to her nervous system."

Labeling herself "a direct victim of the acts and omissions" of the defendants, Laura, too, asked for similar damages, including compensation for the "services of physicians, psychologists, counselors and related incidental services."

According to Laura, she was "severely hurt and injured in her health, strength and activity in that she contemporaneously observed the traumatic collapse and near death of her husband."

Although Herman was not aware that Laura and Lew had filed a malpractice suit, she said she was not surprised.

"If she was trying to fix blame on her problems with somebody else, [filing a lawsuit] makes sense," said Herman.

Then, just two weeks after filing suit, Laura and Lew felt well enough to sign purchase papers on a vacation house on Bay Road in fashionable Lake Arrowhead, California.

Still, between caring for Lew and Deryk, and working her shift at KFI, Laura pretty much left the management of *The Dr. Laura Schlessinger Show* up to Fuller. Laura felt Fuller was a loyal friend who would take care of her interests as well as his own.

She also had her hands full promoting *Ten Stupid Things Women Do to Mess Up Their Lives,* which had just been published by a division of Random House in February 1994. Laura went on a tour that winter to promote the book, leaving her own show with reruns. Laura knew from personal experience what could happen when someone filled in for an absent talk-show host, and she was adamant that the same thing would not happen to her. One of Laura's stops on her promotional tour included a gig in Denver, Colorado.

A talk-show psychologist named Dr. Audrey Brodt had just taken over for Andrea Van Steenhouse at KTLK in Denver, after having been a fill-in for her on occasion. In this case, Van Steenhouse had chosen not to move from one station to another, so Brodt was hired instead.

During her second week on the air, Brodt was informed by management that a guest was coming to promote her new book, and that that guest was Laura Schlessinger. Brodt had never heard her before and thus, as she put it, "I had no frame of reference."

"So, she arrived at the station and I went in to greet her. I'm this pathetically nice person, and I say, 'I'm sure you were expecting to be interviewed by Andrea,' and then I go on to explain what happened at the station. I was trying to be gracious and nice.

"She looks at me," continued Brodt, "and you know how you can [beckon] someone over with your fingers . . . that little motion. Well, she took me to the corner of the room and said, 'You're new at this. Let me give you some advice. Never, never, never, never let anyone fill in for you.' I just looked at her. Then she said, 'How did you get this job?'"

Acknowledging that it was a point well-taken, Brodt said that Laura then went on to say that she never let people fill in for her, having them rerun tapes instead.

But the bombshell, for Brodt, came when Laura gave her the second piece of advice.

"She said, 'And number two, always, always, always, always call yourself "Doctor."'"

"At that time," concluded Brodt, "I didn't know she wasn't a doctor [of psychology or psychiatry]."

Brodt said she cannot understand how Laura gets away with calling herself "Dr. Laura."

"It is considered unethical to call yourself Dr. so-and-so if you are presenting information and your doctorate is not in that field. When I was on air I checked her out. I called the licensing board in California and she has a license as a marriage and family therapist. So yes, she has education in the field. I'm not saying that she doesn't. I just question whether it is ethical to use 'Doctor' when your doctorate is not in psychology or psychiatry."

Brodt also was unimpressed with how Laura answered a caller on her own show that same day back in 1994.

"You have to understand," explained Brodt, "that I was so new in the spot [of hostess]. We get on the air, it's a new station, and I'm grateful when we get a call. This guy calls, I don't remember his name, but he is the first call of the day. He starts out by saying, 'You know, I've lived in Denver for a year now, and I think the women in Denver are very unfriendly.'

"[Laura] jumps right in, and she says, 'It's not the women, you're the problem, and you've probably always had this problem.' I am, like, dying. I can't believe this woman. She didn't even ask him any questions. A guest usually defers to the hostess—but she just jumped right in. I was so mortified."

Brodt said her own style was quite different. "If I am on the air as a mental health professional," she explained, "I have a responsibility to model appropriate behavior. What we know about human behavior is that what is modeled is the most powerful influence."

Then Brodt laughed.

"Of course," she concluded, "she is nationally syndicated, and I'm off the air."

And in truth, the Dr. Laura phenomenon was continuing to swell.

The book tour had heightened her national image, and the book itself not only ended up on the *New York Times* bestseller list but also garnered a number of reviews, most on the positive side.

The Orange County Register, for example, bottom-lined *Ten Stupid Things* with the words: "Good, solid advice—if you're brave enough to take it."

Meanwhile, back on the radio side, while Laura was the creative talent, Fuller was the man behind the scenes. Together with Radio Today, he was putting together a media and marketing blitz aimed at top talk-radio stations throughout the United States and Canada.

In less than a year, Dr. Laura had become a recognized name. She was then on air in over a hundred markets, including most of the major ones, and her show was generating advertising revenues in the millions.

In April 1995, the radio trinity of Dr. Laura, Fuller, and Shanahan decided to add merchandise as well. Together they formed Worldstar Productions, Inc., to distribute a wide variety of Dr. Laura–branded items, such as "I Am My Kid's Mom" T-shirts, sweatshirts, and hats, as well as a Dr. Laura newsletter. This time, the split was to be in equal thirds.

But, with added success came added problems, in the form of a producer-manager.

"Throughout late 1995 and early 1996," Laura would write in a declaration she gave as part of a mid-1996 lawsuit, "I had numerous discussions with Mr. Fuller about the extension of my employment contract with SBI.

"Early on, whenever I would ask Mr. Fuller about the status of my contract, he told me that the contract was being held up by Mr. Shanahan. He explained to me why there was a delay signing an extension of my contract with SBI because, according to Mr. Fuller, Mr. Shanahan would not give him what he wanted in his contract. Mr. Fuller told me that he was trying to get an ownership interest in SBI. Mr. Fuller described Mr. Shanahan as unfair because he would not give him [Mr. Fuller] an ownership interest; I wanted to be loyal to Mr. Fuller so I waited."

At the same time, Laura and Lew were still in the midst of their malpractice suit.

The attorney for Sylmar Medical Center filed a total of twenty so-called wrongful death interrogatories, seeking more detail from Lew and Laura concerning their alleged injuries, medical history, employment, and loss of earnings. Sylmar requested copies of bills, invoices, receipts, accounting records—any evidence of the kind and amount of expenses the couple incurred after Lew's heart attack.

Reportedly, Lew and Laura objected to the phrase "wrongful death" (since no one had died), even though both it and the questions Sylmar asked in the interrogatories were warranted according to the state code of civil procedure.

By July 5, 1995, when there was still no response from Lew and Laura's attorney, Sylmar's lawyer asked the court to compel them to respond to the request for documents, and asked for a monetary sanction of $254 to cover "reasonable expenses and attorney's fees" in connection with the proceeding.

On August 15, 1995, the entire case was dismissed—with prejudice, which essentially means the suit cannot be refiled.

Also dismissed, with a different sort of prejudice, was Laura's ex-mentor, Bill Ballance.

In December 1977, Ballance left KABC, having been replaced by one of his resident sages, Dr. Toni Grant. The next month, he moved to a station in San Diego where he broadcast six nights a week for the next fifteen years. By 1995, however, he was hoping to land a spot on Laura's station, KFI.

According to a report first published in *Biography* magazine in 1997 and later corroborated by both Ballance and Dr. Norton Kristy, Laura was not happy about the thought of Ballance working at KFI. She reportedly wrote him a letter saying, "If KFI hires you, I will resign."

That, of course, never happened.

CHAPTER

FIFTEEN

Nobody is normal.

—DAVE BARRY

DAVE BARRY TURNS 50

At 4:31 A.M. on January 17, 1994, Laura and Lew, like thousands of other residents in the San Fernando Valley, were sleeping when the world started quaking around them. With their eight-year-old son, they dodged falling objects in their newly remodeled ranch house as they withstood the gyrations of an earthquake that later would be measured at 6.6 on the Richter scale.

Though its initial jolt lasted ten seconds, followed by thirty seconds of ground shaking, the quake was one of the largest ever to hit metro Los Angeles. Laura and Lew's house lost electrical power at the same moment as 82,000 other houses in the valley. Many people also faced disruptions in water and phone service, which remained jammed throughout the city.

Meanwhile, outside it was pitch black.

"All the alarms went off when the earthquake hit, and not one light was on," recalled Vern Buller, whose house is in the same area as Laura and Lew's. "All you could hear were car alarms and home alarms going off.

"Everybody was out in the street," said Buller, "walking around like zombies. It was hard to conceive of what was going on. You could tell by looking at us that we were bewildered. It was so scary."

Laura conveyed similar feelings to John Griffiths of *People* several months later, describing that night as "chaotic."

Jack Warford, who lived directly across the street from Laura and Lew's old house, remembered people standing out in their yards, yelling over fences, "Are you okay? Are you okay?"

Within seven minutes of the first shock there was an aftershock with a 5.0 magnitude. Throughout the day, the aftershocks, hundreds with a magnitude of 3.0 or greater, continued to shake the San Fernando Valley, the epicenter of the earthquake.

"When the shock waves hit, they roll just like ripples in water. They hit something, and then they bounce back and reflect. Where you had crests coming together, in most respects, that was where you had the most serious damage. It was like you could almost draw a line where the heaviest damage was," explained Warford.

"The damage varied, from the house on the corner, which was condemned," recalled Warford, "to most of the other houses that had chimneys that fell down, and cracks in the plaster. And, of course, everything fell off the shelves, but that was about it. The only ones [on Laura and Lew's block] who had to move out were the people on the corner."

In comparison with the upheaval Laura and Lew experienced in 1993, the year when their house caught fire and Lew had his heart attack and subsequent health problems, the earthquake was noteworthy but not as damaging—either physically or mentally.

Less than six months after the earthquake, in June 1994, Laura sat for her first interview with *People*. John Griffiths, the correspondent who visited their Woodland Hills home and spoke with Laura, Lew, and Deryk, recalled that it seemed their life was finally coming back together.

Griffths described the place as a rambling ranch-style house with a huge backyard and a ranch-type fence out front. "It was not extremely well-kept, manicured, or green," said Griffiths. "It was not glamorous. Her taste, at the time, was kind of like a Valley housewife, which was, in a way, refreshing. It was nice to know she didn't have this 'Jim and Tammy Fae' lifestyle."

Griffiths saw Laura herself as almost a pert little housewife, "with a Donna-Reed-on-speed sort of quality."

He was, of course, referring to her high energy level and fast talk.

"She's a mile a minute," remembered Griffiths. "I got the feeling she likes to hear herself talk, so she talked a lot. She also self-congratulated . . . patted herself on the back a lot. She is very proud of her accomplishments."

Still, Griffiths sensed a vulnerability in her boastfulness.

"Maybe it comes from the pain again, like she has to reaffirm who she is with herself. She is a tad defensive, like she is ready to be punched a little bit.

"My instinct is that she is not cynical. I think she wants to help people," he said. "She's got this strident quality that seems to mask some pain. Some people wallow in it; some people deal with it in therapy. I think she kind of decided . . . to move on, almost in a way like not dealing with the past."

An able interviewer with thousands of hours of tape-and-pencil time spent looking into the lives of personalities, Griffiths makes his living thoughtfully observing people. He was struck by the relationship between Laura and Lew.

"There was real love between the two of them," recounted Griffiths. "I talked to him on the phone again a few days later. I've interviewed people where there is a personality like hers and a personality like his and they seem a little exasperated. I didn't get the sense of that.

"I remember Lew as very mild-mannered, extremely low-key, and a good guy. They have a good relationship. He takes her motor mouth, her craziness, in stride.

"I think there is genuine love in her eyes when she looks at him. She feels safe and warm. That's where the woman who collects teapots and has these cute, fringed, Donna Reed–type curtains in the kitchen looks at him like, 'I have a loving husband who is just great.'

"She seems to get out of herself with Deryk and with her husband," said Griffiths.

"She was always looking around [during the interview], saying, 'Where is my son?' She did listen to him, but she was very righteous about her motherhood powers. I don't know if she spoils him, but she certainly dotes on him."

Certainly, Laura took pride in Deryk's accomplishments—encouraging him, for example, in his entrepreneurial efforts.

Jack Warford, the neighbor who then lived across the street, was impressed when, earlier that year, Deryk started a recycling business. According to Warford, Deryk walked the neighborhood and placed a little note on every door.

"Deryk said he would collect all the recyclable aluminum cans people had and take them to the store, where they had a recycling machine. He would put the cans in the machine, then come back and split the money. He did that about five or six times I guess," revealed Warford.

Shelley Herman, who first met the family in 1983, said she had always known Deryk to be a "polite, articulate child." "He tends to have his mother's opinions," she added, "but he can state them well."

A broadcast journalist who interviewed Laura around the same time agreed with Herman's assessment of Deryk. This reporter visited Laura's radio show to do a story about child care, in the course of which she asked Laura how she would expect single mothers to choose between feeding their families and placing their children in day care.

"Her son called just then," remembered the journalist, "and she said, 'Let me ask him. He would have a great answer to this.'"

Laura then handed the phone to the broadcaster, who found herself speaking with Deryk personally.

"He was very articulate and said something to the effect that there are always ways to make do without having to put your child in the care of strangers. I think he was about nine at the time. He was amazingly articulate. He definitely has her frame of thought that you are not supposed to warehouse your children in day care," recalled the broadcaster.

When Griffiths did his interview with Laura in 1994, he, too, noticed her obvious pride in Deryk, going on and on about how Deryk could convey his feelings to others and help others.

According to Griffiths, Lew even acknowledged that Deryk was going to be just like his mother, and when Griffiths asked Deryk what he wanted to be when he grew up, Deryk promptly replied, "A psychotherapist."

In all, Griffiths remembered Laura as "boastfully happy," both about her son and her life. "She was proud," he concluded, "to be living life on her own terms."

And lucky that the money was finally rolling in.

One of the couple's first major purchases that summer was a second home, situated in the ritzy mountain community of Lake Arrowhead. The resort is located just ninety miles east of Los Angeles, up a winding highway where endless lines of tall pines, cedars, and other dense vegetation hug the road's edge. Only thirty minutes from San Bernardino by car, it seems light-years away from the harried L.A. lifestyle.

The lake itself, 784 acres of crystal-clear mountain water, is man-made. Except for some 10 percent of land, primarily around the lake, the area is completely surrounded by the San Bernardino National Forest.

Lake Arrowhead is the kind of community where celebrities are regular commodities. It is not unusual, for example, for Roseanne to wander into the bakery in the Village Square, dressed in a T-shirt and shorts, her young son and her husband, Ben, in tow. Or for Kurt Russell and Goldie Hawn to sun themselves in the white plastic chairs at the Belgian Waffle restaurant, located dockside near the lake. Patrick Swayze has spent time there, and Mark Harmon and Pam Dawber are regulars, along with Frankie Avalon and Herb Alpert.

In 1994, when word spread that Dr. Laura was buying a house, many of the locals said, "Who?"

"We don't get her radio station that easy up here," explained a local store owner who lives at the lake year-round. "So most of us had never heard her on air."

The first property Laura and Lew purchased was a $220,000 house off Bay Road.

And then they bought a boat. It was a Cobalt, considered by many in the business to be the Mercedes of speedboats.

"Once they bought it," recalled a former employee of Mile High Marine Storage, Inc., in Lake Arrowhead, "it was like they didn't feel they had to pay any bills that came up on the boat. They took anywhere from six to nine months to pay their bill, and then they refused to pay any late interest. I saw the invoices."

The ex-employee also said Laura and Lew were "very demanding" about service.

"We had four hundred and fifty boats we put into storage, and everybody wanted them by the three-day weekend in May. So if you didn't make advance reservations for that, we couldn't get it all done. [Laura] would call two days before and expect you to drop everything and service her. It's not fair to the other customers.

"We dealt with lots of celebrities. Mark Harmon had been a customer for about ten years. We had Patrick Swayze for several years, and Frankie Avalon. They are the most pleasant, unpretentious people. When they call to ask for something, they actually come out and tell you, 'I don't expect preferential treatment because of who I am.' That's what they all say. 'Just put me in line like everybody else.' Mark Harmon even works on his own boat. They have never demanded to be put ahead in the line because of who they are. They are like regular people."

Not so, Laura and Lew.

"Her husband came in one day to get the boat out, and when the owner's wife explained she couldn't do it because they didn't have their advance registration in and that would mean another customer wouldn't get their boat when it was promised, he got really huffy.

"He said to her [the proprietress], 'I am so tired of you petty little mountain people. [Laura] busts her butt for [the community]. She donates her time and she was in the Christmas parade, and she speaks at the hospital. Nobody does anything for her. You just take advantage of her.'

"It's like, donating your time at the hospital doesn't excuse you from paying your bills," he said. "She doesn't feel that she should have to follow the rules, and, because she is a celebrity, they should just be forgotten."

Then there were the bubbles.

Laura, the ex–marina employee explained, kept Lew calling about the bubbles around her boat.

"This is going to sound really dumb, but she kept calling and saying that the bubbles that come up from the back of her boat didn't look like everyone else's bubbles. Somebody said to her, 'Remember, when you are looking at other people's bubbles, you're looking at them from the back of the boat, *outside* of their boat. When you're looking at the bubbles behind *your* boat, you're looking down, overboard. You have a side view, so they are going to look different looking overboard.' She kept insisting there was something wrong with this boat because of the bubbles, and she wanted the owners to take it back.

"The owner kept checking it. Finally she meets the owner at the marina so he can ride with them and see what the problem is. Laura shows up with a bunch of kids and her husband. The owner gets in the boat, and he says, 'Okay, you drive it so I can see what you're doing.' There is a five-mile-an-hour buoy, and after that you can hit the gas and go. [Laura] tootles on out to the five-mile buoy sign, and makes a little stop, and then she says, 'Okay, is everybody ready?' Then she punches the engine and goes flying up out of the water. The first wave she hits, she smashes. 'Now,' she says, 'the rule is, whenever we hit a wave, everybody throws their hands up in the air and yells, Wheee.' Then she lets go of the steering wheel, jumps out of her seat, and everybody is doing this 'whee' thing. It was a clear violation of lake rules.

"They have a very arrogant air about them. They don't feel that any rules apply to them. They [rules] apply to everyone else but them, and that's exactly how they talk to you," he said.

It was also apparent to many in the Lake Arrowhead community that Laura wears the pants in her family.

"He does all the phone calling and all the talking," recalled the former Mile High employee, "but you know what's coming out of his mouth came from hers. You can tell the difference between when he is demanding things and when he is just talking like a regular person. She very rarely calls to handle anything. It is always through the husband."

In 1996, Laura and Lew purchased another boat, an even bigger and more expensive Cobalt, somewhere in the $40,000 to $45,000 range.

"She gets a lot of buyer's remorse," believed the former employee. "They have had this big one a second season, and I hear they want to get rid of that and get a pontoon boat. She is constantly changing her mind.

"Then, when they came in to buy the boat," added the former employee, "he stood back quietly and let her do all the talking. When they were outside, she and her son would climb in the boats, and he stayed on the side with the salesman.

"Her and the son are like the main things in the family, and the husband is just kind of there," believed the employee.

And it is not just store owners who have felt the wrath of Dr. Laura; Lew has gotten it as well. Publicly.

"A couple of years ago they were pulling their boat into a dock at

Woody's [a popular restaurant on the lake]. They were coming in too fast, or something like that, and hit the side of the dock," recalled a resident who witnessed the event. "They [Laura and Lew] were there with some friends, and Laura started yelling at him [Lew]. I mean, loud. Pretty soon he was yelling back. The whole thing was completely embarrassing."

Still, since moving into the community, Laura and Lew have also tried to contribute.

Laura has broadcast her radio show from the plaza in the village square and also from outside the Belgian Waffle restaurant on the dock, a favored eatery for the family.

"Every year, the beginning of December, we do this little Christmas parade, and Dr. Laura was like the grand marshal that first year she lived up here," recalled another resident. "She sat in a little car and waved."

Then, in August 1996, the Mountains Community Hospital Foundation at Lake Arrowhead asked Laura to participate in a fund-raiser to garner money for renovations to the hospital.

"It was our capital improvement program, Project 2000," recalled Chris Klein, executive director of the Mountains Community Hospital Foundation, "and we asked Laura to be our featured speaker at a black-tie dinner. She was the hostess and took questions from the crowd. Her husband, Lew, was there, and her son, Deryk, collected all the questions on notecards from the crowd. She did like she does on her show."

In addition to Laura's talk, the foundation auctioned off hospital rooms to be named after the highest bidder after remodeling. According to Klein, Laura waived her standard speaking fee, and instead asked that the hospital name a room after her.

When the renovations were completed, in December 1996, the birthing rooms at Mountains were fitted with a brass plaque that read: "The Dr. Laura Schlessinger Obstetrics Department."

It was an apt title for a woman who was just celebrating a rebirth of her own.

CHAPTER

SIXTEEN

The best of all the preachers are the men
who live their creeds.

—EDGAR A. GUEST

(1881 1959)

Given that Laura's first experiences with people of the Jewish religion were not altogether pleasant, her conversion to Judaism was surprising to some.

Laura was, after all, raised by a Jewish father whom she did not particularly admire and a Catholic mother who was verbally attacked by her in-laws for not being Jewish. Laura herself told reporters that when the family moved to the suburbs of New York, her mother was snubbed by Jewish neighbors. Indeed, when Laura was in her teens, both her parents joined the Unitarian Church. And the man whom Laura met, married, and divorced in New York was also of Jewish descent.

It must have been harder still for a scientist like Laura, whose intellectual development was moored in biological principles and theories that often contradict conservative religious viewpoints, to take the leap into Orthodox Judaism.

Yet, despite her history, despite the fact that (as Laura has repeatedly said) she was raised with virtually no religious orientation at all, she went on to claim what she perceived as her religious heritage.

She has said that the impetus for her to become a Jew came in 1991 or 1992, when her son was watching a program about the Holocaust. Never particularly good with dates, Laura has told various publications both that Deryk was six and that he was five when they saw the program on the Holocaust. But, if the date was not important, the event certainly was. Watching television one rainy Saturday morning, Laura recalled her epiphany exactly.

"Suddenly we're hearing Elizabeth Taylor's voice-over as they're showing actual footage of the Nazis lining up women with their babies, and mowing them down into a pit. My son says, 'What is this? Who are they?' And I say, 'Those are Nazi soldiers.' And he says, 'What are they doing?' And I say, 'They're murdering Jews.' He says, 'What are Jews?' And I say, 'Our people.' He turns to me and says, 'What are you talking about?' And at that moment I thought, It's time I claim my heritage. Because frankly, without religion, life has no meaning." That was how Laura described the event to Mary Mohler of *The Ladies' Home Journal.*

Earlier, she had told another publication that her interest began even before that. "We had our son," she told the *Ethnic Newswatch,* "[and] family religion became an issue."

She went on to say that even though she "identified Jewishly," she really did not know the meaning of Judaism. To find out, Laura said, she studied theology, and came away "impressed with Jewish thinking."

Then, in the 1998 video on the Ten Commandments that Laura did for PBS, at least partially as a fund-raiser for public television, she added yet another reason.

First airing in late summer of 1998, her presentation started off by chronicling Laura's own religious evolution. She retold the story of seeing the PBS special on the Holocaust with Deryk, and then related another anecdote, involving Lew, about the absolute moment she realized there was a God. Laura said Lew and Deryk were watching a program about biblical history and archeology when suddenly Lew, who was raised Episcopalian, turned to her and said, "'Odd, don't you think?' and I said 'What, dear?' and he said 'How many cultures, for four thousand years, have tried to eliminate this tiny group of people, and they are still here.'

"I dropped the book [she was reading] and I started to cry. I said, 'Oh my God, the covenant must be true. There is a God, because that was the deal made at Sinai.' I am walking around the house infused with this realization I don't know what to do with, and this sense of acceptance. It was at once for me very peaceful, very nice, very comforting and very confusing. What do I do with this now? That was the genesis of reading Torah [the Jewish Bible] and studying it," Laura told the studio audience.

In 1995, when she went to check on joining Temple Aliyah, a 2,000-member Conservative synagogue near her home in Woodland Hills, she discovered that, for purposes of determining who is Jewish, descent is traced through the mother rather than the father. Since Lundy was Catholic, Laura was not automatically Jewish, and would have to convert.

To prepare, Laura and Deryk underwent a Conservative conversion program through the University of Judaism in Los Angeles. For over a year, they studied Hebrew, Jewish history, the Bible, and how to make the Jewish law part of their everyday life before finally going to mikva—a ritual bath marking their religious transformation—in April 1996.

Lew did not go through the conversion with his wife and son.

In January of 1997, he told Rebecca Johnson, writing for *The Independent* (London), that he had not yet converted. When she asked him why, he responded that he had been "busy" managing his wife's career and then added, "and there are some things about it I'm still struggling with."

When Johnson asked him what he was struggling with, Lew replied, "Oh, the problem of evil."

But Lew kept with it, with personal help from Reuven Bulka, an Orthodox rabbi, author, and radio personality from Ottawa, Ontario, Canada.

In the acknowledgments to the book she published in 1998, *The Ten Commandments,* a book she wrote with Rabbi Stewart Vogel, Laura wrote that Bulka had faxed her after hearing her program in Ottawa, and eventually began to mentor the family's Judaic studies. Rabbi Bulka appeared to be equally taken with Laura, praising her highly in the 1998 *Vanity Fair* article.

"To call her America's conscience," said Bulka, "is not an exaggeration."

Within the Jewish religion, Orthodox Jews (as opposed to Conservative and Reform Jews) interpret and adhere to the laws and rituals more rigidly as defined in the Torah and in oral teachings.

Judaism is based on the premise that God created humanity out of love and out of a desire to give to humankind. Accordingly, the ultimate goal of a Jew is to be in an intimate, detailed, close relationship with God. Orthodoxy sees that as the ultimate purpose of Jewish ritual—to connect with God by attempting to observe all of the 613 commandments that Orthodox Jews believe were given by God.

Laura told the *Ethnic Newswatch* that her family started with the ritual of keeping kosher, even before they attended their first class at the University of Judaism.

According to the Torah, only certain foods are fit for eating, and procedures for preparing them are carefully spelled out in both written and oral teachings. The practice of keeping kosher is about holiness. There are certain foods not to be eaten at all because they are not holy, and other foods that God has commanded to be prepared only in certain manners, for the same reason.

Thus, Orthodox Jews do not eat certain species of animals, specifically animals that both chew their cud and have a split hoof; thus pigs are not kosher. Nor are predators. Jews eat sheep, goats, cows, birds that were eaten historically by their grandfathers, and fish that have both fins and scales, which eliminates lobster, shrimp, and crab. In addition, food animals must be ritually slaughtered in a prescribed, humane manner.

Meat and dairy foods are never eaten or cooked together, nor are fish and meat. Those foods are not cooked in the same pan, nor are they served on the same plates. Processed kosher foods, rigidly inspected by an authorized or recognized authority, such as the Va'ad Hakashrus, may be used only if they feature a hechure symbol. The Ⓤ hechure is the most widely recognized.

Within Orthodoxy there appear to be differences in how families practice the teachings regarding how observant they are in keeping kosher rules. Laura told the *Ethnic Newswatch* in April 1997 that she was "95 percent" kosher when she eats out.

Taking another step, Laura said, the family then began to observe Shabbat, the Sabbath.

Shabbat is the holy day, which for Jews is Saturday. Shabbat begins eighteen minutes before sunset on Friday and runs through sundown on Saturday. Most Orthodox Jews attend services in their local synagogue on Friday night, Saturday morning, and late Saturday afternoon. Men and women pray separately.

No work is done on Shabbat. That means, for example, that observant Jews do not drive (even to synagogue), shop, cook, or even flip on light switches.

Laura confessed to the *Ethnic Newswatch* that Shabbat was, at first, difficult for her. "For me you get up on Saturday, eat breakfast and go to the mall. All week you work your brains out; this is the reward. The first couple of Saturdays, I literally stayed in bed," she said.

Laura told her rabbi that she didn't particularly like Shabbat, and he encouraged her to keep trying.

"I have two and a half million obligated behaviors or prayers, plus candles and more prayers, and synagogue, and more prayers," Laura told *The Ladies' Home Journal*. "I am immersed; it's like being back in the womb."

But Laura admitted that there are still temptations.

"We'd been observant for about a year when a tennis club invited my son to play in a Saturday tournament. I felt terrible for him. Then he said, 'It would be okay if we hit some balls as a family, but to be out there competing, wanting to beat somebody else—that doesn't sound holy.' The point is, he grasped it, he embraced it," she told Mohler.

An important part of keeping Shabbat has to do with the formal Friday meal. When the holy day begins, at eighteen minutes before sunset, the females in the family light candles; dinner follows when the family returns from synagogue. The meal starts with traditional blessings and the singing of Shabbat songs.

"We're good at it," Laura told the *Ethnic Newswatch,* though she admitted they still used sheet music.

Laura was not quite so good at following other laws surrounding Shabbat.

When John Dart, a religion writer for *The Los Angeles Times-Valley News,* interviewed Laura in September 1998, she admitted to driving to services at the West Hills synagogue, and to flipping on her closet light switch to find clothes to wear to services.

"We don't live in a neighborhood where we can walk [to synagogue], and we regret those breaches," Laura told Dart, adding that her family was "slowly moving toward expressing" the commandments laid down by Orthodox law.

Traditionally, most Orthodox rabbis have said Jews should refrain from driving on the Sabbath. Also, the Torah forbids Jews to "kindle a fire on the Sabbath." And while there is a divergence of opinion among Conservatives on whether that should be held to include the use of electricity, most Orthodox rabbis believe that electricity and fire are similar, and therefore ban the use of electricity, even when flipping on a light switch.

By May 1998, Lew had completed his conversion, and, Laura told John Dart, the whole family then underwent an Orthodox conversion in Ottawa, conducted by Rabbi Bulka. That same month, Laura and

Lew were remarried in the Orthodox tradition, with three rabbis performing the ceremony.

"It was wonderful," Laura told Dart.

Then, in the introduction to her book on the Ten Commandments, Laura also revealed that the family was planning to visit Jerusalem in 1998 for Deryk's bar mitzvah.

On air, Laura is careful never to mention God's name, and in *Ten Stupid Things Men Do to Mess Up Their Lives,* she renders "God" as "G-d."

In Orthodox Jewish tradition, to write out the word "God" is like taking God's name in vain. For people in the observant community, that means not writing God's name at all, or else changing it a little. Hence, "G-d."

And, while Laura's practice may not always be strictly in accordance with Orthodoxy, many Orthodox Jews would not fault her.

"I want to be clear that I don't condemn people's inconsistencies," said one Orthodox Jew, who asked not to be identified. "I just think it's important to call things what they are. If someone were to ask me if I'm Orthodox, I would probably tell them that my theology is Orthodox— I believe that the Torah is G-d's word and that the interpretations apply for all time. However, I would say that my practice is growing towards being more consistent with Orthodoxy. So, I don't know where Dr. Laura stands. She may mean by saying that she's Orthodox the same thing I do. I can't judge her."

In fact, Laura has often said—for instance, in her book on the Ten Commandments—that she is "a serious Jew, not a perfect Jew."

Laura told *U.S. News & World Report* that after reading a passage in Genesis concerning God's covenant with man she ran downstairs to Lew and said: "Lew, I'm a priest and my mission is to help God perfect the world."

Then, to Janet Wiscombe of *The Los Angeles Times Magazine,* Laura twice spoke of herself as a prophet.

"I bash everyone," she told Wiscombe. "I want to make an impression. I have to get people's lives on track. I am a prophet."

Most Jewish educators would think that calling oneself a prophet would probably be going too far. "Prophets are considered designated by G-d," said one.

Kathryn Levy Feldman, writing in the summer 1998 issue of the Jewish publication *Inside,* noted that even though Laura wears "a diamond Star-of-David pendant, keeps kosher (even while admitting to missing bacon), refuses to travel or work on the Sabbath and sends her son to a Jewish day school, the gospel she preaches derives from the Judeo-Christian tradition.

"The Rev. Gregory Adkins, pastor of the Washington Street United Church in Alexandria, Va., recently posted the following on his signboard, 'If you think that Dr. Laura Schlessinger is judgmental, moralistic and helpful—you should listen to Jesus Christ.' Someone sent her a photo of the signboard and she shared it with her listeners. 'I don't consider that blasphemy,' she laughed," wrote Feldman.

With respect to homosexuality, Laura at first seems to have drawn a line, albeit with a few hedge marks, between her views and Orthodox Jewish law. Orthodox Judaism is very precise in that it condemns the act, although not the person. However, Laura told *U.S. News & World Report,* "[This] is something that God and I will work out later."

She explained her views on the subject more fully to *Good Housekeeping* in March 1996:

"It is my professional opinion that one does not choose to be homosexual or lesbian. I cannot, in good conscience, tell someone that they cannot have a lifelong companion of love and affection. I go after people if they are frivolous about their sexuality."

But, two years later, in August 1998, Laura was being more definite with regard to homosexuality and Jewish law. When a twenty-three-year-old gay man wrote to Laura's nationally syndicated newspaper column that he was "confident in my sexuality" but shopping for a formal religion, Laura made it quite clear that Jewish law and tradition forbid homosexual acts.

"I appreciate that for some this presents a dilemma and a struggle," wrote Laura. She then named two organizations that assist people "desiring to restructure their sexuality from homosexuality to heterosexuality.

"And of course," she concluded, "there is always abstinence."

Laura draws another line, this one in concrete, with respect to children.

"Individual homosexuals and lesbians are as capable of functional, important, creative, loving lives as are individual heterosexuals," she wrote. "But to suggest that this state of being is equivalent morally or practically to heterosexuality is taking an advocacy to the degree of being destructive to children's development."

In fact, according to Laura, the only station that ever canceled her program did so because of her stance on homosexuality.

"They dumped me because they said, 'She talks to homosexuals as though they were human.' I got a better station across town, so I worked out okay," Laura told *Newsday*.

Questions concerning the Jewish ideal of modesty were raised by some Orthodox Jews who have seen Laura attired, as she was in a *Vanity Fair* picture, with her shoulders fully exposed. Generally speaking, the more observant, ultra-Orthodox Jews deem that all females should wear long-sleeved dresses and never wear slacks. Many married ultra-Orthodox women also wear a headcover.

Like many religions, Judaism teaches forgiveness; for this and other reasons, Laura decided to contact her mother.

She told Larry King on his show in 1998 that she had attempted to contact her mother, and she told the same thing to Shelley Herman in August of the same year.

"She said to me they hired a private investigator. They found her mother and they sent a letter to her, and she sent it back as undeliverable," said Herman.

If it is true that Laura has tried to contact her mother, they are not attempts Laura has talked about in her book, *The Ten Commandments*, whose longest chapter is devoted to the fifth commandment, "Honor your father and your mother, so that your days will be lengthened upon the land that the Lord, your God, gives you."

Nor did Laura mention in the book that she has been estranged from her mother for more than fourteen years, though she has publicly discussed her problems with her mother elsewhere. She did explain, however, how she interpreted the commandment.

"We are not commanded to respect our parents, in terms of holding them in high regard," wrote Laura. "Instead, we are commanded to behave in a certain way toward them that reflects their status as parents, sometimes in spite of our opinions and emotions about them."

Then, when discussing the fact that some brides and grooms dishonor their parents when they do not invite them to their wedding, Laura added that such "dishonoring," "in fairness, . . . is not always the fault of the child. Some parents create so much tension with their children that they make it a matter of self-defense to be excluded, as is the case with an addicted, violent parent. When the parent is a disappointment or annoying, as is the case with an immature or self-centered parent, I suggest that the invitations be sent anyway—there are some circumstances that simply must be accepted and with which we must cope."

Laura told John Dart of *The Los Angeles Times-Valley News* that her mother was not invited to her and Lew's Orthodox wedding. Nor had Lundy been present for the original wedding in October of 1984, in front of a justice of the peace.

Orthodox Judaism also has a taboo, although not an actual commandment, against sex before marriage. Of her own history, Laura has said that being in college in the sixties, exposed to what she calls "secular feminism," had a profound effect on her actions, as did her parents' "inter-faithless marriage."

"Had I, in my 20s, had the perspective I now embrace, I would not have had sex outside of marriage," she wrote in her syndicated column. "I am proud of the journey I have taken toward a more holy life, and I realize I have miles and miles to go." That column appeared on September 6, 1998, shortly after the article in *Vanity Fair* hit the newsstands.

Dr. Norton Kristy, who admittedly has not seen her in a dozen years, nonetheless guesses that she was sincere in her conversion to Judaism and in her belief that she has "found the light, the road, or the path to all truth."

"The fact that it answers a basic question for her, I think, is secondary," said Kristy. "It frankly does not surprise me at all that Laura has come to a passionate belief in religion and in morality that she would like to hang on to, or hold very, very tightly to her, because she was pretty much lacking a moral and ethical compass when I first met her twenty-three years ago."

"There is a huge thing about discipline with Laura, and I think that is why she embraced the Orthodox faith. There are rules, hard-and-fast rules, and she functions real well in that kind of environment," said Herman, who also happens to be Jewish.

According to Herman, the last time she spoke with her, Laura was thinking of hiring a "legal couple" (kosher) to live on her property and do the cooking, so as to keep the kitchen truly kosher.

"I think religion has wonderful things to offer," Laura told a Montreal paper in 1997. "It makes you stop and think about whether what we are doing is right or wrong, as opposed to secular law, which makes you wonder whether what you are doing is going to get you arrested or not."

For Laura, 1996 was truly a year of new beginnings. Not only did she convert to Judaism, but in April she and Lew also bought a new house, located in a gated community called Hidden Hills, just around the corner from Woodland Hills. Laura and Lew sold the Woodland Hills house for $2,023,636; they paid only $1,275,000 for the new house, which was over twice as big. Both houses had swimming pools, but the new house had one more bedroom and two more baths, as well as three fireplaces. For the decor, Laura selected soft colors: peach and turquoise.

The Hidden Hills house was clearly a step up in size; at the same time, it enabled them to buy a larger property in Lake Arrowhead, worth $1,350,000. In August 1997, Lew and Laura finished remodeling their new house there, with its dock right on the lake.

"It's much larger and more prestigious [than their previous Lake Arrowhead house]" was how one town resident describes Laura and Lew's latest purchase.

To christen the new abode, Laura had it completely wired as a broadcast studio so that she could spend the month of August doing her show from the comfort of her vacation home.

Laura has said that she was warned not to come out on her radio show as religious.

"Everybody said it would destroy my show," she told *The Ladies' Home Journal.* "And anti-Semitism would come out of the woodwork. The irony is that my biggest supporters have been the Christian community. The president of a Bible college told me, 'I just love your show, and I'm so glad you're Jewish. If you were Christian, you would be instantly discounted as a right-wing fundamentalist maniac.'"

Laura has said that her show switched from "mental health to moral health as I evolved religiously."

"I'm more of a Jewish mother," she told *Publishers Weekly* in 1998. "I nag."

And nagging, it would seem, was working. Laura's talk-radio show was clearly soaring into the big time.

The reality is that one can believe and live by standards . . .
but imperfectly. That is not hypocrisy, that is the reality of
the limitations of all human beings to attaining divinity.

—DR. LAURA SCHLESSINGER

THE TEN COMMANDMENTS: THE SIGNIFICANCE OF GOD'S LAWS

IN EVERYDAY LIFE

Whether in spite of her religious conversion or because of it, Laura's audience continued to multiply. By the late nineties, the estimate was 18 million listeners on 450 stations; between 52 and 54 percent of those listeners were men.

Laura told *Psychology Today* the reason she has such a high male listenership has to do with "men-bashing," which she does not do.

"Historically," she said, "shows dealing with relationships were men-bashing. That's why the men weren't listening. And I came along and I bashed whoever needed it. Nondenominational bashing. And the men found a place where they could be comfortable. I hit them over the head when I think they've done something wrong. But they see a fairness."

However, not every person sensed that same fairness. Laura was having difficulties with others on the broadcasting front.

In August 1996, Shanahan Broadcasting, Inc. (SBI), the production company for *The Dr. Laura Schlessinger Show,* fired producer Alan L. Fuller for allegedly increasing his own salary by $100,000 a year without authorization and misappropriating company assets. Fuller, who had worked with the show for over two years and had been quoted in newspaper and magazine articles as president of SBI, filed suit in 1996 against Laura Schlessinger, the SBI firm, and several individuals; he claimed that, under his contract, he was owed 20 percent of *The Dr. Laura Show*'s net profits.

"Although I, like Mr. Fuller, was only an SBI employee and had nothing to do with the decision to terminate Mr. Fuller, I am named as the lead defendant in that lawsuit," said Laura in her statement to the court. "Based on our relationship, Mr. Fuller knew that naming me as the lead defendant would upset me."

As part of that lawsuit, Fuller was allowed to depose Laura, which he did on Sunday, April 27, 1997. During the deposition, Laura said Fuller asked her "questions about the future plans for ownership, production and syndication of the Dr. Laura Schlessinger Show, including whether SBI was canceling its contracts with various affiliates which now carry my show."

Since parting ways with SBI, Fuller and a partner had formed a new company, Netstar Seven Entertainment Group International, Inc., to market a competing talk show hosted by Dr. Toni Grant, a former colleague of Laura's. (Back when Laura was getting started at KABC in Los Angeles, she did a Sunday seminar with Grant, Bill Ballance, and Dr. Norton Kristy.)

"Dr. Toni Grant is also a person in talk radio" is how Laura described her in the lawsuit, "although inactive for some seven years since KFI, the Show's current flagship station, fired Dr. Grant.

"Years ago, I had a week-end radio talk show at the same local radio station, KABC, where Toni Grant had a week-day radio talk show. Dr.

Grant is fiercely competitive and apparently was threatened by the success of my weekend show and my fill-in appearances on her program. According to a sales executive, at the time, she insisted that the radio station fire me and agreed to a cut in pay or other consideration in exchange for the radio station's agreement to fire me. Mr. Fuller is aware of these facts."

In the "trade secrets" lawsuit filed by Laura and SBI, Fuller was alleged to have "misappropriated certain trade secrets and proprietary and confidential information owned by SBI," including customer lists and the dates and times Dr. Laura's show was broadcast. These, the suit alleged, gave Fuller "an unfair competitive advantage."

Because SBI and Laura had just sold the production and syndication rights of her show to Synergy Broadcast Investment Enterprises, her affiliates were about to be asked to sign new contracts. According to court documents filed by her attorneys the day after Laura's deposition in Fuller's suit, dozens of her affiliate stations received faxes from Netstar, urging them to drop Laura for Toni Grant. The faxes read as follows:

"Now that Laura's terminating you, you have a choice! Don't be pressured into signing a new contract; secure the talk show opportunity of the year, Dr. Toni Grant, for your station before your competition does!

"She's back and taking the country by storm! Dr. Toni is America's original radio psychologist who has an established, loyal following and is winning the hearts of new listeners since her return to radio just one month ago. She'll be in your market soon—don't let it be on someone else's station." The flyer continued on how to obtain a demo kit.

Laura, by all accounts, went ballistic.

In court papers, she called Fuller's action "a vindictive attempt by Mr. Fuller to interfere with my relationship with the affiliates stations which now carry the Dr. Laura Schlessinger Show and encourage those affiliates to discontinue the Dr. Laura Schlessinger Show in favor of Mr. Fuller's new venture, the Dr. Toni Grant Show. Of course, by his acts, Mr. Fuller also is hoping to interfere with and adversely affect the relationships that have been developed with the sponsors of the Dr. Laura Schlessinger Show."

In addition, Laura was "outraged" by Fuller's allegations that he was the "founder, creator, and executive producer" of her show.

"These false assertions have the potential to, among other things, impair my credibility with my affiliates and sponsors because they will think that I and the Dr. Laura Schlessinger [Show] are the creation of Alan Fuller and that the continued success of the Show is in jeopardy because Mr. Fuller now is affiliated with Dr. Toni Grant."

More of the same fax went out from Netstar the following day. Laura's attorneys were already preparing a "trade secrets" lawsuit, seeking to bar Netstar from sending any more faxes, and asking, among other things, for compensatory and punitive damages.

The request for a restraining order was dropped just three months later. In the meantime, none of the parties involved could say how or why the lawsuit was settled because of a confidentiality agreement.

Regardless of what dollar amount was settled upon, though, Laura no longer had any financial problems. The rewards of her labors were providing Laura with an increasingly more comfortable lifestyle, for which she did not apologize. During 1998, Laura frequently said on her show that people should not have to apologize for having money. She certainly didn't.

Then, on May 27, 1998, she announced on air that her family was moving that day to a new house. The excitement was evident in her voice, although she didn't mention to her listeners the lavishness of her new digs.

Located in the same gated community of Hidden Hills, Laura and Lew's spread, purchased for $3.6 million, was a two-story stucco with a tile roof, five fireplaces, and the mandatory swimming pool. With 9,427 square feet of living space, including four bedrooms and seven and a half baths, the family members would have to do their best to find one another.

Life was good.

In addition to her fourth book, *The Ten Commandments: The Signif-icance of God's Laws in Everyday Life,* appeared on September 9, 1998, and immediately hit the *USA Today* and *New York Times* bestseller lists. Laura also had a children's book in the hopper for April 1999, to be published again by HarperCollins.

"It's a story about a little boy," explained Daniel McFeeley, the graphic artist who worked on the book with Laura and her co-author, Martha Lambert. "Basically, the gist of it is that when a child is angry with you, the child hates you and wants you dead. So, of course, the child thinks the parents think the same thing about the child. This is Laura's attempt to quell that and quiet a child's fear about that. The analogy in the book is that love is like the sun behind a cloud. Even though a cloud may drift through every once in a while, the love, like the sun, is always there."

McFeeley, who was first brought to the proposed book project in 1991, was introduced by Shelley Herman, then a mutual friend of his and Laura's. The project lay dormant for nearly seven years and was finally resurrected in April 1998.

"I was working on a movie, *The Addams Family,*" recalled McFeeley, "and they wanted me right away. It was like, Come hurry up. I finished up the last two weeks of the movie, which was really nice of them [Laura and Lew]; they could have kept shopping.

"She had me over to her house and told me that the publisher insisted that they use their own illustrator, but she had a deal with me, and she really wanted my stuff. Laura said, 'No, I'm sticking with my guy.' She was really loyal to me.

"Since then we have had a little back-and-forth time, decisions about the book, and she has faxed me on every little thing . . . little colors and what kind of doll the boy was going to have when he went to bed or what kind of typesetting for the cover of the book. And Laura said, 'Do what he [McFeeley] says.'"

McFeeley added that when they first began the project in 1991, Laura was not nearly as well-known as she is now.

"We all signed equal payments contracts, so whatever was made on that book, we were all going to share equally on profits . . . and [Laura] stuck with the original contract. She's really come through," said McFeeley.

Besides radio and print, there was the persistent rumor that a television show was also in Laura's future, although Laura told Steven Cole Smith of the *Fort Worth Star-Telegram* in 1996 that she did not like TV.

"I disdain regular television," she said. "It's candy for the eyeballs. What I can do on radio is infinitely more profound and meaningful. You could never get me away from radio.

"Many have tried," she continued. "I've been offered infomercials, I've had major companies offer me television shows [she declined to name them]. I get offers on a daily basis that would make me a millionaire [although she already was]. And I turn them down. I'm not tacky."

One of the "major unnamed companies" Laura was referring to was Universal Studios, which in the fall of 1994, did, in fact, come to Laura with an offer. Back then, at least one of the executives at Universal Television was a great admirer of both Laura's books and her shows.

"I do admire her," said one executive, who asked not to be identified. "It was [for] that reason that I phoned her initially."

So Laura was called in to talk with Universal about doing a project that might appeal both to her and to the studio. The show she was initially interested in doing, *Rant N' Rave,* was not a television version of her radio program. Rather, Laura would first stand up and "rant and rave about an issue that was bugging her," and then answer questions from the audience.

"There were also sketches in the show," said one executive, who added that they actually shot a long pilot that was then culled down into a shorter version.

Universal hoped to take the pilot to syndication. Then local television stations throughout the United States would sign on to broadcast the program on a daily basis.

"The good news was we tested it [the pilot] in front of audiences that had nothing to do with the television business but were users of daytime television, and they liked it a lot," revealed the Universal executive.

Still, the studio wanted to see a few changes, which Laura reportedly did not want to make.

"One night Laura told me, 'I don't want to do the show. I don't want to do television; I've got too much on my plate,'" explained a Universal executive, adding that Laura made her decision sometime that winter, and delivered it "very cordially."

And, even though company executives tried to talk Laura into rethinking her decision, she had, once again, made up her mind.

"She very nicely agreed that she would not do another show with anybody else without our consent given that we risked the money on her going to series," explained a company executive. "We had made a good-faith business arrangement with her."

According to that Universal executive, they did not want to put Laura in "involuntary servitude," so they placed a cap on the time limit, which expires, he thought, sometime in the year 2000.

Then, in early 1998, Laura was approached by CBS's Eyemark Entertainment about the possibility of doing a pilot for another television show. Despite her earlier trepidation, Laura elected to speak with CBS.

According to well-placed sources at CBS, however, she "was made aware when she first began talking with us that we were developing a show with Howard Stern."

"We were in discussions with Laura and ultimately the type of program she envisioned and the type of program we envisioned, weren't the same" was the official statement from an Eyemark Entertainment spokesperson.

Sources said that CBS was aware that Laura was still under some sort of obligation to Universal.

"What happened with us," said a source at CBS, "is that Laura was interested in doing the show. We had ideas as to what kind of show we wanted it to be, and she had very strong ideas as to what kind of show it should be and the amount of control she had in that show. It didn't get as far along as it might have been made out by the mainstream media. It did appear, at one point, that we were heading in the direction toward a deal. There was a sense all along on the production side that Laura didn't necessarily have her heart in it, that maybe she was getting cold feet. It couldn't really be proven one way or the other, except she was stalling.

"She was also still under contract [to Universal], so we would have had to get her out of that contract. It's not like we were two minutes away from making an announcement," said the source.

"In syndication, there is no such thing as 'a show in the works,'" continued the source. "What you do is you develop show ideas pending on whether you are going after a program that is driven by a host with the name attached to it or whether you are going for a show that is driven by format. We wanted to do a talk show that had a problem-solving element in it. We had approached a couple of people who we thought might be suitable, Laura being one of them. Laura just happens to be the one whose name leaked out, and the other names didn't.

"We were still going along," concluded the source, "and then she went public saying she didn't want to do business with a company that was doing business with Howard Stern."

In mid-April 1998, someone—although decidedly not someone from the CBS camp who thought negotiations were still under way—leaked the information that Laura had broken off talks with Eyemark after Laura learned they were going to do a show with Stern.

"Insiders say Dr. Laura . . . didn't want to be associated with a company that would do such a thing," wrote *The Arizona Republic,* one of many mediums that aired the report.

Time magazine even cited Laura as one of their "Winners" of the week for exhibiting such high moral standards.

As for Howard Stern, he, not surprisingly, spent the next two weeks blasting Laura on his show, calling her "less than a nobody."

"I don't think she had the right to make the CBS deal," said the Universal executive. "When I read about it in the paper, I said, 'She does not have a right to do a show with CBS without coming to us.'

"I have a feeling that although she used Howard Stern as the lightning rod to change her mind, I have a feeling she realized she had to come to us and get our okay on it. And I'm not saying [we] wouldn't have granted it, by the way. It would have depended on circumstances."

On September 28, 1998, Eyemark announced its choice to host the new show—basically, the show they had wanted from the beginning. According to well-placed sources at CBS, the talent they ultimately selected was the same person CBS had been speaking with even before Laura: Dr. Joy Browne.

An established talk-show host with a three-hour daily radio program based in New York and syndicated in 300 markets, Browne has a Ph.D. in psychology. In addition to being a licensed clinical psychologist who sits on the board of the American Psychological Association, Browne has authored five books.

With past experience as a guide, Laura may well have thought that she and Browne were not in competition, since Browne did a show with a psychological bent while Laura offers moral advice. Indeed, according to the California Board of Behavioral Science Examiners, Laura even chose to put her MFCC license into "inactive status" as of December 13, 1997.

"That means she has paid her required fees and can renew at any time, but at this point, she cannot practice," said the board's executive officer, Sherry Mehl. In other words, Laura cannot see patients privately, though that doesn't affect what she does on the air.

Meanwhile, though, in the press release announcing the introduction of *The Dr. Joy Browne Show* for September 1999 Eyemark's president, Ed Wilson, said the company wanted a host "who could look at subjects in a balanced, multi-dimensional way and serve as a truly qualified voice of reason.

"Dr. Joy," continued Wilson, "has expertise unmatched by any other host in broadcasting today, along with warmth, humor and a distinctive point of view. We've long been impressed by her proven skills on radio and the genre she's inspired, and we're thrilled to be building an equally-powerful opportunity for her on television."

According to the press release, each episode of Browne's show would "explore a single topic—including the personal, provocative stories of diverse people confronting them."

"What distinguishes single-issue talk shows is how you handle the subjects, and our goal is to offer a series that fixes problems rather than creates them," noted Jim Dauphinee, senior vice president of programming and development for Eyemark.

The press release also quoted Browne as saying, "I'm in the business of helping make lives better, not by bashing but by teaching people how to take responsibility for their behavior."

So what did Browne's intro into the CBS syndication lineup mean for Laura?

"The Laura deal is dead," said an industry source who asked not to be named. "The take is now that there is not an opportunity for [her] to get into television."

This does not apply, however, to public broadcasting. In the past few years, Laura has done PBS specials—*Dr. Laura on Character, Courage, and Conscience,* and *The Ten Commandments: The Significance of God's Laws in Everyday Life*—in connection with two of her books.

And, although she may not host a show of her own anytime soon, Laura will likely continue to appear as a guest on national shows like *Oprah, Today, The View,* and *Larry King Live.*

In fact, it was on her September 16, 1998, visit to Larry King that she broke from her usual stance against commenting publicly about political issues. With the Kenneth Starr report in on President Bill Clinton and Monica Lewinsky, she said, Clinton should resign for "moral reasons."

In the past, Laura has adhered to a longtime policy of not commenting about politics. When Debra Saunders of the *San Francisco Chronicle* asked her in September 1997 whether she was a conservative politically, Laura answered, "I don't talk about politics. The focus of my show is moral behavior."

Then, when Saunders went on to question why she would not talk about her own politics, Laura said "That's personal and not relevant to what I do.

"On some issues," Laura expanded, "I might seem more conservative, on others more liberal. I'm hard to thumbtack down. So groups with an agenda have a hell of a time getting real mad at me because the next day I'll say something they like."

In July 1995, though, she admitted to Walter Gottlieb of *The Washington Post* that she was a "six to ten" on a scale of one to ten, ten being the most conservative.

She does support ultraconservative groups that she feels mirror her views. For example, the Promise Keepers organization proudly cites her in its public relations material. Under the heading, "What Women Are Saying About PROMISE KEEPERS," Dr. Laura is quoted as saying that the group "is a Christian organization that's re-igniting men's involvement and respect for family, marriage and children. That same sort of thing is needed for our teenagers today."

Meanwhile, according to voter registration records, Laura herself is a registered member of the Independent-American Party. In truth, Laura very likely did not realize when she checked the box on her voter registration form that the group is far from the independent she probably thought she checked.

For example, according to the *Las Vegas Review-Journal* (July 9, 1994), the Independent-American Party was trying to get an initiative on the ballot that would bar homosexuals from obtaining spousal status and also would forbid government agencies and schools from teaching that homosexuality is the "equal of race, gender, and religion in regard to minority status."

This was hardly a viewpoint that Laura would be likely to support.

CHAPTER

EIGHTEEN

Everybody thinks of changing humanity and nobody thinks
of changing himself.

—LEO TOLSTOY

(1828–1910)

To Laura's credit, awards and honors in praise of her endeavors have
been coming in on a regular basis in the past few years.

She has been lauded by such groups as Mothers Against Drunk
Driving (MADD); Women in Need Growing Strong (WINGS); Los
Angeles Women in Advertising (LULU); and Fairness for Fathers, to
name but a few.

Starting in March 1997, Laura also began what has become an annual celebration of her fiftieth birthday (which is really in January)
with a bash aptly called "Blast to the Past." The fifties dance, to which
Laura, Lew, and Deryk come decked out in fifties regalia, raises money
for ChildHelp USA, and Laura, who ironically did not have as much
fun in the real 1950s, now dances the night away.

ChildHelp USA awarded Laura its Children's Friend Award in 1996, thanks in part to the woman Laura named in her last book as her "dear friend" and "spiritual soul-sister," Patti Edwards. In *Vanity Fair,* Edwards called Laura's radio show "one of God's blessings."

Then, in 1997, Laura earned what some might consider the radio equivalent of an Emmy or an Oscar: the National Association of Broadcasters' Marconi Radio Award as the top syndicated personality of the year. She was the first woman ever to win.

Yet, even with all the adulation and attention directed her way, as well as the more intense media scrutiny that naturally comes with fame, Laura, a part-time journalist herself, remained thin-skinned.

Walter Gottlieb of *The Washington Post* noted in 1995, for example, that Laura once asked a reporter at the end of an interview, "You're not going to write anything that will hurt my feelings, are you?" and complained she was becoming "very cynical."

When *The Post,* in an effort to get both sides of Laura's family story, told her they were attempting to contact her mother and sister, she refused any further cooperation and, "in a subsequent conversation, hung up on a reporter."

That attitude has carried over into the broadcasting arena as well.

A television correspondent and part-time anchor, who prefers to remain unnamed, recalled an interview she did with Laura in 1996.

"Dr. Laura was downright nasty to my cameraman," claimed the correspondent. "He moved a cup on her desk when she was on the air to get a better shot of her in this little radio studio, and she glared at him. When we were in a break she turned to him and said, 'Don't you *ever, ever* move anything on my desk again.' She was so rude. Actually, the whole tone [of the interview] was kind of like that."

When *Minneapolis Star Tribune* columnist Kristine Holmgren criticized her in 1997, Laura responded with a ten-minute on-air tirade, according to the Long Island newspaper *Newsday.* She called Holmgren, who is also a Presbyterian pastor, "a liar, and ripping feminists and journalists."

And, following her Texas turmoil in March of 1997, she verbally bashed national columnist Marlyn Schwartz, whom Lew had phoned to complain about her column criticizing Dr. Laura's behavior at a Jewish Federation dinner in Dallas.

Then Laura took a second hit at Schwartz, blasting her in Wiscombe's 1998 *Los Angeles Times Magazine* article nearly a year later.

She said Schwartz was "immoral" (although she never explained just how) and added that because of her religion she could not defend herself against "vicious attacks."

"I have to eat a lot of shit," Laura told Wiscombe. "It makes you want to get vengeance, but I control it."

Schwartz, who had not written a line about Laura since the March 1997 events in Dallas, was surprised by Laura's attack.

"I was appalled to read what Dr. Schlessinger said about me . . . that 'she [Schwartz] is a terrible woman,'" said Schwartz, referring to Wiscombe's article. "'She preaches morality but she is not moral.' The only contact I've had concerning Dr. Schlessinger is a story that I reported on. I was not preaching. My story was fully substantiated and I have at least a thousand witnesses who were at the dinner where she was called rude, arrogant, and insulting. Many of them walked out. The pious Dr. Schlessinger then explained she could say more about me but it was against her religion. Perhaps she had forgotten the ninth commandment: Thou shalt not bear false witness."

As Laura's media consultant, Keven Bellows, told Wiscombe, "[Laura] is panicked about what people will say about her."

Bellows, who was then with GCI Communications in Los Angeles, has since left the organization and was hired by Laura's syndicator, Premiere Radio Networks.

Although she did not mention it in her story, Wiscombe also witnessed firsthand Laura's need for approval. Wiscombe had been interviewing Laura in her Hidden Hills house while Lew was out buying groceries for the family. When he returned he walked into the room and Laura asked him a question about Deryk.

"She said something [to Wiscombe] about what a cool kid Deryk is and she turned to Lew, who had just walked in the room, and said,

'Isn't that true?' And he said, 'Yes. You have really done good.' It was like she had to have that. She couldn't exist for another minute without being reminded that she's okay. That's the way it felt to me," said Wiscombe.

"I think she is very, very unsure of herself. I remember when she mentioned a couple of television shows and movies she had seen, and she said right away, 'Of course, you wouldn't know about them.' She was making the assumption my taste would be of a higher quality than hers. She really does carry around the feeling that, in some sort of way, she is not at all comfortable with who she is and what class she's from. I still think she had a feeling, for whatever reason, that she didn't quite come from the right family.

"I think [Bellows and Laura's public relations firm, which she hired after the Dallas fiasco] made a huge difference . . . telling her she can't be out there trashing people [publicly]," said Wiscombe.

But even the well-respected Keven Bellows could not stop Laura from being nasty to another national journalist. In May 1998, Leslie Bennetts became interested in doing an article on Laura for *Vanity Fair.*

According to Bennetts, her interest in Laura began in about 1996, when she casually walked into a New York bookstore and happened to see a huge display of Laura's new book, *How Could You Do That?: The Abdication of Character, Courage, and Conscience.*

"I thought, 'Great. Finally somebody has written a book about this.' It really intrigued me, because it was obviously a countertrend phenomenon," recalled Bennetts. "It was about personal responsibility, being a grown-up and taking personal responsibility for your actions . . . all of which I think are salutary messages. That was the first I had heard of her. I live in Manhattan, and we don't drive, so we don't sit in our cars for hours listening to radio, the way people in a lot of other places do.

"Then [in April of 1998], when *The New York Times* ran this piece saying she was now the number one radio program in the country and the fastest growing, and had outstripped Rush, I thought, 'This is really a story.' I proposed it to *Vanity Fair.*

"At that point, I had listened to her show—and again, I think it is hard to quarrel with her basic message, which is 'Grow up, live up to your commitments, take responsibility for your life, do the right thing,' that kind of thing. It is sort of indisputable that the world would be a better place if everybody was doing that," thought Bennetts. "I didn't know anything about her personally. I came in with no prejudices—and, if anything, a positive image because I thought the message of her book was a worthy one."

Bennetts proposed the story to *Vanity Fair,* and even though her editor had never heard of Laura, Bennetts was armed with the *New York Times* clip, so she got the go-ahead.

Thanks to a positive, longtime relationship with Keven Bellows, Bennetts was given an interview with Laura. So, the first part of May, 1998, Bennetts flew to Los Angeles. "I spent three days sitting with her for three hours during the taping of the show, and interviewing her during all the breaks, and then for several hours after that each day," explained Bennetts. "Plus I did a huge amount of reporting [with other people] and then went back to her on the phone.

"It is certainly true [that] from the very beginning, I was fighting against my own feelings of what quickly became dislike for her. She was cold, very condescending. Laura's assumption walking into a room is that she is a lot smarter than anyone else in the room, which is a dangerous way to go through life. She was very defensive. I found that if I asked her anything, even the most innocuous questions, she would lash out at me. I'm not talking about challenging things," revealed Bennetts.

"As a reporter, you need people to articulate things. So I asked her what she meant by the slogan 'I am my kid's mom.' She acted sort of very contemptuous that I would ask her that. A few days later, when I was back home, I turned on the radio and heard her going to town on me. 'There was this reporter here, and she was so *stupid,* can you believe she asked me such a *stupid* question?'

"She went on and on about what a stupid question it was. I'm sorry, I still don't think it was a stupid question. I needed her to say what it meant to her . . . which is that her child is her first priority and so on and so on. Yes, I could deduce that or surmise that, but it's not the same as verifying it. Even at that level, where I am asking her to elaborate on her own words, it seemed to trigger a really angry reaction when she felt challenged, and she seemed to feel challenged on the least provocation.

"On another day I asked her about Orthodox Judaism, and the fact that many Jewish women feel that there are many elements in Orthodox Judaism that are sexist. And she just rejected that out of hand. Her Orthodox Judaism is so selective—and once again, I didn't even get into that with her. I knew I wasn't going to have the space. But just asking her if she had any concerns about sexism in this tradition she had chosen. Once again, I turn on the radio a few days later and she is trashing me, saying how ignorant I was and what a moron I was for asking these questions," continued Bennetts, who said that although Laura did not identify her by name, she was clearly the subject of the tirade. "Her voice was so filled with venom and contempt. I was really shocked; there was a whole series of these things."

But most surprising of all was what Bennetts found out about Laura from other people.

"I was absolutely shocked. I had no idea. I've been a reporter for twenty-nine years, ten years at *The New York Times* and ten years at *Vanity Fair.* I have obviously written about a lot of famous people. I don't think I have ever encountered a situation where there was such rage and bitterness toward someone I was writing about as there was in this case," revealed Bennetts.

"Laura's explanation of this is that these people are just jealous of her. Of course, what I said in my piece was that the only problem with this explanation is that they have all hated her since long before she became successful. They hated her when she was a total nobody, and not only didn't have millions of dollars, but had to worry about the bank foreclosing on her house. So that explanation doesn't wash," she added.

"She is Clintonesque. There were times when she told me absolutely mutually exclusive things," said Bennetts. "She either claims not to remember things or denies [them]. She mostly pleads bad memory. I found her evasive at best, and dishonest often.

"Laura dismissed all criticism—not just criticism, but when people come forward and say, 'She did X, Y, and Z to me.' She dismissed anything negative as being lies, gossip, rumor, and innuendo, and acts as if it is beneath contempt, but she never addressed the substance of what people were actually saying.

"My piece was no hatchet job; every single substantive accusation was on the record from a fellow professional in the radio industry, many of whom had reason to fear for their candor, because it's a very incestuous industry and some of their stations carry her show. I think it took a lot of courage for these people to come forward and actually speak on the record about things she had done to them.

"Originally, when I asked for a list of Laura's friends to interview, I asked for about fifteen or twenty, and Laura had a fit. She said, 'I wouldn't even think of giving you that list.' So she gives me this pathetic little list of six people. She gave me one person who is a friend, one a former co-worker, two current co-workers, and two rabbis. I protested that this was not nearly adequate, that I wanted to talk to a lot of people who knew her well and were close to her. She seemed almost angry that I had asked. When we were closing the piece, she started coming back to me and saying, 'You have to talk to people who have positive things to say about me,' and my response was, 'This is a little late; I asked you for that about a month and a half ago.'

"The striking thing to me was that, of the list she originally gave me, everybody had known her for such a short amount of time. Patti Edwards . . . had known her a year and a half. This is not my idea of a longtime friendship," added Bennetts.

"Laura has been going into these diatribes on the radio, trashing the press. But nowhere does she really ever deal with the substantive questions of the things she has done in her life. The main point here is that almost everything about the way she has lived is contrary to her message: She doesn't take responsibility for what she's done; she hasn't lived according to the values she professes to have. I think people have a lot of tolerance for someone who says, 'Yes, I used to do such and such, but I have really changed and grown and matured over the years, and I've come to a religious faith and I live differently now.' People have asked me, 'Isn't that the case with Laura?' Well, judging by my experience with her, no.

"I think character is destiny, and I think that Laura's appalling conduct toward people she has worked with is the real Laura Schlessinger.

"You know, it's one thing to forgive youthful indiscretions, 'I did X, Y, and Z,' and 'I was under the influence of the sixties,' which is what Laura said. But the awful things she did to colleagues . . . she was in her forties. This is a grown woman. At what point do you become responsible? That's way past the point, in my book.

"She thinks I'm a terrible person, I'm sure, for having reported all this, but I went in with no ax to grind—and, in fact, a favorable impression—and I learned all of this stuff. What was I going to do, not report it? To me, the facts speak for themselves.

"She's got about as much nerve interpreting the Ten Commandments for us as I don't know what," concluded Bennetts.

Some of those who had spoken to Bennetts suffered fallout from the *Vanity Fair* article.

Bennetts got in touch with Laura's longtime friend Shelley Herman, who checked with Lew before talking with the reporter. She reached him on his cell phone at one of Laura's speaking engagements.

"He was kind of whispering in the background while he was at her speaking engagement," recalled Herman. "Lew said, 'Go for it; we have nothing to hide.'"

After Herman heard some of the questions Bennetts was asking, she said she contacted Lew again, to let him know Laura could be in trouble.

"I said, 'Lew, this is not going to be a puff piece. [Bennetts] has talked to people; it's not pretty.'" She suggested that they get some of Laura's friends to talk with Bennetts to help change the article's slant. "When I talked to Lew, they contacted Keven Bellows. Then I talked

to Laura on the phone and she asked me to come down [to the studio].
It was at Laura's invitation.

"I hadn't seen Laura in a couple of years. This was before the article
came out, maybe two or three weeks before then," said Herman. "I saw
her and had what I thought was a very pleasant visit with her, again
saying, 'Why don't you call your friends?' Laura said she was reluctant
to have her friends contribute to the article, because they often get mis-
quoted. I told her, 'I can't say what is going to happen with me, but I
am going to tell you these are the questions Leslie asked.' I didn't have
to tell her anything, Laura already knew everything.

"Laura told me she wasn't going to read it. I said to her, 'I know this
is going to be bad. The day the article comes out, you surround yourself by friends, you have a little party at your house, and you celebrate
your accomplishments. Don't let an article get you down.'"

Then the Monday before the article officially hit the newsstands,
Herman said she was sitting at home when she got a call from Lew
Bishop.

"I said, 'Hi, hon,' and he said, 'Don't "Hi, hon" me,' and I said,
'What is it?' He said, 'Is it true you said that I morphed into Laura?'
And I said, 'Read me the whole thing in context,' and he read me like
a sentence of it. I said, 'I have to see the whole thing, Lew. I can't just
go by that. What I did say was [that even though] Laura . . . talked
about how much she disliked feminism in her own life, . . . the two of
you have your own roles that you play in the household. In some way,
you've switched roles, where you do the cooking and run things in the
home and she is the one out working in the workplace.' I said, 'Parts of
your personality have morphed . . . where one person leaves off, another one begins.'

"And then Lew said, 'And is it true that you said nice things about
Laura's mother?' I said, 'Read it to me,' and he read me the quote. I
said, 'Well, yes . . . I did say that about her,' and Lew said, quote,
'When you say nice things about Laura's mother, it makes Laura look
bad.'"

Before she hung up with Lew, Herman asked him to fax her the article, which Lew said he had received, by fax, from someone in Chicago. He never did. Instead, Herman ended up going on a late-night *Vanity Fair* hunt so she could reply to Lew.

"I have not heard from them since, and I do not know why they would be upset with me, since supposedly they never read the article," concluded Herman.

What Herman was referring to was a story that ran August 30, 1998, in *The Orange County Register*:

"Early reports tipped Schlessinger it would be a negative article," wrote columnist Gary Lycan. "To this day, her husband said neither one has read it, although they've been told about the contents."

Marilyn Kagan, a colleague for six years on KFI, also felt Laura's wrath in connection with the *Vanity Fair* piece. When Bennetts asked Laura to respond to what Kagan had said to the reporter about her, Laura called Kagan "a lying bitch."

"How can somebody call somebody else a lying bitch and then turn around and say they are a moralist?" questioned Kagan. "There is a blind spot there. I don't think Laura gets it.

"It is hard to express the venom and the nasty, hurtful body language, the silence, the judgmentalness that actually comes from this little woman," added Kagan.

Kagan said she has watched Laura become much more conservative over the years.

"She very wisely chose to go down that [conservative] path as she followed Rush Limbaugh [on the air] in the morning, and she very wisely began to pull herself away from therapy and into moralizing."

Laura also had problems with listeners who criticized her.

Burt Sukhov, a retired pharmacist and writer from San Jose, California, faxed Laura a message in 1996, "rebuking her for using her professional prestige, through her young son, to do a radio commercial for a phonics reading program.

"The first line of my letter was 'How Could You Do That?'—the title of her second book. She phoned me personally within an hour and excoriated me bitterly, calling me 'a mean man,'" recalled Sukhov, who added that Laura hung up on him before he could proffer an explanation.

Later, when the *San Jose Mercury News* published Sukhov's letter to the editor regarding Laura's behavior, he faxed the contents to Laura at her studio.

"She faxed it back with a nasty little comment. It said, 'Thank you for sharing your 15 minutes of fame with me.' And the '15 minutes' was crossed out and written 'seconds' instead," recalled Sukhov.

And Sukhov is not alone.

Norm King, a government worker from Ottawa, said he once wrote to Laura, calling her "a hypocrite for espousing moral values on the one hand, yet making her living by exploiting people's problems for the entertainment of others on the other.

"In reply," related King, "I received a handwritten note [on 'Go Take On the Day' letterhead] which said—I'm paraphrasing slightly—'I wonder what could be in the heart of a person that would make them write such a mean letter.'

"I think . . . she doesn't take criticism as well as she dishes it out," said King.

And, among some of her professional colleagues, Dr. Laura is also not universally admired.

Dr. Carole Lieberman is an assistant clinical professor of psychiatry at UCLA and a diplomate of the American Board of Psychiatry and Neurology; she also wrote a celebrity psychoanalysis column for one of the tabloids. She was a featured guest on the station where Laura was broadcasting in 1996. After listening to Laura's show, Lieberman labeled her "an embarrassment to the station."

"I believe she is a hypocrite and a fraud," said Lieberman. "Even if she doesn't like to say she does therapy on the air and even if she calls herself a prophet, in fact she still goes by 'Dr. Laura,' not 'Prophet Laura' or 'MFCC Laura.' Clearly she is perpetuating a fraud on the public by leading them to believe she is either a psychologist or a psychiatrist."

Furthermore, "How can she possibly tell anybody how to relate to parents and siblings when she doesn't have a relationship with her own mother and sister?" questioned Lieberman. "That's hypocritical.

"In my article I called her a menace to society. She doesn't listen to the people. She has her own agenda after they say a few words, and then often gives advice that doesn't relate to their problem."

In Lieberman's estimation, the problem is Dr. Laura herself.

"She reacts to callers based upon her own problems, her childhood," said Lieberman. "In psychotherapy, when any kind of therapist reacts to a patient in a way that is coming from the therapist's head and not the patient's, it is called countertransference. In other words, when a therapist has significant people from their childhood interact with them in a certain way, which causes them problems, they [the therapist] can transfer their feelings toward a significant person in their past onto the patient. When her callers say something to her that triggers a memory from her past, she reacts to them in an emotional, out-of-control way that, I think, relates to her childhood. She is this tremendously angry, rageful woman, and she has this forum to dump it on people.

"Dr. Laura has a lot of demons that are hidden, suppressed," concluded Lieberman. "Some she is keeping secret from herself, and many she is keeping secret from her listeners."

Early on, Laura told *The Los Angeles Times* that there is "a lesson in everything."

"I always look for it," she said. "One of the ways I survive is, I look for what I can get out of this, how I can be a little stronger from this point on, what can I learn to be better."

Later in the interview she added: "So if somebody criticizes me, 'Gee, you were too tough on that call,' you know, maybe I was. But all in all, my heart's in the right place. So I forgive myself that I can't be right on in everybody's estimation of what I should be all the time, even my own."

Dr. David Levy, an associate professor of psychology at Pepperdine University, author of *Tools of Critical Thinking,* as well as two other books, and a scientific researcher who has done two studies of radio talk-show hosts, believes on-air advice in general is not necessarily helpful.

"It can be helpful," he explained. "But we have to keep in mind that they give very personal advice over a very impersonal medium in a very brief segment of time. And all of that happens without any real opportunity for systematic follow-up. So a major concern would be accountability. How do we know the impact that it's having, both on the callers and the listening audience as well?

"To my knowledge," he said, "there have been no systematic studies that actually follow up the callers, and I certainly don't know of any in terms of the listening audience."

In 1989, Levy did the nation's first empirical study using members of the American Psychological Association (APA) to assess the helpfulness of responses by radio psychology-talk-show hosts. Although Levy's study looked only at on-air psychologists—which would not include Dr. Laura, because she is not a psychologist and no longer even calls what she does therapy—the results indicated that "radio psychology talk shows (in general) may be a moderately valuable source of social support both for callers and for the listening audience."

According to Levy, over the years the APA has relaxed its standards concerning what on-air therapists and psychologists do and say, but has always made clear "that therapy should not occur over the air."

"Most media psychologists are very careful to say it is not 'therapy' but 'personal advice,'" he said.

"The research I conducted indicated that the hosts in general tend to give a great deal of advice, but [the experts] determined that the quality of the advice was not particularly good."

Of particular concern to Levy was the fact that there does not appear to be a clear distinction between "therapy" and "advice."

"Some theorists may have different opinions about what constitutes therapy versus advice, but there are a number of commonly accepted forms of therapy wherein providing personal advice is the primary component of that therapy," he said. "So it may be it doesn't go along the lines of classic Freudian analysis, but there are many forms of professionally accepted therapy that do involve giving advice. The distinction might look clear on paper, but in real life it is anything but clear."

Still a larger concern, Levy believed, is the public perception of what therapists do.

"I think it [the psychology talk show] can provide an unrealistic and distorted perception of how mental health professionals operate. People who are genuinely in need of help may avoid seeking therapy. They may think, 'Why should I spend my money or my time if that kind of approach and this kind of advice not only doesn't help me, but would make me feel worse about myself?' It also might deliver the message that most people or everybody can be helped in the same manner or the same kind of style or approach, which might not allow for individual differences," he explained.

Like Laura, however, Levy laid at least partial responsibility on the callers and listeners themselves.

"I think we do have to keep in mind 'caveat emptor,'" he said. "These are people who are listening to the radio of their own free will, and if they are adults and they choose to take the advice of somebody over the airwaves in that brief segment of time, to some degree, they have to be held accountable for their own behavior."

In his study, Levy drew this conclusion: "Even at worst, such programs appear to be a relatively benign phenomenon. They may be especially beneficial to those individuals who have a limited social network."

Levy believed there were several reasons for Dr. Laura's increasing popularity.

"One of them that I think is appealing to people is the notion of taking responsibility, of not passing the buck, of not saying, 'I can't do anything about it' or 'It's not my fault; it's somebody else's fault.' Some people get tired of hearing excuses for people not assuming responsibility, so I think that kind of direct approach is appealing; maybe more appealing to hear it used on somebody else rather than oneself.

"Another reason, I think, is the fact that she presents herself as a moralist, and even if people agree or don't agree with her morals, I think people are looking for a sense of moral and ethical structure. It may fill the same sort of void that people who look to New-Age metaphysics, or to therapy, or even to Eastern philosophies are attempting to make moral and ethical sense out of their lives. To that degree, I think it's appealing to people.

"The third factor is that, I think, certainly we don't want to make things more complex than they are. Einstein once said, 'Things should be made as simple as possible, but not simpler.' And I think that what she might provide is a sense or idea that there are simple answers, or simpler answers, even in the face of seemingly very complex life decisions. People certainly crave, 'What do I do? What is the answer?' They would like to be able to reduce the complexity of life into more simple, straightforward answers.

"And fourth, certainly we can't factor out that many people find it entertaining. They might not necessarily agree with what she's doing or like it, but people watch a lot of things, or listen to things they may not agree with that they find entertaining.

"Let me add a fifth. With the death of Princess Diana, I think there is something applicable. A show like Dr. Laura's gives people a feeling that they are part of something bigger, and the bigger her audience is, there is probably a greater sense of community, at least for those people who follow it. It's like you have something in common with people in New York and California or wherever else the show is, and it is something to talk about, whether over the water cooler at work or over the Internet. That need to be part of something bigger does speak to a very important human need.

"I think it can be a concern when anybody, whether a licensed mental health professional or not, holds themselves out as the dispenser of a truth or wisdom. It can be a bit paradoxical when you tell someone to take responsibility and then tell them how they should do it.

"Chances are most people could predict what is going to happen and what's going to be said, so it's interesting to me why people would keep calling. It might not even be about the advice per se, but more about the contact. And, as she becomes more famous, now we're getting into people needing to be close to celebrity, which is a factor to consider as well," concluded Levy.

Dr. Norton Kristy wondered about Laura's future.

"Laura was an uncommonly neurotic person when I knew her well, twenty years ago," said Kristy. "Ironically, she has not, to the best of my knowledge, sought psychotherapy or any remediation of that historical pain. I have to believe that she still carries a good deal of it with her. She has some new things in her life that seemingly are important to her. She has her religion now, and a husband and a child and a very great deal of fame and money. Those things act as buffers and aids to coping in a world that otherwise triggers painful responses in her.

"It is my hunch that her relationship with Lew has helped her a great deal. He is a very, very kind, tolerant, what you would call an easygoing type of person. I think both her husband and her son have given her enhanced credibility as a woman and that success that she has had is a shtick that the listening public was very much ready for. I think all of these things have tended to mellow her, although she is very thin-skinned, even now. I think her particular ancient buckets of pain are still there."

Michael Harrison, the editor of *Talkers* magazine, tended to agree that Laura is thin-skinned.

"She has a tendency to take things personally," said Harrison. "She would rank as one of the two thinnest-skinned in the industry, with the other one being Rush Limbaugh. They are amazingly sensitive when it comes to taking criticism . . . shockingly sensitive. They can dish it out, but they can't take it, which only makes them bigger targets for their critics."

At the same time, Harrison does not discount the talent it takes to stay "on" in front of a radio mike.

"It takes a colorful, charismatic, attractive, complex personality to be a talk-show host," described Harrison. "You have to come across as real, uninhibited, and up-front with opinions. You have to seem to have lived; have experience to draw upon. And you have to have something intangible that makes you interesting.

"To be a successful talk-show host also takes a huge ego," concluded Harrison. "And another common trait: insecurity. Most of them are amazingly insecure."

But, regardless of Laura's nature or her behavior off the air, there are others who feel Dr. Laura is fulfilling a societal call for clear standards of right and wrong. In June 1996, for example, the nationally syndicated newspaper columnist Clarence Page clearly caught the vibes when he humorously nominated Laura as "National Mommy."

"Most people know what the right thing is," wrote Page. "It is just that some of us feel so tempest-tossed and out-of-control that we need someone else to tell us to do it.

"That's when I decided Dr. Laura should be our National Mommy, not the coddling kind, but the no-mollycoddling, eat-your-broccoli kind," concluded Page.

Others seem to feel the same, including the television correspondent who witnessed Laura's rudeness firsthand.

"I don't like her because of what I've seen," said the correspondent, "but I think part of her message is a good one. . . . A lot of times what she is saying really hits the mark."

"She is serving a very useful purpose, which in earlier times would have been served by a rabbi or priest or wise woman, who wasn't interested in empathy, but in helping people solve their ethical dilemmas," William Doherty (the director of the Marriage and Family Therapy Program at the University of Minnesota and author of the book *Soul Searching*) told the magazine *Family Therapy Networker.*

"[Schlessinger] is one of the forces making it possible to bring moral and ethical issues openly into the discussion of personal and family life," said Doherty. "Those who dismiss the importance of Dr. Laura or who attack religion are missing an important lead about this culture."

Some of Laura's friends wonder how she is able to bear all of the potshots that have been taken at her, beginning in earnest after the Dallas incident in 1997.

"I can see where she can come off as being harsh," explained Daniel McFeeley, the graphic artist who worked with her on her first children's book. "Laura is so focused. She is very quick."

As an example, he recalled how, at one meeting about the book, she told McFeeley she was concerned that the name of the boy, Tyler, was "too yuppie."

"I started telling her about my friend. I said, 'He's got a son named Sam.' And she said, 'Sam, that's it.' And I said, 'Oh, you like that name,' and she said, 'That's the name.' I said, 'Okay, we'll consider that,' and she said, 'No, that's the name.'

"She probably does that a lot in her life, and that's probably what keeps people away a bit. She is a boulder running down a hill. She has to do this to get to the next thing.

"When I first met [Laura's assistant], I asked her what it's like to deal with Laura every day. I said, 'Sometimes she can be a little harsh, especially to Lew.' Sometimes I've heard her say things that I thought were kind of curt. On her show she can be kind of curt, and I heard her be curt to Lew.

"And [her assistant] said, 'Oh, when Lew was sick, Laura was as tenacious as a bulldog, making sure that everything Lew needed was taken care of.' That was Lisa's experience," said McFeeley.

"I think people, in their lives, do things as a growth process. I think that is what Laura is about. Laura is a work in progress. She is becoming the best she can possibly be. Everybody has done things they are not particularly proud of at some point in their lives. They figure it out that these weren't the best things. It must be very difficult for Laura to have made this conversion to Judaism. I think, in a way, it is one of her attempts to make things right."

McFeeley said that he and Lew once talked about whether the money was worth it.

"He said it was better than being poor, of course, but he was really kind of getting weathered by all these shots. As a matter of fact, I was thinking about it this weekend when I saw the show *Private Ryan* [*sic*]. I kind of pictured their life as being a little bit like when they hit the beach at Normandy—remember the *ping, ping, ping?* I wonder how thick her skin is to have that constant *ping, ping* . . . to all the time have someone saying something negative about her."

But is she happy?

Herman remembered how she responded when asked that question about Laura.

"I said, 'I'd like to think she is, but I don't think so because she is constantly putting the bar higher. Every time she gets accomplished at something where a person would take joy out of the experience— whether it be her knitting, her bike riding or exercising or whatever she is doing—she isn't satisfied just doing that. She has to look for new challenges.

"I know that the life she is living now is indeed the life she speaks about," continued Herman. "She really has not acknowledged the past at all. She is almost like Bill Clinton in being a master of semantics. Unless a direct question is asked to her, she will not answer it forthcomingly. For Laura's new moral code of living, that works."

E P I L O G U E

The educational accomplishment I am most proud of is
learning from my mistakes.

—DR. LAURA SCHLESSINGER
AMERICA ONLINE, 1997

During the pre-Deryk, pre-Judaism days of 1979, Laura was on a
Santa Ana radio station on Sunday evenings for three hours. Back
then, *The Los Angeles Times Home* magazine described Laura's talk-
radio style as that of "a sensitive, sympathetic counselor who believes
in the therapy of humor."

"I know I'm helping people," Laura said then, "and sometimes I
find that laughing with them—certainly not at them—is the best way
to go."

By late 1989, Laura was broadcasting weekday mornings on some
eighty stations across the United States. She was juggling her work
schedule to meet the needs of a four-year-old son, but had not yet
found religion. She was still comfortable with the "therapist" title, al-

though certain callers could cause her to shed that mantle and digress about responsibility and moral choices.

Still, in 1990 she insisted to David Wharton of *The Los Angeles Times* that she could help her callers.

"I don't do shtick on the air," she claimed.

Not quite ten years later, she had completed her conversion to Judaism, and her daily radio show had gone mainstream on more than 450 radio stations in the United States and Canada, with a weekly audience estimated at 18 to 20 million listeners. The diva of talk was now nagging more, listening less, and urging callers to help themselves.

Dr. Laura had concluded her metamorphosis from therapist to moralist.

Laura told Walter Gottlieb of *The Washington Post* that it was her listeners who "trained" her to be tougher.

"At first," Laura said, "I was more careful. 'Oh my! How do you feel?' Then I realized there had to be a right and a wrong."

It was on CNN in November 1996 that Laura first christened her new brand of talk radio.

"I pretty much preach, teach, and nag," she told Miles O'Brien. "It's not pop psychology at all. If anything, it's a new genre, and I'm naming it today. . . .

"It would be pop morality," she said. "I really work on morality and ethics and principles as guidelines for how to make decisions in life, as opposed to pop psychology, which is pretty much on your feelings."

Dr. Laura's evolution has been profitable.

On September 10, 1997, Synergy Broadcasting, Inc., which owned her show, sold it to Jacor Communications for $71.5 million.

Jacor's Premiere Radio Networks now syndicate the show throughout the United States and Canada, with hopes to expand soon into both South Africa and England.

With her ratings, as of April 1998, surpassing Rush Limbaugh's, it was still extraordinary that her show was sold for $22 million more than Jacor paid for Limbaugh's in 1996, even though Limbaugh was contracted for fewer years. Even more incredible, however, was the fact that *The Dr. Laura Schlessinger Show* had only been syndicated nationally for three years prior to the sale.

Steve Lehman, president of Premiere, told *Broadcasting & Cable* magazine that he planned to launch a sixty- to ninety-second "mini-feature" of tough-love advice from Dr. Laura, which would air each weekday in addition to her regular show.

Lehman labeled her show "advertiser-friendly," telling *The Los Angeles Times* that "nontraditional radio advertisers gravitate toward her."

While John Shanahan of "Hooked on Phonics" fame held 51 percent of Synergy Broadcasting, 49 percent was controlled by Laura and Lew. On August 13, 1997, Lew filed papers to make Dr. Laura her own corporation. As Lew later told *The Los Angeles Times,* "for tax purposes . . . now, the corporation loans her out to the radio show."

This was a break they probably needed, in that their personal take on the Jacor deal was a tidy $35 million. The sale, according to *The Los Angeles Times,* reportedly did not include Laura's salary, meaning she still picks up an annual paycheck estimated to be in "the mid-seven-figure range."

And, according to well-placed industry sources, Laura also scored a real bonus in a deal that was not made public: namely, that Premiere would not syndicate, for the run of her contract, any other talk-show personality with a similar format.

"She is with a powerhouse radio syndicator," said one source. "It is the difference between being a show distributed by Warner Brothers or by the Joe Smith Company. Who can throw the weight behind it?

"If she is number one, she has no competition. She won't permit her own company to take on anybody else, and the company that is number two in that end of the business is sort of a minimized number two," believed the source, who therefore thought it would be unlikely that Laura would be dethroned anytime soon.

And besides the dollars, Laura also picked up another perk: her own studios. In early 1998, Premiere moved her out of KFI, where she had done her show for the past seven years, and into a broadcasting facility that was crafted for Laura and her staff.

In addition to her radio show, Laura has written three best-selling books—*Ten Stupid Things Women Do to Mess Up Their Lives, How Could You Do That?: The Abdication of Character, Courage, and Conscience,* and *Ten Stupid Things Men Do to Mess Up Their Lives*—that, in total, have now sold over 2 million copies. By April 1998, her first book had 1.2 million copies in print, according to *Publishers Weekly.* Laura's second book popped into third place on the nonfiction best-seller list in its first week on sale, and five printings later had sold nearly half a million copies. Then, despite some less-than-glowing reviews, her third book did equally well, with a first printing of 350,000.

On September 9, 1998, HarperCollins published a book she co-authored with Rabbi Stewart Vogel. It was originally going to be entitled *The Ten Commandments: What's in It for Me?* The advance printing of the hardcover was 250,000 copies, and *Publishers Weekly* reported that the advertising budget was $250,000. By the time the book actually reached stores, however, its title had become *The Ten Commandments: The Significance of God's Laws in Everyday Life.* Regardless of its handle, the book climbed to number 5 on the *New York Times* bestseller list after only two weeks on the market.

In addition, reportedly at least sixty newspapers across the country publish Dr. Laura's weekly column.

Through her 1-888-DRLAURA number and her Dr. Laura website, she still markets "The Dr. Laura Collection," including everything from "I Am My Kid's Mom" items to Dr. Laura workout wear and "Go Take On the Day" paraphernalia, not to mention her books and videos. And she also hawks her monthly newsletter—now in magazine form: $39.95 a year.

Besides her retail line, Dr. Laura is on the Internet via AudioNet (http://www.audionet.com) out of Dallas, which multicasts her program on-line for those in-office types who don't have access to a radio. The

Long Island newspaper *Newsday* reported in October 1997 that Laura's website crashed earlier that spring "when 310,000 people hit at once."

She also commands $25,000 to $30,000 per speech, plus expenses. Laura is nondenominational when it comes to speaking, with repeat performances at places like the Reverend Robert Schuller's Crystal Cathedral and the Catholic Archdiocese's Religious Education Congress, both in Los Angeles.

And through it all, she is still doing it her way.

Each weekday from eleven A.M. to two P.M. PST, Laura sits behind a control panel at her studio in Sherman Oaks, California. She puts the headphones over her ears, and flips on her computer, connected with her producer's, Carolyn Holt, a former customer-service representative for a credit card company. It is Holt who answers the phone calls and screens the callers who might ultimately make it through. Perhaps eighteen of 50,000 or 60,000 estimated callers each day actually get to speak with Dr. Laura.

Holt, on the other hand, converses with between 100 and 200 callers daily. She types the particulars on to the computer screen—searching, she once told writer Rebecca Johnson, for listeners "who have a dilemma, a conflict, something that will make good radio[,] but not anything too dark like suicide or sex abuse." Once she has the nominees, Dr. Laura herself acts as the final screener, selecting which calls she will take.

Laura told *Psychology Today* that Holt asks callers, "What moral or ethical dilemma are you struggling with?"

"And," she said, "if their problem doesn't fit into that format, they don't get on the air."

"We don't take vulnerable people and put them on the air and exploit them," Laura told Debra Saunders of the *San Francisco Chronicle*, "because this is not entertainment, it is not the 'Jerry Springer Show.'"

When Saunders asked her whether someone was "putting her life in your hands" when phoning in for personal advice, Laura answered no.

"I have an influence," she told Saunders. "I have no power. People call and ask my opinion. They can do what they will with it."

Perhaps, but those who doubt her ability to move someone to action need only contact Marilyn Beck and Stacy Jenel Smith, who write an entertainment column for the *Chattanooga Times.*

Dr. Laura was among the people nominated for their "Tacky Taste Awards" of 1998. Laura told her national audience she wanted to win "because those who would vote her Tacky must be against morals, values, ethics, religion, and God."

Laura then asked her listeners to cast ballots for her.

According to Beck and Smith, they got "thousands of responses"—and "hundreds" repeated Dr. Laura's words verbatim, "like robots."

Laura told *The Dallas Morning News* in 1995 that she was very comfortable with the impact she has on people, as well as with the success she has earned:

"I think I deserve it and I earned it," she said. "I've worked very hard."

And, by all indications, she will persist in working hard.

"She is still going to grow," predicted Michael Harrison of *Talkers* magazine. "I think mathematically there is still room for growth. But even if she peaks, she will still go for years."

So, as our "National Mommy," Dr. Laura will undoubtedly continue, well into the next century, to reap the rewards of dispensing tough moral prescriptions to millions of devout listeners, perhaps even staying on the air long enough to evolve into our "National Nana."

Only time—and ratings—will tell.

N O T E S

I repeatedly tried to interview Laura Schlessinger, Lew Bishop, and other Schlessinger family members. Schlessinger and Bishop did not respond to interview requests, nor did several other members of their immediate families.

Included here are references to the sources used in writing each chapter. Although the notes are not all-inclusive, they do give an overview of the people who were interviewed, the documents that were obtained, and the publications that were utilized in researching material for this book. For detailed annotations, please refer to the bibliography on pages 243–250.

I wish to acknowledge, once again, and sincerely thank the individuals listed in the notes for their many contributions to this work.

CHAPTER I

The events that took place between March 3 and March 13 were reported in newspapers, and by radio and television stations, throughout the United States. My primary sources, however, were the *Dallas Morning News* articles and columns written by Marlyn Schwartz, as well as my interviews with those who attended the events.

Dr. Laura's conversation with one of her callers, Jennifer, took place on her May 15, 1998, show.

Among those interviewed were D. J. Kassanoff; Phyllis Davis; Rose Saginaw; Dr. Adele Hurst; Marlyn Schwartz; and others who asked not to be identified.

Primary publications used included *The Dallas Morning News,* March 1997, and *The Atlanta Journal and Constitution,* March 1997.

CHAPTER 2

Background on the Schlessinger family comes from *New York Times* obituaries, immigration ship manifests, and, where possible, birth, marriage, and death certificates. (New York state law prohibits anyone who is not a relative from obtaining birth and death records, and marriage certificates that are less than fifty years old.)

Research on Russian Jews and their immigration to the United States comes from Ira Rosenwaike, *Population History of New York City;* Abraham Shulman, *The New Country: Jewish Immigrants in America;* Harry Golden, *The Greatest Jewish City in the World;* Hyman B. Grinstein, *The Rise of the Jewish Community in New York 1654–1860;* and Alfred J. Kolatch, *The Second Jewish Book of Why.*

Information on Orthodox Judaism, especially as it relates to females, was provided by detailed interviews with an Orthodox Jewish educator in Denver, Colorado.

The anecdote about Monty Schlessinger leaving his family's Passover celebration comes from the introduction to Laura Schlessinger and Stewart Vogel's *The Ten Commandments.*

Monty Schlessinger's military record was provided by a Statement of Service from the U.S. Army Personnel Division. Most of Monty's military records were housed in the St. Louis, Missouri, National Personnel Records Center, which was heavily damaged by fire on July 12, 1973.

Information about Lundy's background came from a distant relative of the family, living on the East Coast, who did not wish to be identified, and from a former neighbor who also did not wish to be named.

Monty and Lundy's California divorce records from Los Angeles County provided wedding dates, birth dates, and other information pertinent to their marriage.

The Schlessingers' addresses in New York were obtained from back phone directories, available on microfiche in the New York Public Library and from the Long Island Studies Institute at Hofstra University.

Interviews with John Fernandez; Gerry Pepper; John Griffiths; Barbara Russell; and two sources, a former neighbor and a distant family member, who did not wish to be identified.

See also articles in *Redbook,* May 1997; *U.S. News & World Report,* July 1997; *Ethnic Newswatch,* 1997; *The New York Times,* 1996; *Newsday* (Long Island), 1997; *The Los Angeles Times,* 1994; and *The Los Angeles Times Magazine,* 1998; and syndicated Dr. Laura Schlessinger's columns, published in the *Minneapolis Star Tribune,* 1997.

The history of the Village of Westbury comes from "Our Westbury Heritage," in the Westbury file housed at the Long Island Studies Institute at Hofstra University, as well as from other clips on file in the Long Island Studies Institute, such as newsletters from the Village of Westbury and from the Westbury School Board.

Television transcript: ABC's *20/20,* January 26, 1996.

CHAPTER 3

Information about Westbury High School was obtained from the yearbook, *Wing & Spur,* and also from Westbury School Board newsletters found in the Westbury file at the Long Island Studies Institute at Hofstra University.

Information about Jericho High School came from the Jericho Yearbook, *Imperator.* Facts about the community were, once again, gleaned from the files on Jericho at the Long Island Studies Institute, including an article in *The Villager,* March 7, 1963.

Details about Cold Spring Harbor Lab came from Wendy Goldstein of the lab's public relations department. Especially helpful was a thirty-five-page history of the lab, "The First Hundred Years," written by David Micklos with Susan Zehl, Daniel Schechter, and Ellen Skaggs.

Interviews were conducted with Ron Estroff; Richard Pasqualetto; Helene Spitzer; Bob Raiber; Arthur Kaminsky; Donna Wolper; David Martin; Miriam Reff; Lois Smith; Lawrence Grobel; Virginia Star; and a former neighbor of the Schlessingers, who did not wish to be identified.

CHAPTER 4

Verification of Laura's high school graduation came from Jericho High School records.

Information about Stony Brook came from "A Brief History," Department of Special Collections at Frank Melville Jr. Memorial Library, State University of New York at Stony Brook.

Information about the scholarships Laura received came from her high school commencement program and from a source who asked not to be identified.

Information about Laura's activities while at Stony Brook came from the college yearbook and the college newspaper, *The Statesman.*

Interviews were conducted with Jack Feirman; John Griffiths; Janet Wiscombe; Joanne Schaedel; Susan Woulfin; Marni Elias; Virginia Star; Dr. Edwin Battley; Mary Bernero; Vincent Cirillo; Lilli Cirillo; Terry Eagle; Howard Posner; and two sources who asked not to be identified.

CHAPTER 5

Laura's graduation from Stony Brook was confirmed by the registrar's office at the State University of New York at Stony Brook.

Information regarding Michael Rudolph's graduation was taken from the 1973 commencement program and also was confirmed by the registrar's office at Columbia.

Data regarding Laura's graduation also came from the registrar's office at Columbia. Information about her thesis came from *Dissertation Abstracts International,* which gives a brief summary of every dissertation written.

Information about where Laura and Michael lived in New York came from past student directories for the university.

Interviews for this chapter were conducted with Joanne Schaedel; Marni Elias; Dr. Edwin Battley; John Griffiths; Dr. David Schachter; Dr. Raimond Emmers; Dr. Viktoria Kohler; Dr. Helena Burrell; Dr. Frank Erk; Richard D. Cassetta; a former Catholic nun who taught at the College of New Rochelle; and two classmates of Laura's and Michael's who asked not to be identified.

CHAPTER 6

Interviews included several sessions with Bill Ballance and Dr. Norton Kristy.

Validation of Kristy's claim that Ballance was one of the first doing intimate talk radio came from Michael Harrison, editor of the industry bible, *Talkers* magazine.

The intimate relationship between Laura Schlessinger and Bill Ballance was documented, in part, by photographs of a sexual nature taken of the couple by Ballance with a self-timer, as well as by various letters and mementos, such as a Valentine's inscription from Laura in a dictionary she gave to Ballance, vowing devoted love. In addition, several individuals quoted in this chapter and the next confirmed that the two were romantically linked.

CHAPTER 7

Information about Monty and Yolanda Schlessinger's divorce comes from divorce records on file with the Los Angeles County courts.

Laura wrote about her reaction to her parents' divorce in her newspaper column of July 27, 1997.

The reference to the cat Bill Ballance gave Laura was made on her radio show during the first week of February 1998.

Interviews included: Bill Ballance; Carol Hemingway; Dr. Norton Kristy; Ray Briem; and John Fernandez.

CHAPTER 8

Information about how Laura and Lew met comes from interviews with Bill Ballance, John Griffiths, two close family members, and a colleague at USC; the latter three asked not to be identified. Some of these same people supplied information about Lew and Jeanne Bishop's relationship.

Lew's degrees were confirmed by the registrar's offices of Brown University and RPI.

Information about Lew and Jeanne's wedding and divorce came from their divorce papers, filed in Orange County, California.

Verification of Lew's doctorate came from Dissertation Abstracts Online.

Information about what Lew taught at USC came from course catalogs in the archives at the university.

Verification that Lew was still married when Laura began dating him came from Bill Ballance, a colleague at USC who asked not to be named, and two friends of the family, who also asked not to be named. In addition, stories that included some of the same details appeared in *Vanity Fair* (Leslie Bennetts, "Diagnosing Dr. Laura"), September 1998, and in the *Palm Beach Post* (Emily J. Minor, "Who Is Dr. Laura Anyway?"), November 23, 1996.

Laura mentioned her "past behaviors" in her June 22, 1997, newspaper column.

Information about the house that Laura and Lew bought on North Irving

Boulevard came from the grant deed, found in the real estate records in Los Angeles County.

Verification of Laura's and Cindy's MFCC licenses came from the Board of Behavioral Science Examiners in California.

Information about how Laura listed herself in the telephone directory came from microfiches of those directories, found in the Los Angeles Public Library.

Rob Lewine was also interviewed.

CHAPTER 9

Information about the classes Laura taught at Pepperdine came from records kept by the psychology department.

Data about Cindy's graduation from Pepperdine came from the registrar's office.

Interviews were conducted with Carol Hemingway; L. James Hedstrom; Dr. Norton Kristy; Bill Ballance; Donna Wolper; Cheryl Saunders; Shelley Herman; and John Griffiths.

CHAPTER 10

The quotation about how Laura came to know she wanted to be pregnant is from her PBS video *The Ten Commandments: The Significance of God's Laws in Everyday Life,* which first aired in the fall of 1998.

Information about Cindy Schlessinger's wedding comes from the marriage records of Los Angeles County.

The grant deed for Lew and Laura's house in Woodland Hills is available at the Los Angeles County Recorder's Office.

Laura spoke about her tubal pregnancy on her program, November 20, 1997.

Details about Deryk's birth came from Deryk's birth certificate, available at the Los Angeles County Office of Vital Records.

Laura's classes at Pepperdine came from employment records archived in the psychology department.

Interviews were conducted with Bill Ballance; Shelley Herman; John Griffiths; and a former patient of Laura's who asked not to be named.

CHAPTER 11

Information about Monty and Raenetta's wedding comes from the marriage records of Los Angeles County.

Two attempts were made to interview Raenetta Schlessinger, who has refused all comment.

Information about Monty's death comes from his death certificate, found at the Los Angeles County Office of Vital Records.

Interviews included John Griffiths; a former patient of Laura's who asked not to be named; Shelley Herman; Gerry Pepper; John Fernandez; Andrew Lisowski; and two other sources who asked not to be identified.

CHAPTER 12

Lengthy interviews were conducted with Shelley Herman; Tom Holter; Tracey Miller; Barbara Whitesides; Fred Wostbrock; Barbara De Angelis; and a former patient and friend of Laura's who asked not to be named.

CHAPTER 13

Information about the fire came from a City of Los Angeles Fire Department field report and interviews with friends and neighbors.

Data about the tax lien came from public records regarding tax liens available through LEXIS Liens Library and other services.

Verification of the Board of Behavioral Science Examiners' complaint against Laura came from letters sent by the board to Laura's former patient.

Verification of Laura's resignation from the Board of Behavioral Science Examiners came from the governor of California, office of appointments.

Interviews were conducted with Shelley Herman; John Griffiths; Janet Wiscombe; Barbara Whitesides; Tracey Miller; Barbara De Angelis; Marilyn Kagan; a former patient of Laura's who did not wish to be identified; and Scott Barton.

CHAPTER 14

The recreation of the scene of Lew Bishop's heart attack draws on Laura's statement given as part of the couple's malpractice suit against Sylmar Medical Center, filed in June of 1994, and from information provided by a source who asked not to be identified.

Information regarding how Alan L. Fuller and John Shanahan came to syndicate Laura's show came from a breach-of-contract lawsuit filed by Fuller against Shanahan and Laura in August 1996.

Data regarding the number of talk-radio shows in the United States came from Michael Harrison, editor of *Talkers* magazine.

The information about the medical malpractice suit Laura and Lew filed in June 1994 comes directly from court documents, including the "Complaint for Damages."

Facts about Worldstar Productions came from the breach-of-contract lawsuit Fuller filed in 1996.

County real estate records were searched to determine when Laura and Lew bought their property in Lake Arrowhead.

Interviews were conducted with Shelley Herman; Tracey Miller; Barbara Whitesides; John Griffiths; Michael Harrison; Dr. Audrey Brodt; Bill Ballance; and Dr. Norton Kristy.

CHAPTER 15

Information about the earthquake on January 17, 1994, came from published reports as well as interviews.

Data about Lake Arrowhead come from the Lake Arrowhead website. I also visited the area.

Interviews were conducted with Vern Buller; Jack Warford; John Griffiths; Shelley Herman; a broadcaster who interviewed Laura; Chris Klein; and five businesspeople in the Lake Arrowhead community who asked not to be identified.

CHAPTER 16

The story of how Laura first turned to Judaism has been repeated by her to a variety of interviewers over the years. The actual quote, however, comes from the interview she gave *The Ladies' Home Journal* (Mary Mohler, "Are There Really Angels?") in April 1998.

Laura's video on the Ten Commandments, which was aired for the first time on PBS in September 1998, was also quoted in this chapter.

Special thanks to Ellyn Hutt, an Orthodox Jewish educator from Colorado, who aided immensely in helping me understand Orthodox Jewish practices, especially as they pertain to females. At no time was Hutt attempting to interpret Jewish law, but rather, like Alfred J. Kolatch in *The Jewish Book of Why* and *The Second Jewish Book of Why,* to explain the reasons behind certain practices. Any errors concerning Orthodox practices are mine.

Data about Laura and Lew's new homes in Hidden Hills and in Lake Arrowhead came from real estate records on file with the county assessor's office.

Interviews included those with Shelley Herman and Dr. Norton Kristy.

CHAPTER 17

Listenership figures come from Michael Harrison, the editor of *Talkers* magazine.

Data regarding Alan Fuller's reasons for leaving SBI came from a trade secrets lawsuit filed by SBI, John Shanahan, and Laura Schlessinger against Fuller in May 1997.

Information about Laura's home in Hidden Hills comes from county real estate records.

Information about *The Dr. Joy Browne Show* came from a CBS Eyemark Entertainment press release, dated September 28, 1998.

Data about Laura's endorsement of the Promise Keepers came from literature provided by the Promise Keepers organization.

Voter registration records in California, which are a matter of public record, provided the information that Laura is registered as a member of the Independent-American Party.

Interviews were conducted with Daniel McFeeley, Michael Harrison, and four radio/television industry sources who asked not to be named.

CHAPTER 18

Information on Laura's awards comes from her résumé, published on the Internet.

Interviews were conducted with Marlyn Schwartz; Janet Wiscombe; Leslie Bennetts; Shelley Herman; Marilyn Kagan; Burt Sukhov; Norm King; Dr. Carole Lieberman; Dr. David Levy; Dr. Norton Kristy; Michael Harrison; and Daniel McFeeley.

EPILOGUE

Information regarding the number of stations on which Laura appears and her listenership comes from Michael Harrison of *Talkers* magazine and from *The New York Times* (Andrea Adelson, "A Dash Past Rush?"), April 13, 1998.

Data on the number of books Laura has sold are from *Publishers Weekly* in April 1998, and February 5, 1996. See also "Laura Schlessinger Wants to Make the Ten Commandments a Blueprint for All" by Sandee Brawarsy.

The fee Laura receives for her speeches is cited in numerous articles surrounding the controversy in Dallas, mentioned in Chapter 1.

Information about items offered through Dr. Laura's 888 number and website comes from her brochure and her website.

Interviews were conducted with Michael Harrison and with four other industry sources, both in television and radio, who asked not to be identified.

BIBLIOGRAPHY

BOOKS

Golden, Harry. *The Greatest Jewish City in the World*. New York: Doubleday, 1972.

Grinstein, Hyman B. *The Rise of the Jewish Community in New York 1654–1860*. Philadelphia: The Jewish Publication Society of America, 1945.

Kolatch, Alfred J. *The Jewish Book of Why*. New York: Jonathan David Publishers, 1981.

————. *The Second Jewish Book of Why*. New York: Jonathan David Publishers, 1985.

Rosenwaike, Ira. *Population History of New York City*. Syracuse, New York: Syracuse University Press, 1992.

Schlessinger, Laura. *How Could You Do That?: The Abdication of Character, Courage, and Conscience.* New York: HarperCollins, 1996.

―――. "Schlessinger, Laura." *Newsmakers 1996,* issue 3. Gale Research, 1996.

―――. *Ten Stupid Things Men Do to Mess Up Their Lives.* New York: HarperCollins, 1997.

―――. *Ten Stupid Things Women Do to Mess Up Their Lives.* New York: Villard Books, 1994.

――― and Rabbi Stewart Vogel. *The Ten Commandments: The Significance of God's Laws in Everyday Life.* New York: HarperCollins, 1998.

Shulman, Abraham. *The New Country: Jewish Immigrants in America.* New York: Scribners and Sons, 1976.

MAGAZINES

"America's Therapist?" *Family Therapy Networker,* September/October 1997.

"Around the Network . . . America's Therapist." *Family Therapy Networker,* September/October 1997.

Bendis, Debra. "A Dose of Moral Adrenaline from Dr. Laura." *The Christian Century,* May 14, 1997.

Bennetts, Leslie. "Diagnosing Dr. Laura." *Vanity Fair,* September 1998.

Berges, Marshall. "Laura Schlessinger." *The Los Angeles Times Home,* July 15, 1979.

Brawarsy, Sandee. "Laura Schlessinger Wants to Make the Ten Commandments a Blueprint for All." *Publishers Weekly,* April 1998.

"Dr. Laura Wants You." *Psychology Today,* January/February 1998.

Feldman, Kathryn Levy. "Calling Dr. Laura." *Inside,* Summer 1998.

Griffiths, John. "Don't Blame Your Flame." *People,* July 11, 1994.

Harrison, Michael. "Talk Radio Audience Expands, Diversifies." *Talkers* magazine, March 1998.

King, Patricia, and Kendal Hamilton. "Listen Up Callers: No Whining Allowed." *Newsweek,* May 27, 1996.

Maryles, Daisy. "Behind the Bestsellers . . ." *Publishers Weekly,* February 5, 1996.

Mead, Rebecca. "The Angriest Woman on the Radio." *Redbook,* May 1997.

Mohler, Mary. "Are There Really Angels?" *The Ladies' Home Journal,* April 1998.

Petrozzello, Donna. "Jacor Pays $71 Million Doctor Bill . . ." *Broadcasting & Cable,* September 15, 1998.

————. "WABC Pulls Dershowitz . . ." *Broadcasting & Cable,* March 25, 1996.

Rich, Laura. "Talk Therapy." *Inside Media,* May 29, 1996.

Rosin, Hanna. "The Moral Dominatrix." *New York,* September 1, 1997.

Schlessinger, Laura. "The Cohabitation Trap." *Cosmopolitan,* March 1994.

————. "Prime-Time Checkup." *TV Guide,* August 30, 1997.

————. "What Is a Well-Lived Life?" *Parade,* March 15, 1998.

Schrof, Joannie M. "No Whining." *U.S. News & World Report,* July 14, 1997.

Scott, Walter. "Personality Parade." *Parade,* August 17, 1997.

Smith, Lynn. "The Shrink's Couch Via the Airwaves." *Good Housekeeping,* March 1996.

"Talk Street." *Talkers* magazine, June 1998.

Williams, Geoff. "Dr. Laura Schlessinger." *Biography,* May 1997.

Wiscombe, Janet. "Dr. Laura Wants You to Stop Whining." *The Los Angeles Times Magazine,* January 18, 1998.

NEWSPAPER AND WIRE SERVICE ARTICLES

Adelson, Andrea. "A Dash Past Rush?" *The New York Times,* April 13, 1998.

Deahm, Terry. "Ethical Conflict: Stern Spoils Dr. Laura's Talks with CBS." *The Arizona Republic,* April 17, 1998.

Beamish, Rita. "The Shrink's Couch Via the Airwaves." Associated Press, July 10, 1982, A.M. cycle.

Beck, Marilyn, and Stacy Jenel Smith. "It's Turkey Time Again: Dr. Laura is Tackiest." *Chattanooga Times,* November 27, 1998.

Beeghly, Art. "Bill Ballance 'Heals' from Coast to Coast." *Modesto Journal,* August 13, 1975.

Berman, Laura. "Commentary: Dr. Laura . . ." *The Detroit News,* March 20, 1997.

————. "Dr. Laura Explains It All." *The Detroit News,* October 18, 1996.

"Best-Selling Books." *USA Today,* September 17, 1998.

"Books & Authors." *The Denver Post,* September 27, 1998.

Bourgoyne, J. E. "Radio Doctor Airs Emotions After Public Scolding." *The Times-Picayune* (New Orleans), March 14, 1997.

Carter, Kevin. "Dr. Laura Speaks Her Mind . . ." *The Gazette* (Montreal), April 14, 1997.

Christopher, Hearne, Jr. "Call-in Therapist Has Herself a 'Killer' Show." *The Kansas City Star,* December 1, 1994.

Cleeland, Nancy. "Fans Eat Up Dr. Laura's Sound-Bite . . ." *San Diego Union-Tribune,* February 23, 1996.

Cornwell, Rupert. "Housewife Makes Waves . . ." *The Independent* (London), May 27, 1996.

Cuellar, Catherine. "Up Close and In Person." *The Dallas Morning News,* February 28, 1997.

Cuprisin, Tim. "Society Has Its Rules: Dr. Laura Has Her Own." *Milwaukee Journal Sentinel,* March 17, 1997.

Dart, John. "Dr. Laura Comes Down with the Commandments." *The Los Angeles Times–Valley News,* September 12, 1998.

———. "Moral Victory . . ." *The Los Angeles Times,* June 21, 1997.

Dell, Maryanne. "A kick-in-the-pants method for avoiding '10 Stupid Things.'" *The Orange County Register,* April 12, 1994.

Dietrich, Matt. "Dr. Laura's Falling Victim to What Happened to Rush." Springfield, Ill., *The State Journal-Register,* March 20, 1997.

———. "Love Her, Hate Her, Dr. Laura Talks the Talk." *The State Journal-Register,* October 6, 1996.

Dolik, Helen. "On Air Therapy." *Calgary Herald,* May 8, 1996.

———. "Radio Psychotherapist Dr. Laura Squeezes Career Around Her Life." *The Ottawa Citizen,* May 12, 1996.

Donahue, Deirdre. "Schlessinger Stakes Out Moral Ground." *USA Today,* February 22, 1996.

Downey, Maureen. "Dr. Laura's Tough On and Off the Air." *The Atlanta Journal and Constitution,* September 30, 1995.

"Dr. Laura Won't Return Fee to Dallas . . ." *The Orlando Sentinel,* March 19, 1997.

Eldredge, Richard L. "Dr. Laura Backs Out . . ." *The Atlanta Journal and Constitution,* March 16, 1997.

Feran, Tom. "Dr. Laura Doesn't Know How to Say I Don't." *The Plain Dealer,* August 21, 1996.

Freeman, John. "Psychotherapist Brings Her Prescription for Relationships to Radio." *San Diego Union-Tribune,* November 24, 1995.

Gallivan, Joseph. "Stop Messing Up Your Life." *The Guardian* (London), August 29, 1995.

Glassman, James K. "A Moralist on the Air." *The Weekly Standard,* May 6, 1996.

Goddard, Peter. "The Dominatrix of Whine Radio." *The Toronto Star,* July 16, 1995.

Gottlieb, Walter J. "Dr. Laura's Dose of Reality." *The Washington Post,* July 26, 1995.

Hampson, Rick. "Images of Takeover, Cigars in President's Office, Fresh After 20 Years." Associated Press, April 16, 1988, A.M. cycle.

Hiaasen, Rob. "Listen Up, Stupid Men: Dr. Laura Has Some Advice."
Raleigh, N.C., *The News & Observer,* October 15, 1997.

Hinckley, David. "Stern Lights Into Dr. Laura for Taking His Name in
Vain." *New York Daily News,* April 14, 1998.

Hinman, Catherine. "Therapist Dr. Laura Brings Her Brand of Ethics to
WDBO." *The Orlando Sentinel,* August 30, 1996.

Janis, Pam. "Hot Air." *The Detroit News,* March 27, 1996.

Johnson, Rebecca. "Beyond Caring." *The Independent* (London), January 19,
1997.

————. "The Just-Do-It Shrink." *The New York Times,* November 17, 1996.

Jones, Rebecca. "Shock Therapy." *Rocky Mountain News,* February 26,
1996.

Keveney, Bill. "A Higher Call-in: Tough Love on the Radio With Dr. Laura."
The Hartford Courant, May 3, 1995.

Kimmel, Michael. "Dr. Laura Takes Guys' Side Even as She Lays Into
Them." *San Francisco Chronicle,* October 16, 1997.

Lacher, Irene. "Dr. Laura's Life Lessons." *The Los Angeles Times,* March 13,
1994.

Longino, Mirian. "On Radio." *The Atlanta Journal and Constitution,* March 19,
1997.

Lorando, Mark. "The Betsy Ross of Radio." *The Times-Picayune* (New Orleans), July 3, 1996.

————. "Dr. Laura: Men Like Her Muscle." *The Times-Picayune* (New Orleans), September 24, 1997.

Lowry, Rich. "An Antidote to Dr. Ruth." *The Wall Street Journal,* June 18,
1996.

Lycan, Gary. "New Diagnosis for Dr. Laura." *The Orange County Register,*
August 30, 1998.

Mahler, Jonathan. "Sparks Fly in Texas . . ." *Ethnic Newswatch,* March 21,
1997.

Manning, Anita. "Dr. Laura Dispenses Morality Over the Radio." *USA Today,*
September 25, 1997.

Matzer, Marla. "Company Town: Vital Signs Are Fine for Dr. Laura
Show . . ." *The Los Angeles Times,* September 11, 1997.

McCoy, Adrian. "Dr. Laura Hammers Away at Liberal Moral Values." *Pittsburgh Post-Gazette,* April 28, 1996.

McEnroe, Colin. "Why Do Women Love This Man? . . ." *The Gazette* (Montreal), March 19, 1994.

Minor, Emily J. "Who Is Dr. Laura Anyway?" *Palm Beach Post,* November 23, 1996.

Moore, Micki. "The Doctor Is In." *Toronto Sun,* September 8, 1996.

"Morning Report." *The Los Angeles Times,* June 11, 1992.

Murtha, Frank. "Beware the Glib McTherapy of Dr. Laura." *The Buffalo News,* June 27, 1997.

Myers, Donald. "Calling Dr. Laura . . ." *Newsday* (Long Island), October 7, 1997.

O'Reilly, Tim. "Therapist Doesn't Baby New Callers." *The Dallas Morning News,* March 9, 1995.

Page, Clarence. "Radio's Know-it-all Talk Show Host Should Be Made National Mommy." Greensboro, N.C., *News & Record,* June 16, 1996.

Patton, Charlie. "Puh-Leese!" Jacksonville, Fla., *The Florida Times-Union,* October 17, 1996.

Pertman, Adam. "Dr. Laura Lays Down the Law." *The Boston Globe,* May 30, 1996.

Peters, Nick. "America's 'Kick-Ass' Agony Aunt . . ." *Sunday Times* (London), July 27, 1997.

Precker, Michael. "So What's Your Problem?" *The Dallas Morning News,* May 30, 1995.

"Public Outcry Over Anti-Gay Ad Supplement." *Las Vegas Review-Journal,* July 9, 1994.

"Radio's Dr. Laura Says She's in a 'Personal & Spiritual Crisis.'" Associated Press, March 14, 1997, P.M. cycle.

Rafter, Michelle. "Rock'N and Roll'N with the Internet." Reuters, October 8, 1997, 3:12 P.M.

Reed, Leonard. "Doc Laura's Advice Can Pack a Very Mean Punch." *The Los Angeles Times,* March 16, 1995.

Reischel, Diane. "Psychologist Knits Herself a Therapy and a Business." *The Los Angeles Times-View,* November 13, 1987.

Richmond, Ray. "Jacor Buys 'Dr. Laura.'" *Daily Variety,* September 11, 1997.

Rosegrant, Susan. "Airwave Psychologists Soothe Psyches." Associated Press, April 28, 1980, P.M. cycle.

Saari, Laura. "Shock Therapy." *The Orange County Register,* November 19, 1996.

Salter, Stephanie. "A Multiplicity of Radio Shrinks." *San Francisco Examiner,* July 22, 1997.

Saunders, Debra J. "The Moral Is the Message." *San Francisco Chronicle,* September 28, 1998.

———. "Values Are Worthy Even When We Fail." *San Francisco Chronicle,* September 18, 1998.

Schlessinger, Laura. "Alcoholic Husband Made Choice." *Rocky Mountain News,* October 19, 1997.

———. "Being Gay Is No Excuse." *Rocky Mountain News,* August 23, 1998.

———. "Hold Dear the Four R's." *Rocky Mountain News,* May 10, 1998.

———. "On Preaching, Judgment and Happiness." *Minneapolis Star Tribune,* June 22, 1997.

———. "On the Holy Path." *Rocky Mountain News,* September 6, 1998.

———. "The Problem with the Kids Is in Your Mirror." *Minneapolis Star Tribune,* March 30, 1997.

———. "Remember, Nobody—and No Family—Is Perfect." *Minneapolis Star Tribune,* July 27, 1997.

———. "Rights vs. Right . . ." *Chicago Tribune,* June 1, 1997.

———. "Rising to the Occasion: Why It's Your Duty to Do the Right Thing." *Chicago Tribune,* February 23, 1997.

———. "Teach Son a Lesson." *Rocky Mountain News,* May 17, 1998.

———. "When Good People Have Bad Thoughts." *The Fresno Bee,* April 13, 1997.

———. "When Morality Needs an Update." *Rocky Mountain News,* June 14, 1998.

———. "Where's the Commitment?" *Rocky Mountain News,* August 16, 1998.

Schultz, Connie. "Hard-Line Counselor . . ." *The Plain Dealer,* September 9, 1997.

Schwartz, Marlyn. "Dr. Laura Had No Latitude When It Came to Her Attitude." *Houston Chronicle,* March 17, 1997.

———. "Dr. Laura, It's the Attitude, Not the Allergies." *The Dallas Morning News,* March 13, 1997.

———. "Two Famous Visitors: Now One's Infamous." *The Dallas Morning News,* March 11, 1997.

Singer, Suzanne F. "Doctor Laura: 'National Mommy' and Jewish Priest." *Ethnic Newswatch,* April 30, 1997.

Smith, Steven Cole. "Dr. Laura Is Talk Radio's Moral Surgeon . . ." *The Austin American-Statesman,* February 24, 1996.

———. "Moral Health Is More the Focus of Dr. Laura Radio Show." *The Albany Times-Union,* February 22, 1996.

Stovall, Waltrina. "Personal Crisis Over Response: . . . " *The Dallas Morning News,* March 13, 1997.

Valeri, Tracy. "Radio Host to Talk at Jewish Temples." *The Daily News of Los Angeles,* January 11, 1997.

Weiss, Patricia. "The Doctor Is On." *The Hartford Courant,* January 7, 1996.

Wharton, David. "Dr. Laura." *The Los Angeles Times,* February 4, 1990.

Whittell, Giles. "A Word from the Mother of All Mothers." *The Times* (London), August 13, 1997.

Zuckerman, Faye B. "Profile." *The Providence Journal-Bulletin,* January 25, 1996.

TELEVISION TRANSCRIPTS

Brown, Bob. "Listen to Dr. Laura." *20/20,* ABC, January 26, 1996. Transcript #1604-2.

Interview: "Dr. Laura Schlessinger, Gary Bauer, Robert Novak, Joe Conason, Gene Lyons, and Christopher Hitchens Debate the Scandals Surrounding the White House . . ." *Meet the Press,* February 15, 1998.

"Dr. Laura Schlessinger, Reverend Jerry Falwell, Mario Cuomo and Representative Jesse Jackson Jr. Discuss Moral Issues Facing the United States." *Meet the Press,* December 21, 1997.

O'Brien, Miles. "Laura Schlessinger Discusses Her Morality Radio Show." *CNN Sunday Morning,* November 24, 1996. Transcript #96112412V46.

INTERNET

Bauder, David. "Has Shock TV Crossed the Line?" AP Online, April 27, 1998.

"OnlineHost." America Online, Inc., 1997.

A

Abbott, Dr. Bernard, 75
Adkins, Rev. Gregory, 190
Advertising Age, 165
Are You the One for Me (De Angelis), 139
Alive and Well, 102
AM Los Angeles, 102
America Online, 96
American Association of Marriage and Family Therapists, 70
American Psychological Association (APA), 219

Antrim, Minna, 63
Arizona Republic, The, 202
Assistance League of Dallas, 8
Atlanta Journal and Constitution, The, 16
AudioNet, 230

B

Bacon, Francis, 53
Ballance, Bill, 64–73, 76–86, 88–89, 99, 108, 131, 171
Barry, Dave, 173

Barton, Scott, 155–156
Battley, Dr. Edwin, 45–46, 56
Beck, Marilyn, 232
Bellows, Keven, 209–211, 214
Bennetts, Leslie, 68, 137, 145,
    210–214
Berges, Marshall, 60
Berman, Laura, 62
Bernero, Mary, 46–48, 50
Biography magazine, 99, 103,
    171
Bishop, David, 89–90, 93, 96
Bishop, Diane, 88, 94, 96
Bishop, Jeanne, 88–90, 93–95
Bishop, Lew
    divorce from Jeanne, 85, 87–
        95
    heart attack of, 158–162,
        166–167, 170–171, 224
    manager of Laura, 15, 105,
        122–125, 128–129, 133–135,
        145, 151, 166, 185–186,
        214–216
    marriage to Laura, 5, 96, 98,
        103, 108, 110, 175–176,
        179–181, 188–189, 222
Bishop, Stephen, 88, 96
Blast to the Past, 207
Blue Key, 34
Breakaway, 102, 104
Briem, Ray, 78
Broadcasting & Cable magazine,
    229
Brodt, Dr. Audrey, 168–169
Brown, Bob, 22, 25
Browne, Dr. Joy, 203–204
Bulka, Reuven, 186, 188
Buller, Vern, 174
Burrell, Helena, 57

C

Cassetta, Richard D., 59–62
CBS, 139–140, 201–204
Ceccovini, Catherine and Joseph,
    19–20
Center for Counseling and Psy-
    chotherapy, Los Angeles, 65
Chattanooga Times, 232
ChildHelp USA, 207–208
Cirillo, Vincent, 47–48
CNN, 15, 94, 228
College of New Rochelle, 59–62
Columbia University, 53–59, 61
Conflict, 104–105
Courage and Conscience, 204

D

Dallas Morning News, 13–16,
    232
Dart, John, 188–189, 192
Davis, Phyllis, 8–9
Davis, Raenetta, 117, 119–121
De Angelis, Barbara, 131–132,
    135–140, 146–149, 153
Detroit News, The, 55, 62, 107
Dimnet, Ernest, 75
Doherty, William, 223
Donahue, 144
Dr. Joy Browne Show, The,
    203–204
Dr. Laura on Character, 204
Dr. Laura Schlessinger Show, The,
    163–167, 196–198, 229
Drexel Elementary School, West-
    bury, 24
Duncan, Deborah, 8

E

Eagle, Terry, 32–33
Edwards, Patti, 208, 213
Elias, Marni, 42–43, 45–46, 49,
    53–54
Emerson, Ralph Waldo, 17
Emmers, Raimond, 56–57
Erk, Dr. Frank, 58–59
Estroff, Ron, 28
Ethnic Newswatch, 21, 22, 25, 109,
    184, 186–188
Eyemark Entertainment (CBS),
    201–204

F

Fairness for Fathers, 207
Family Therapy Networker, 223
Federated Societies of Biology
    and Medicine, 61
Feldman, Kathryn Levy, 190
Feminine Forum, 66, 71, 97
Fernandez, John, 19, 85, 118–
    121
Fierman, Jack, 39–40
Fort Worth Star-Telegram, 67, 162,
    200
Friedman, Judith, 111, 114
Fuller, Alan L., 163–164, 169–
    170, 196–198

G

Gambrell, Richard, 44
Gateway Educational Products,
    163

GCI Communications, 209
General Hospital, 155–156
Geraldo, 144
Good Housekeeping, 190–191
Gottlieb, Walter, 205, 208,
    228
Grant, Dr. Toni, 66, 70, 73, 118,
    137, 171, 196–198
Griffiths, John, 21–22, 25, 40,
    56, 58, 62, 87, 103, 113,
    120–121, 123, 144, 162,
    174–177
Grobel, Lawrence, 35
Guest, Edgar A., 183

H

Hampson, Rick, 55
Harris, Brad, 101, 111
Harris, Cindy Schlessinger, 25,
    29, 83–85, 101–102, 111
Harrison, Michael, 164–166,
    222–223, 232
Hedstrom, L. James, 98, 101,
    103
Hemingway, Carol, 76, 97
Herman, Shelley, 102, 104–105,
    109, 111–113, 121–123,
    126–128, 131, 134, 140–141,
    144, 160, 166–167, 176, 191,
    193, 199, 214–216, 225
Holmgren, Kristine, 208
Holt, Carolyn, 231
Holter, Tom, 128–131
Hooked on Phonics, 163–164
How Could You Do That?
    (Schlessinger), 95, 127
Hurst, Adele, 12

I

Independent, The, 185
Inside Media, 165

J

Jacor Communications, 228
Jericho High School, 29–41, 100
Jewish Federation of Greater
    Dallas, 10–15
John Davidson Show, The, 102
Johnson, Rebecca, 185, 231

K

KABC, Los Angeles, 64, 66,
    73, 76, 78–79, 97, 171,
    196–197
Kagan, Marilyn, 152–155, 157,
    216
Kaminsky, Arthur, 30–33, 37–38
Kamrava, Dr. M. M., 111
Kassanoff, D. J., 7, 10–13
Kazarian Spencer & Assoc., Inc.,
    134
KFI, 131–132, 135–140, 146–147,
    149, 153, 156–157, 160–161,
    166, 171, 230
KGBS, 66
King, Larry, 191, 204
King, Norm, 217
Klein, Chris, 181
KMPC, Los Angeles, 84
Knit Names, 121–124
Kohler, Viktoria, 57
KOST, 133

Kristy, Dr. Norton, 64–66, 69–73,
    76, 78–79, 82–84, 99–100,
    171, 192–193, 222
KRLD, Dallas, 9, 14
KTLK, Denver, 168–169
KTRB, Modesto, 68–69
KWNK, 127–128

L

Lacher, Irene, 26, 111, 141
Ladies' Home Journal, The, 184,
    187, 194
Lambert, Martha, 199
Las Vegas Review-Journal, 205
Lasswell, Marcia, 70–71, 84, 99
Leikus, Tom, 137
Levy, Dr. David, 218–222
Lewine, Rob, 90–92
Liberty Lobby, 131
Lieberman, Dr. Carole, 217–218
Lisowski, Andrew, 118–120
Longino, Mirian, 16
Los Angeles Times, The, 57–58,
    111–112, 130, 150, 218,
    228–229
Los Angeles Times Home maga
    zine, 24, 35–36, 60, 90–92,
    227
Los Angeles Times Magazine, The,
    23, 77, 189, 209
Los Angeles Times-Valley News,
    The, 188, 192
Los Angeles Times-View, 121–122,
    124
Los Angeles Women in Advertis-
    ing (LULU), 207
Lycan, Gary, 216

M

Marconi Radio Award, 208
Marcovitch, Dr. Rhoda, 111, 113, 114
Martin, David, 33
McClintock, Barbara, 37
McFeeley, Daniel, 140–141, 199–200, 224–225
Mead, Rebecca, 22
Mehl, Sherry, 148–149, 203
Mendoza, Anne, 149–150
Merv Griffin Show, The, 102
Michener, James, 143
Mid-Morning LA, 102
Mile High Marine Storage, Inc., 178–181
Miller, Tracey, 131–133, 137, 145, 152, 160–161
Minneapolis Star Tribune, 208
Mohler, Mary, 184, 188
Mothers Against Drunk Driving (MADD), 207
Mountains Community Hospital Foundation, 181
Myerson, Mort, 10

N

National Association of Broadcasters' Marconi Radio Award, 208
Netstar Seven Entertainment Group International, Inc., 196–198
New Country: Jewish Immigrants in America (Shulman), 18
New York Times, The, 22

Newsday, 22, 191, 208, 230–231
Newsweek, 162

O

O'Brien, Miles, 94, 228
Orange County Register, The, 169, 216

P

Page, Clarence, 223
Pasqualetto, Richard, 29, 31–32
Paton, Alan, 97
People magazine, 21, 58, 87, 103, 120, 144, 162, 174–177
Pepper, Gerry, 118–119
Pepperdine University, 98, 101, 103, 113, 124
Posner, Howard, 48–50
Premier Radio Networks, 209, 228–230
Psychology Today, 28, 195, 231
Publishers Weekly, 194

Q

Quantum Leap, 155

R

Radio Today, 164–166, 169–170
Raiber, Bob, 30, 32, 38
Rant N' Rave, 200–201
Redbook, 22, 92

Reff, Miriam, 34
Rich, Geoff, 165–166
Richter, Jean-Paul, 117
Rudolph, Michael F., 57–62, 100
Russell, Barbara, 24

S

Saginaw, Rose, 9, 13–14
Sally Jessy Raphael, 144
San Francisco Chronicle, 204, 231
San Jose Mercury News, 217
Sandburg, Carl, 107
Santa Barbara, 155
Sarnoff, David, 127
Saunders, Cheryl, 101
Saunders, Debra, 204–205,
    231–232
Saunders, Laurie, 133
Schachter, Dr. David, 56, 61
Schaedel, Joanne, 41–42, 44–45,
    47–49, 53–54
Schlessinger, Cindy. *See* Harris,
    Cindy Schlessinger
Schlessinger, Deryk Andrew, 5,
    112–115, 120, 125–126,
    132–133, 176–177, 184–185,
    189, 209–210
Schlessinger, Dorothy Singer, 18,
    20
Schlessinger, Dr. Laura C.
  adolescence of, 27–40
  birth and childhood of, 21–26
  courtship and marriage to Lew
    Bishop, 12, 87–96, 98, 108,
    110, 175–176, 188–189, 222
  family therapist, 93–94,
    99–101, 113–115, 124–125
  heritage of, 17–21

Judaism and, 3, 7, 10–11,
    13–14, 183–194, 212
  KABC and Bill Ballance and,
    65–73, 76–86
  marriage to Michael Rudolph,
    58–62, 67, 71
  motherhood and, 5–6, 11–12,
    107–115, 125–126, 132–133,
    176–177
  national radio program of,
    6–7, 14
  public image of, 207–225
  quotes by, 5, 27, 39, 87, 159,
    195, 227
  radio syndication of, 127–141,
    144–158, 163–171, 195–205
  teaching career of, 59–62, 68,
    75, 84, 98–101, 113–114
  university education of, 40–51,
    53–59, 93
Schlessinger, Monroe "Monty"
  Laura's adulthood and, 68,
    82–85, 104, 117–121
  Laura's childhood and, 24, 26,
    40
  Laura's university years and,
    40, 42–43, 47–48, 53, 61
  marriage of, 19–21
Schlessinger, Ralph, 18
Schlessinger, Yolanda Ceccovini
    "Lundy," 1–3
  Laura's adulthood and, 82–85,
    102–104, 117, 191–192
  Laura's childhood and, 21–26,
    28–29, 34
  Laura's university years and,
    40, 42–43, 47–48, 53, 61
  marriage of, 19–21
Schrof, Joannie M., 113
Schwartz, Marlyn, 14–16, 209

Science Research Program, Cold
    Spring Harbor, 36–37, 40
*Secrets About Men Every Woman
    Should Know* (De Angelis),
    139
Shanahan, John M., 163–164, 166,
    170
Shanahan Broadcasting Interna-
    tional (SBI), 163, 170,
    196–197
Shapiro, Bob, 147
Shulman, Abraham, 18
Singer, Suzanne, 21
Smith, Lois, 34–36
Smith, Stacy Jenel, 232
Smith, Steven Cole, 67, 71, 162, 200
Spitzer, Helene, 30
Star Trek, 155
Star, Russell F., 37, 43–44, 46
Star, Virginia, 37
State University of New York at
    Stony Brook, 40–51
Statesman, The (SUNY Stony
    Brook), 49
Stern, Howard, 201
Students for a Democratic Soci-
    ety (SDS), 50
Sukhov, Burt, 216–217
Sun Radio Network, 128–131
Sylmar Medical Center, 166–167,
    170–171
Synergy Broadcast Investment
    Enterprises, 197, 228

T

Tacky Taste Awards, 232
Talkers magazine, 164–165, 232
Temple Aliyah, 185

Ten Commandments, The
    (Schlessinger), 103–104, 186,
    189, 191–192, 199, 204, 230
*Ten Stupid Things Men Do
    to Mess Up Their Lives*
    (Schlessinger), 15–16, 189
*Ten Stupid Things Women Do to
    Mess Up Their Lives*
    (Schlessinger),* 48, 62, 75,
    134, 167–169
Time magazine, 202
Toll, Dr. John S., 49
Tolstoy, Leo, 207
Tools of Critical Thinking (Levy),
    218
Toronto Sun, 92
Torres, Annabelle, 61
20/20, 22, 25
TV Guide, 156

U

U.S. News & World Report, 22,
    113, 189–190
Universal Studios, 200–202
University of California at Los
    Angeles (UCLA), 114, 122
University of Southern California
    (USC), 62, 68, 75, 84, 88–89,
    93, 107

V

Van Steenhouse, Andrea, 169
Vanity Fair, 68, 77, 89, 137–138,
    145, 186, 191–192, 208,
    210–214
Vogel, Rabbi Stewart, 186, 230

W

Warford, Jack, 174, 176
Washington Post, The, 103, 205,
        208, 228
Westbury High School, 27–28
Westbury Junior High, 24
Wharton, David, 228
Whatley, Suzanne, 160
Whitesides, Barbara, 132–133,
        137, 145–146, 151–152,
        155–158, 161

Wilson, Ed, 203
Wilson, Pete, 150
Wiscombe, Janet, 23, 40, 189,
        209–210
Wolper, Donna, 32, 100
Women of KFI, The, 152
Women in Need Growing
        Strong (WINGS), 207
Worldstar Productions, Inc.,
        170
Wostbrock, Fred, 134–136
Woulfin, Susan, 42, 45, 48–50